BUKOWSKI
AND THE BEATS

BUKOWSKI
AND THE BEATS

A commentary on the Beat Generation

Translated from the French
by Alison Ardron

Followed by

AN EVENING AT BUK'S PLACE
—AN INTERVIEW WITH CHARLES BUKOWSKI

Jean-François Duval

2002
Sun Dog Press
Northville, Michigan

BUKOWSKI AND THE BEATS

Translated from the French By Alison Ardron

Cover design by Grey Christian

Book design by Judy Berlinski

The publisher is especially grateful to Judy Berlinski for her invaluable contribution in editing, graphic concepts, and text design.

A special thank you to Michael Mehall for his professional guidance and patience in the preparation of this book.

Warmest thanks to Linda Lee Bukowski for providing photos from her personal archive.

Grateful appreciation to John Martin of Black Sparrow Press for kindly given permissions.

Originally published in a different version as *Buk et les Beats*, Paris: Editions Michalon, 1998

Library of Congress Cataloging-in-Publication Data

Duval, Jean-François
   [Buk et les Beats. English]
   Bukowski and the Beats : a commentary on the Beat Generation / Jean-François Duval ; translated from the French by Alison Ardron ; followed by An evening at Buk's Place : an interview with Charles Bukowski.—1st ed.
      p.cm.
   Includes bibliographical references.
   ISBN 0-941543-30-7 (alk. paper)
      1. Bukowski, Charles. 2. Bukowski, Charles—Interviews. 3. Authors, American—20th century—Biography. 4. Authors, American—20th century—Interviews. 5. Beat generation—Interviews. 6. Beat generation—Biography. I. Bukowski, Charles. Evening at Buk's Place. II. Title.

PS3552.U4 Z6313 2002
811'.54—dc21
[B]
                                                            2002017708

Printed in the United States of America   First Edition

To my son Matteo

BY THE AUTHOR

Les Proscrits, récits
L'Aire, 1986

La Voix fantôme, roman
Zoé, 1993

Buk et les Beats
essai sur la Beat Generation
suivi de
Un soir chez Buk
entretien inédit avec Charles Bukowski
Michalon, 1998

Boston Blues
Routes de l'inattendu
Phébus, 2000

CONTENTS

Charles Bukowski *himself!*

FOREWORD

There are several reasons for this book. The principal one is pleasure. The pure pleasure of returning to Charles Bukowski and to the Beats, of dipping a little into their legend, particularly as the Beat movement is now enjoying renewed attention through new editions, appearances of previously unpublished material, exhibitions and other events. There is also the pleasure of rediscovering Charles Bukowski, cult author whose reputation continues to grow steadily in America, Great Britain, Germany, France, the Eastern European countries, and even in Japan. Buk has long been popular in Germany and France, but fifteen or so years ago he had limited recognition in the USA. Over the past fifteen years, largely thanks to the release of Barbet Schroeder's film *Barfly* (for which Buk wrote the screenplay) he has been acknowledged in his homeland as one of the greats. Now, some compare his imposing presence of stature with that of Hemingway.

After his death in 1994, recollections and small testimonies were published, such as the *Charles Bukowski: The Second Coming Years* by A. D. Winans (1996), *Spinning Off Bukowski* by Steve Richmond (1996), *Charles Bukowski: A Sure Bet* by Gerald Locklin (1997), and *Bukowski Boulevard* by Joan J. Smith. Neeli Cherkovski, his official biographer, believes he erased too many of Hank's characteristics from his work while Buk was alive (and Buk commented: "I wish you had put in those wilder stories!"). In 1997 he updated his book *Hank: The Life of Charles Bukowski* which had been published in 1991 with the title *Bukowski: A Life*. In 1996 German readers discovered *Das War's: Letzte Worte mit Charles Bukowski* by Gundolf S. Freyermuth. In the United States, Gay Brewer gave us a close study of Buk's work in his *Charles Bukowski* (1997). And more recently, in Great Britain, Howard Sounes published *Charles Bukowski: Locked in the Arms of a Crazy Life*, a well documented biography, with photographs of Hank's childhood, friends and women (1998), which was followed two years later by *Bukowski in Pictures*

(2000), a remarkable pictorial biography with some two hundred photographs. Later in the same year, Jules Smith's *Art, Survival and So Forth: The Poetry of Charles Bukowski* and even a *Bukowski for Beginners* translated from the Spanish were to be found in bookshops. The beginning of the year 2001 saw the publication of a collective tribute book, *Drinking with Bukowski: Recollections of the Poet Laureate of Skid Row*, at Thunder's Mouth Press.

In almost every issue, magazines such as Kevin Ring's *Beat Scene* (G.B.) frequently associate Buk with the Beats; Hank regularly rubs shoulders with Kerouac, Ginsberg, Burroughs, Cassady, Corso and the rest. There are Internet sites devoted entirely to him. In America, books autographed by Buk (nearly always accompanied by small drawings or paintings) sell for hundreds of dollars.

Buk's correspondence, like Flaubert's (though obviously in a completely different style), is particularly outstanding. Four volumes (*Screams from the Balcony, Living on Luck, Reach for the Sun* and his correspondence with Sheri Martinelli, *Beerspit Night and Cursing*) have already been published. An unknown Buk is revealed there: he is in brilliant form—human, too human, sometimes mentally conversing with Henry Miller, Hemingway and the Beats. As Robert Crumb puts it: "He was a great letter writer and related to fellow human beings far better through the medium of the typewriter."

In 1997 Black Sparrow Press also indulged itself in a limited edition of his previously unpublished journal—brilliantly illustrated by Robert Crumb, at $650 per copy (not bad for the diary of an ex-bum). The journal had one of those titles to which Buk holds the key: *The Captain Is Out To Lunch And The Sailors Have Taken Over The Ship*. It was made accessible to everyone with a paperback edition in 1998. At the start of 2001, *The Cruelty of Loveless Love*, a portfolio of 18 poems and photographic portraits of Bukowski was even offered to collectors by Kunst Editions, New York for $1000 dollars per copy!

Charles Bukowski's growing reputation discredits Allen Ginsberg's view several months after Hank's death in 1994: "Bukowski? I think his star probably will fade a little. Maybe there will be a couple of poems in an anthology of great poetry, I'm not sure," he told me.

Furthermore, I believe a whole field has remained widely unexplored, until now— Buk's links with his cousins, the Beats: Kerouac, Ginsberg, Cassady, Corso etc. This book is an invitation to explore and discover it. Therefore, I have provided useful information as found in travel guides, technical manuals and other practical books (as the Beat movement was not only a literary vision, but also intended to help people find their way in the world).

The notes and a selected bibliography enable the reader to get his bearings in the realm of Buk and the Beats. There is a Who's Who, which seemed a necessity as the Beat legend is at times labyrinthine. Who is who? Literature and life were never really separate for the Beats (they were on the road, never shut away for very long, Virginia Woolf-style).

The Who's Who shows which person in real life inspired which character in "The Duluoz Legend"—the title Kerouac wanted to give the entirety of his work, his "Balzacian" *Comédie Humaine*. The fact that it was never published as such does not detract from the pleasure; indeed quite the opposite is true. Kerouac's work can be read as a giant jigsaw in which each piece represents a form of literature, a different attempt to reconstruct life artistically.

The recording of the interview with Charles Bukowski, *An Evening At Buk's Place*, is carefully stored in my archives next to a series of photographs taken

Allen Ginsberg, New York, November 1994.

11

that evening without a flash; paradoxically the alcohol helped me to stay totally still. I was certainly blessed that night. I had always thought that the interview could be the subject of a book as it followed the classical unities: the unity of time (it all happened on one evening); the unity of place (Charles and Linda Bukowski's house in San Pedro); the quasi-dramatic progression of the action under the influence of alcohol and Buk's slow, sure, rhythmic voice which seemed to echo an art and vision of life. Leaving Buk, I almost felt as if I was carrying away a small play—and I would like to make you the audience.

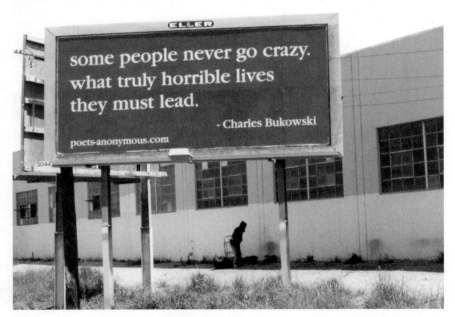

Los Angeles billboard, 1999.

BUKOWSKI
AND THE BEATS

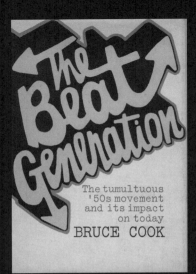

The Beat Generation

The tumultuous
'50s movement
and its impact
on today
BRUCE COOK

Here are the most vital
and controversial writers
on the American scene

35¢

THE BEATS

Raw, penetrating stories,
poems and social criticism
by JACK KEROUAC
NORMAN MAILER
ALLEN GINSBERG
LAWRENCE FERLINGHETTI
and many others

Edited by Seymour Krim

Hal Chase, Jack Kerouac, Allen Ginsberg, and William Burroughs
in one of the first photos taken of them as the Beat Generation in
the year they met, 1944.

THE BEAT REVIVAL

The growing interest in Charles Bukowski's work is not the only piece of good news: since the 1990s, the Beats are definitively back! At the beginning of the new millennium, and more than 50 years after the birth of the movement, young people faced with a rise of fundamentalist, neoconservative and politically correct trends are rediscovering the movement's breath of inspiration—freedom of thought, speech and behavior.

In the USA from the East coast to the West, the Beats' books are back on the displays and cult shelves of bookshops where high school kids and students hang out. Not only Kerouac, Ginsberg, Burroughs, and Neal Cassady are rediscovered, but a whole constellation of authors whose names are going to stay, like Gregory Corso, Michael McClure, Philip Whalen, Gary Snyder, Lawrence Ferlinghetti, Diane DiPrima, Carolyn Cassady, Hettie Jones, Jan Kerouac, and many more. At the Whitney Museum in New York, the exhibition *Beat Culture and the New America: 1950-1965* enjoyed resounding success from the end of 1995 right through 1996, before it went to San Francisco and Minneapolis. Among other treasures, it was a pleasure to see for the first time the 119-foot roll of teletype paper—finally released by his literary agent, Sterling Lord—on which Kerouac wrote the first draft of *On the Road* (his editor altered the version that we know). Christie's sold this scroll on May 22, 2001, for 2.4 million dollars, an auction record for a literary manuscript. Each year we see new books, biographies, correspondence, testimonies, essays, anthologies, books of photographs published on the Beats by authors on both sides of the Atlantic, in Great Britain, France, Italy, Czech Republic . . . This is evidence that Beat literature is around to stay.

Censorship has its say too. *Howl*, Ginsberg's poem-manifesto, published in August 1956, one year before *On the Road*, caused a scandal on the grounds of obscenity and in the 1990s it was once again banned from American radio and television! A fine blow for a movement which transpired more than half a century ago from the explosive encounter of a few young guys in Times Square, New York: Herbert Huncke, poet and junkie who fascinated William Burroughs; Lucien Carr whose friend Edie Parker later introduced to Kerouac (Edie herself became Kerouac's first wife); the disturbing William S. Burroughs, grandson of the inventor of the first adding machine; and 17-year-old Allen Ginsberg, the youngest and most restless of them all, who became the catalyst of the whole movement—a movement whose heroic character par excellence was Neal Cassady, who seduced all of them.

In the 1950s the boost given by the core members of the Beat movement unleashed the baby-boom generation's revolt against the conventions of a rigid society, fossilized in its terror of the cold war, prudish, materialistic and alienating. A society which would also be challenged by Brando and James Dean's films and Presley's music.

Indeed we owe much to the Beats—Dylan, the Beatles, beatniks, hippies, LSD, Katmandu, protest, "Make love not war," Woodstock, demos, punks, renewal of interest in the East, in Buddhism and ecology, not forgetting grunge and Kurt Cobain. Perhaps it isn't too much of an exaggeration to state that the second half of the 20th century bears the Beat imprint—freedom of morals, music, literature, the way we dress, love, travel, are politically active and live.

Since 1993, magazines and dailies like *Time* and *The New York Times* have devoted cover stories and long articles to the Beat revival. Commerce and merchandising are getting in on the act; old photographs of Kerouac and Ginsberg adorn khaki jackets and trousers found at The Gap. Rumor has it that Francis Ford Coppola may finally produce *On the Road*, to which he has held the rights for twenty years. The press fêted Allen Ginsberg—"probably the most famous American poet"—to the crowd that welcomed him on the 40th anniversary of the bookshop City Lights (mecca for Beat culture, founded in 1953 in San Francisco by the poet Lawrence Ferlinghetti). Stanford University bought Ginsberg's correspondence for one million dollars—300,000 pieces including tapes of his conversations with Burroughs and jam sessions with Bob Dylan—surprising official recognition from this reputedly conservative university of a movement that was the basis for the 1960s counterculture!

Is it just a fad? A fashion craze? Allen Ginsberg would have none of it, and in January 1995 told the French newspaper *Libération:* "Young people have freed themselves from simplistic ideologies, from simplistic capitalism, from simplistic Marxism, from simplistic neoconservatism. When all these encroachments expired, when brainwashing failed, the human element and the experiences of life and writing of the '40s and '50s were rediscovered. Exploration of consciousness, spontaneity, was also rediscovered."[1] The new "beatniks" of the virtual age are regular travellers on the information superhighways on rollerblades and skate-boards with a laptop under their arm. Some believe these techno-bohemians are casually creating a new counterculture, capable in its turn of shattering a number of our cultural and social frameworks.

One man was completely convinced that the Internet age was, to a certain degree, part of the underground movement.

That man was Timothy Leary who, in the years that preceded his death, became one of the chief icons of cyber-culture. At the beginning of the sixties, this outstanding Harvard professor introduced Ginsberg, Cassady and Kerouac to psilocybine. As the "high priest" of the pop and hippie generations, he was later considered by President Nixon as "the most dangerous man in the USA." Leary also resurfaced between 1990 and 1996, although he had never really disappeared. While others dreamed nostalgically about the '60s, the pope of the psychedelic and anti-establishment counterculture of the '60s was travelling in cyberspace accompanied by young switched-on disciples; only a few ini-

Timothy Leary and Jean-François Duval at Leary's home in Beverly Hills, 1995.

tiates and magazine readers in the know were aware of it. Leary reappeared like a whale that suddenly resurfaces and breaks out into the open, only to publicly announce his next departure. The climax of this comeback was Leary's spectacular statement in 1995 about his imminent death. In November 1995, in a dispatch circulated throughout the press by *The New York Times Service*, he rejoiced that "dying is the most fantastic experience in life. It's a hip, chic, vogue thing to do. It's the most elegant thing you can do. Even if you've lived your life like a complete slob, you can die with terrific style. I can't wait for this moment." William

Burroughs immediately phoned him to congratulate him for this "great" statement.

All the ex-fans from the '60s then real-ized that 75-year-old Tim Leary, at the point of death, was back. Better still, he was hip again. *Time* confirmed it. The switched-on cyberpunk Californian magazine *Mondo 2000* went wild with his contributions. His book *High Priest* had just been republished. As Tim's health was not good enough for him to travel by air, he addressed 3000 young people from his home in Beverly Hills. They hung on his every word in  London (in 1995) and Amsterdam (in 1996) at massive raves via huge screens. Even more surprising was that Leary was writing and publishing underground books of disturbing style with the aid of a cybernetic staff. The most striking of these titles is *Chaos & Cyberculture*, which was published by Ronin in 1994 and which proved that Leary had forgotten nothing. Promoted to cyberpunk icon he endeavored to link his present status with his past status by forming links between the different stages of post-war counterculture, noting four fundamental periods that spawned each other in several mutations:

The Beats (1944-1959): cool jazzy, hip bohemians, attracted by Buddhism, not really inclined towards the tech-nical.

The beatniks and hippies (1959-1975): detached, peace-loving, tolerant, anti-intellectual, intuitive and mystic.

The punks (1975-1990): lugubrious, gloomy, destroy, fun-damentally pessimistic, reject western culture.

The cybernauts (1990-2005): alert, eclectic, confident, surf the waves and networks, individual, Zen opportunists, designers of chaos.

BUKOWSKI, THE COUNTERCULTURE'S DISSIDENT

In 1994, the year that saw the renewal of interest in the Beat generation, Charles Bukowski died in San Pedro, California. He was a notable figure of the counterculture. Many newspapers—in Europe particularly—were a bit too quick to present him as Kerouac and Ginsberg's successor. Charles Bukowski would probably better rank in the third section of Leary's classification (as discussed above)—the post-Beat punk era. There is no doubt that Bukowski's "destroy" mythology—dirty and perpetually drunk, surrounded by a pile of beer bottles and boxes—matched the punk aesthetic more closely, and it is probably no accident that Buk's international recognition in the '70s coincided with the advent of *No Future* philosophy.

When he was interviewed in 1978 in Paris by the chief editor of *Paris Métro*, Bukowski made this clear: he declared "that he felt closer to the punks than to the beatniks," and he added: "I'm not interested in this bohemian, Greenwich Village, Parisian bullshit. Algiers, Tangiers that's all romantic claptrap."[1] Back in 1967 when an American magazine associated him with the beatniks' heroes—"Timothy Leary, Norman Mailer, William Burroughs, Jean Genet, Henry Miller, LeRoi Jones, Lawrence Ferlinghetti, Bob Dylan,

Bertolt Brecht, John Cage, Eugène Ionesco, W. H. Auden, Anaïs Nin, Allen Ginsberg and Charles Bukowski"—Buk felt an affinity with only a few of these big names. He clarified this in a letter to his German translator, Carl Weissner: "Genet in portions when he doesn't creampuff out in love with his writing, Brecht in portions, and the very early Auden."[2]

Let's take for instance the way he reports his "encounter" with one of the most famous Beats. In his novel *Women* he tells of a reading that Chinaski, his alter ego, agreed to give in the North. "It was the afternoon before the reading and I was sitting in an apartment at the Holiday Inn drinking beer with Joe Washington."

Suddenly Joe, the event organizer, glances through the window and calls out: "Hey, look, here comes William Burroughs across the way. He's got the apartment right next to yours. He's reading tomorrow night."

Chinaski gets up, goes over to the window and says: "It was Burroughs all right . . . We were on the second floor. Burroughs walked up the stairway, passed my window, opened his door and went in."

Joe suggests a meeting with Burroughs. Chinaski declines. All the same Joe goes to Burroughs and thinks he is doing the right thing in telling him that Chinaski is in the next room; he doesn't have much success. Burroughs barely gives a terse "Oh, is that so?"

A little later, when Chinaski leaves his room to look for an ice machine, he cannot fail to catch a glimpse of the great Bill: "As I walked by Burroughs' place, he was sitting in a chair by the window. He looked at me indifferently."[3]

Fact or fiction (but more fact than fiction, according to his last wife Linda Lee Bukowski), the whole scene is very accurate and the two men are perfect in their respective roles. Burroughs and Bukowski have just one thing in common: a completely mutual indifference. Buk hits home in his description: Burroughs in an armchair in his motel room, stripped of expression, as silent and still as a figure in an Edward Hopper painting.

Burroughs appears here as if in a photographic negative (no meeting, nothing, zero communication). To a certain extent the "Burroughs motif" in this piece has no other function but to give Bukowski the opportunity to explain his link with the Beat writers, via the link's very absence. Burrough's personality, at that moment, reinforces this void: Victor Gioscia described Burroughs at that time as entirely cerebral, becoming more and more like "a vast computer running all the time, making arcane comparisons silently."[4] This is the Burroughs that Buk/Chinaski probably saw through the motel room window.

Bukowski certainly didn't think too much of the Beat writers.

For this reason it seems incongruous to come across him years later, in 1992, on a film and a CD-ROM entitled *Poetry in Motion* principally devoted to the Beats.[5] It is a collection of readings given (sometimes in front of 3000 people) by poets like Ginsberg, Burroughs, John Cage, Robert Creeley, Diane DiPrima, Michael McClure, Gary Snyder, Anne Waldman, and most unexpectedly, Charles Bukowski. The CD-ROM is even introduced by Bukowski who "after drawing a passionately eloquent sketch of Beat poetry, regained his self-control to say that everything is just beer shit. Then he knocked back a glassful of port & got pixelated Quick Time."[6] According to the poet Anne Waldman, Bukowski's role in the film was to represent the opposite standpoint: "He is kind of the voice of dissension, in that film documentary, he is used in this way, as a kind of gallery commentaire, and that commentary is amazing, it's funny his role in there, that kind of growl, it is the slightly bitter but very funny commentator on the scene."

Indeed, the whole of Buk's correspondence between 1960 and 1970 reveals his ambiguous attitude towards the Beat writers (the first volume, *Screams from the Balcony*, was published in 1994, and the second, *Living on Luck*, in 1995). But there was a dilemma—how could he stand apart and remain aloof from a movement that was the basis of a counterculture to which he subscribed? How could he claim a similar aesthetic and state of mind, when there was no way he would fit into a group that had been seminal to the whole underground movement? On one side there was the constellation of Beat writers—Kerouac, Ginsberg, Burroughs, Gary Snyder, Philip Whalen, Gregory Corso, Michael McClure, Philip Lamantia, etc.—a literary movement that linked the West coast to the East coast. On the other side there was a loner, a rebel for all causes, a total dissident even within the counterculture. Bukowski alone embodies the most deprived, most hard-working, most popular fringe of the system's rejects, of the poor in spirit, in literature and in poetry.

Russell Harrison, the author of *Against the American Dream: Essays on Charles Bukowski*, a study that mostly refers to *Post Office* and *Factotum*, notes that Buk was probably the only American poet who addressed the nonintellectual classes and whose poetry related to the concrete and everyday realities of the world of work (although, it was pointed out, he was not really interested in the working class as a group, only as individuals).[7] Those realities he experienced through the hundreds of dead-end jobs, reluctantly toiled at for forty years around the country. It is no surprise his first novel told of his life at the post office (writing *Post Office* inspired Buk in 1969 to leave his job of the past 11 years): the sorting office, the horrors of routine work with no creative outlet, hell for the soul of an artist . . .

The Beats were more up-market; bums, but heavenly bums. They, too, put their hand to a range of jobs, led a bohemian lifestyle and spent time in prison. Kerouac went to sea with the Merchant Marines, worked in a ball bearings factory and was a brakeman for Southern Pacific Railway as was Cassady. Ginsberg was involved in journalism and advertising. Like Buk, they were no angels. Herbert Huncke was a junkie and notorious thief. Neal Cassady boasted of stealing more than five hundred cars before he was twenty; not for the money but for the pleasure of going for a spin in the Rockies near Denver. Burroughs inadvertently gunned down his wife Joan while acting out William Tell in Mexico, and spent two weeks in prison before being released on bail. Lucien Carr was imprisoned for two years for the murder of a professor who was sexually harassing him. And Kerouac, who helped Carr conceal the knife, only narrowly avoided prison by marrying Edie Parker with two policemen as witnesses.

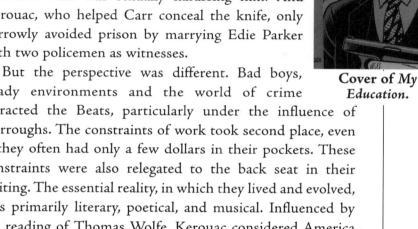

Cover of *My Education.*

But the perspective was different. Bad boys, shady environments and the world of crime attracted the Beats, particularly under the influence of Burroughs. The constraints of work took second place, even if they often had only a few dollars in their pockets. These constraints were also relegated to the back seat in their writing. The essential reality, in which they lived and evolved, was primarily literary, poetical, and musical. Influenced by his reading of Thomas Wolfe, Kerouac considered America principally as a poem. When Ginsberg, aged 17, first met Kerouac he confided that he wanted to study law to help the working classes, Kerouac gently pointed out: "You have never worked a day in your life in a factory, you have no idea about labor."[8]

Kerouac himself was rather removed from the hardships of the world of work, to which he looked at primarily as a poet. In a long article about the Beat revival which appeared in 1996 in the French newspaper *Le Monde*, Samuel Blumenfeld wrote: "During a reading of 'October in the Railroad Earth'[9] in a piano bar in 1959, Kerouac openly scorned the commuters with their tight collars obliged to catch the 5:48 train at Millbrae or San Carlos to go to work in San Francisco, while he—a son of the road—could watch the freight trains pass, take in the immensity of the sky and feel the weight of ancestral America."[10] Carolyn Cassady in *Off the Road* tells of "the extent Kerouac was really keen on the comfort of her home, perfectly ordered, with a bourgeois interior, whose view," Blumenfeld reports sarcastically, "looked over the same Bayshore Freeway that took these commuters with tight collars from their homes to San Francisco." In fact, Kerouac romanticized the people at the bottom, as James Campbell put it rather severely: "The difference between the Beats and the bums they imitated is that the latter would have got off skid row if only they could: their failure had made them beaten, and they wouldn't have cared anything for 'beat,' which it would have been their rights to consider a white middle-class invention."[11]

Bukowski lived in a totally different world to the Beats, alternating long periods as a bum with temporary work. At the beginning of the '70s he said: "At one time I had this idea that one could live on a bus forever: travelling, eating, getting off, shitting, getting back on the bus. . . . I had the strange idea that one could stay in motion forever."[12] But he worried about work all the time and he was unable to apply the Beats' carefree attitude to his obligations. He wrote about it (starting his sentence as usual in the lower case, a question of aesthetics): "the years I have worked in slaughterhouses and factories and gas stations and so forth, these years do not allow me to accept the well-turned word for the sake of the well-turned word."[13] He would often tell journalists ironically: "It beats the eight hour job, doing what you are doing. It's better than the eight hour job. Don't you think?" In many respects writing was a way out of this fate. While the Beats

26

danced along the road composing a hymn to their freedom from social proprieties, Buk put in forty years to free himself from the shackles which alcohol and poetry alone helped him to forget at times. As an echo to Kerouac's lyrical motto "the only people for me are the mad ones, the ones who are mad to live, mad to talk," Bukowski, in a letter reproduced in *Reach for the Sun*, in 1992, two years before his death, states: "Thank the gods that the first 50 years of my life were spent with the Blue Collars and the truly mad, the truly beaten."[14] There is no lyricism in his vision of the road. The same year, he writes to an unknown correspondent: "I didn't want the road, I wanted to write so I needed some walls for that."[15]

For Bukowski, America was much more unsentimental than a lyrical poem in Kerouac's style. When he got off the bus in New York, he thought the city seemed more brutal than anywhere else in America. "When you have only $7 in your pocket and look up at those huge buildings . . . I went to every town broke in order to learn that town from the bottom. You come into a town from the top—you know, fancy hotels, fancy dinners, fancy drinks, money in your pocket—and you're not seeing that town at all."[16]

Nevertheless, the Beats were a frequent reference point for Bukowski. Much of his correspondence from the '60s highlights his necessity to place himself in relation to the Beat movement. In 1962 he wrote: "Now, the original Beats, as much as they were knocked, had the Idea. But they were flanked and overwhelmed by fakes, guys with nicely clipped beards, lonely hearts looking for free ass, limelighters, rhyming poets, homosexuals, bums, sightseers—the same thing that killed the Village."[17]

In a letter in October 1963 he noted: "Ginsberg has gotten out of it somehow so he has time to write even if he ends up writing badly. It's a gathering of dust and electrodes and a vomiting out, later. But he's got a better chance than if he was working in a Chinese Laundry or as Secretary of State—IF HE REMAINS UNPROFESSIONAL."[18]

Oct. 29, 1962

Dear Jon:

Got your long letter, and it is better to be plugged than
buried alive, but to me Art (poetry) is a continuous and continuing
process and that when a man fails to write good poetry he fails to
live fully or well. I have long been blessed by the gods both with
a late start in writing and a late type of semi-recognition. This
has kept me a workman and a human-being. By workman I do not mean
a time-clock puncher, of course., I have seen too many men wilt and
go silly under a little light, and then they continue to write and
get published, turning out pure crap under a name that has become a
bad habit. The next poem is all that counts. You can't stand on
past poems.

I hope that I d o not sound like a 42 year old crank but one
cannot be too careful. Being a nurse, you see a lot of decay and
death ####### physical and being an editor you also see the #####
psyche shit the sheets and Frost-out.

Anyhow, I am glad you found 6 poems that you could use.

Yes, do send me a copy of the present GALLOWS when it appears.
My thanks.

I do not have anything on hand # right now, and have not written
for a month or so, but will ship you more for a looksee in time.

As per publication, I am in present EPOS, NORTHWEST REVIEW,
MIDWEST, TARGETS, renaissance, and THE BLACK CAT REVIEW. Also
things to appear in future MIDWEST, ### BLACK CAT, renaissance,
SIGNET, RONGwRong or BRAND x, WORMWOOD REVIEW, EMERSON REVIEW,
EL CORNO EMPLUMADO, QUICKSILVER, maybe TARGETS (at least he still
holds one accepted); THE OUTSIDER, and maybe some I have forgotten.
Yes, I've thought of some more: COASTLINES and ###### NOMAD and
also MICA, and then EPOS is to bring out a special number containing
my poems which will be issued (I'm told) about mid-November. I
don't want to appear indifferent to acceptances but I do not write
them down.

Thank you for the good letter and the boosts.

Now I've thought of some more. I am in present OUTCRY with work
accepted for future issue. Then there is also SCHIMARTY or however
the hell you spell. They hold future work. Then there are some
mags that have accepted but have never appeared. Well, hell.

Luck and courage to you in re-adventure of GALLOWS.

                    hail,
                    Charles
                    Bukowski

Charles Bukowski
1623 N. Mariposa Ave.
Los Angeles 27, Calif.

A PROBLEM OF TEMPRAMENT

I played the radio all night the night of the 17th.
and the neighbors applauded
and the landlady knocked on the door
and said
PLEASE
PLEASE
PLEASE
MOVE,
you make the sheets dirty
and where does the blood come from?
you never work.
you lay around and talk to the radio
and drink
and you have a beard
and you are always smirking
and bringing those women
to your room
and you never comb your hair
or shine your shoes
and your shirts are wrinkled,
why don't you leave?
you are making the neighbors
    unhappy
you are making me
    unhappy,
please make us all happy
and go away!

go to hell, baby, I hissed through
the keyhole; mah rent's paid 'til
Wednesday. Can I show you a watercolor
nude painted in 1887 by an unknown German
artist? I have it insured for
$1,000.

Ungratiating, she stamped down the hall.
No artiste, she. I would
like to see her in the nude, though.
Perhaps I could paint my way
to freedom? No?

August 15, 1965: "It's a shame but—Ginsberg, Corso, the rest have been sucked in playing their entrails across the applause of the crowd, and they are dead and they know that they are dead, it's useless, they've skipped across, listened to the applause of half-drunk freaks too long too long, too long have they taken the bait."[19]

However, in a letter dated the previous day, when noting the books that he did not possess and that he would like to see republished, he begins his list with *Howl, On the Road, Gasoline* (by Corso) and *Naked Lunch*. These books were actually available, but he wasn't aware of it.[20] And he could at times show some admiration. In the second issue of the magazine *Ole* he confessed: "I've never said that before but I am now high enough as I write this to perhaps say that Ginsberg has been the most awakening force in American poetry since Walt W."[21] But recovering his self-control on October 25, 1965: "This is what disgusts me with the Ginsburg/Corso mob. they suck to the human adulation bit and are soon swallowed."[22]

The balance was evened out again when Buk wrote to his German translator, Carl Weissner, who also translated for Ginsberg and Burroughs: "How does it feel to be communicating with the Lights of the Age, and also with me. B. and G. have disappointed me at times, but let's admit that they have done things, and that no man creates pure Art day after day."[23]

Bukowski hinted that perhaps jealousy did play a part. "Corso? Ginsberg? maybe I am jealous of the big cats? they've got one thing I got—clarity of style, but they got a little too much the sweet tooth for their own soul (soul importance)."[24]

Very early on Bukowski had a reputation for downgrading others' work in order to show his own merits in a more favorable light. The fact that no one found favor with him—except himself occasionally—shouldn't be taken too seriously. This would miss the point that Bukowski was an artist of the grotesque. He magnified features, inflated, insulted and exaggerated. His writing parallels his drunken brawls in the backyards of sordid bars. Buk took on the world. Sometimes with fists, but particularly with words. Provocation, though, had one virtue in him—it put him in a combat situation, in the state for writing. Buk literally fought with words. His taunts aimed beyond the Beats, Henry Miller, Faulkner, etc. at the very status of the writer, even the status of writing. "I fired from both guns hoping to wake up the show," he writes in 1992. "An act of desperation against life and literature?"[25]

In his striking correspondence—and God knows that loner loved to correspond—it is as if he was directing a small interior play, where he could take people aside and complain and hurl abuse. He acts silently as if indispensible (but would Miller, Ginsberg and Corso have paid any attention to Bukowski's jabs as he was still totally unknown?). They were cutting remarks for his own personal use. He did not exclude himself from this fate, as a letter in February 1967 testifies: "I am not so worried about whether I am writing any good or not; I know I write a valley of bad stuff. but what gets me up is that nobody is coming on that I can believe in or look up to."[26] Bukowski never mocked himself as much as when he was boasting.

Recall Bukowski in the company of Anne Waldman and she paints you a strikingly accurate portrait (she is co-founder, with Ginsberg, of the Jack Kerouac School of Disembodied Poetics in Boulder, Colorado, and author of the collection of Beat poems, *Fast Speaking Woman*). She excels at putting each of the Beats in the correct part of the picture. Timothy Leary—the rogue, charlatan, fox. Burroughs—the man in the background, invisible, the secret agent. Ginsberg—the old mad man who right to the end of his life jumps up in the air, dancing and singing fearless of ridicule. Where does Bukowski figure in the picture? "He is like the ugly old man, the dirty old man, almost like out of a Grimm's fairy tale! You know, the myth of the gnome, or the hunchback, or the ugly father figure, who has also this very purulent side, and sexual side. That's very attractive, it's part of our psyche to be attracted to that. But he is also the artist and the writer, he is articulate, he can express this vision of the world . . . He is amazing, really, because he has a beat on some mystery of the American consciousness and psyche, he has got some beat on that . . . the low life, the quality to strip bare all the weariness of the world."[27]

Stripping reality bare was Buk's objective. He refused to be taken in and rejected even the myth of the writer, all the more so when the writer claims to be "committed." In a letter he wrote: "Pros seem to turn to pricks, finally. See Mailer, Genet, Burroughs, Ginsberg, who the hell else? showing at the Chicago Yippie thing. As giants of Humanity? Bullshit. As Giants of Publicity."[28]

The "big yippie thing" was the huge demonstration in Chicago on the fringe of the Democratic Convention August 24-29, 1968. Norman Mailer who was covering the event for *Harper's* wrote that it was only one of the events "which took place during a continuing five-day battle in the streets and parks of Chicago between some of the minions of the high established, and some of the nihilistic of the young."[29] In April the assassination of Martin Luther King Jr. had led to riots throughout the USA; Robert Kennedy was assassinated on June 6; the mayor of Chicago feared the worst—and 10,000 young people had turned up in his city. Among them were Ginsberg, Burroughs and Jean Genet.

Ginsberg feared the Maoïst elements would get out of hand and he asked the authorities to install a system of amplifiers and microphones in Lincoln Park so that he could address the crowd if necessary. In an attempt to keep the peace Ginsberg got on the stage and sang Hare Krishna for quarter of an hour accompanying himself on the harmonium, interpreting William Blake's "Grey Monk" that he had set to music.

Ginsberg at a Vietnam Peace Rally, New York City, March 26, 1966.

© Fred W. McDarrah

Suddenly there was an inexplicable rush from the police. Panic. The demonstration erupted. Ginsberg climbed to the

top of a small mound and sat in the lotus position chanting the mantra "Ommm." Others joined him. The long vibration—which helped Ginsberg restore his inner peace—grew louder, taken up by thousands of voices! The chant—Ooommmmmm Ooooomm—lasted seven hours! Ginsberg finished it in a kind of ecstasy. "If there'd been any panic and police clubs I don't think I would have minded the damage. Clubbing would have seemed a curiously impertinent intrusion from skeleton phantoms—unreal compared with the natural omnipresent electric universe I was in . . . The fear of death was gone . . . I was in a revolutionary mass of electricity. I was in a dimension of feeling other than the normal one of save-your-own-skin. . . . This was the most interesting thing that happened, for me, in Chicago."[30]

Allen Ginsberg on the scene with the Grateful Dead in Golden Gate Park, February 1967.

It really is difficult to imagine Bukowski indulging in this, however excessive he could be. Shortly after the event, and in complete contradiction with the opinion at the time, he expressed his astonishment in the underground newspaper *Open City*: "the thing in Prague has dampened a lot of boys who have forgotten Hungary. they hang in the parks with the Che idol, with pictures of Castro in their amulets, going Ooommmmm Ooooooommm while William Burroughs, Jean Genet and Allen Ginsberg lead them . . . it's one thing to talk about Revolution while three jackass writers of international fame have you dancing to the Oooooooooommm game; it's another thing to bring it about, it's another thing to have happen. Paris, 1870-71, 20,000 people murdered in the streets, the streets as red with blood as with rain, and the rats coming out and eating at the bodies."[31] He finished his attack with: "there is only one place to write and that is ALONE at a typewriter. a writer who has to go INTO the streets is a writer who does not know the streets." A year earlier he had already written to Weissner: "no school, ho, no politic, just the typer and the walls."[32]

Jack Kerouac draped in the American flag at a gathering
with Ken Kesey and the Merry Pranksters, 1964.

KEROUAC,
BEAT AND REACTIONARY

It was when Kerouac held himself at a similar distance from the '60s that he possibly related to Bukowski. Kerouac generated the whole movement. Bukowski mocked it, and claimed to put a definitive end to it. Neither felt close to the beat scene. As for underground events and antiestablishment activities in the '60s, both remained apolitical and claimed their sole capacity as poet and writer.

Towards the end of his life and until his death in 1969, aged 47, Jack watched the children of the '60s from afar. He considered the beatniks, hippies, proto-hippies, Maoïsts, protesters and '68ers as strange descendants that he could not have created; in no way could he believe that they had come from him (paternity was not his strong point—he never recognized Jan, the daughter he had during his short second marriage to Joan Haverty). He would probably have been very skeptical about virtual reality, cyberspace, the Internet and e-mail, extolled by Leary. In *The Dharma Bums* of 1958 he caricatured a world cut off from its intimate links with nature, completely media-orientated, and eventually embodied it in the global village of McLuhan. He expressed his bitterness towards all the houses lined up on the roadside: "with lawns and television sets in each living room with everybody looking at the same thing and thinking the same thing at the same time while the Japhies of the world go prowling in the wilderness to hear the voice crying in the wilderness, to find the ecstasy of the stars, to find the dark mysterious secret of the origin of faceless wonderless crapulous civilisation."

Originally "Beat" was an imprecise term created in Times Square, New York by the poet and thief Herbert Huncke. Kerouac took the term and gave it content. At the beginning, the expression was quite meaningless—"Man, I'm beat," Huncke would say. He hadn't a cent to his name, he slept in the Underground, it didn't really bother him that nothing ever went right. Straight away, seeing the light in Huncke's eyes, the light that radiated from him, Kerouac understood that "beat" didn't simply mean worn out, but also blessed— blessed because he was worn out. This light contradicted the apparent state of degeneration that the expression entailed.

In 1948 John Clellon Holmes (future chronicler of the movement) asked how Kerouac would characterize the term, and conscious of Huncke's words he replied: "I guess you might say we're a beat generation." Holmes used the expression for the first time in a famous article in *The Sunday Times* on November 16, 1952, and also in his novel *Go* in which he used Kerouac's material (but obviously not his innovative strength!)—*On the Road* appeared only five years afterwards in 1957.

In its simplicity, beat is a word rich in potential. Kerouac, as we attribute the label to him, thought of several other expressions before settling on beat—without giving it too precise a shape. Beat may mean weariness, disenchanted rejection of a conformist society and material values, but Jack gave it an essentially positive value. From 1954 onwards he gave the word a spiritual connotation in order to avoid being confused with the young delinquents and rebels fashionable because of *The Wild Ones* and *Blackboard Jungle*. He associated beat with Buddhist beatitudes, then with Christian beati-

Kerouac as he leaves a party at the Artist's Club,
New York City, New Year's Eve, 1958.

tudes, a reflection of his Catholic childhood—he constantly recalled these dimensions of the term, particularly from 1957 onwards when the Beats came to public attention. The meaning of the word beat was constantly twisted, often redefined in complete contradiction to the sense that Kerouac had given it.

Ken Kesey, Eugene, Oregon alongside his psychedelic bus Furthur, 1998.

While a whole antiestablishment generation laid claim to him, Kerouac very quickly felt that his intentions were generally misunderstood. Ginsberg told of Jack's stupor in July 1964 when Kesey's psychedelic-colored bus stopped in the middle of the night in front of him in Northport. Kesey was the most colorful and craziest of the hippie movement. Tom Wolfe, author of *Bonfire of the Vanities*, devoted a whole book to him in 1968 entitled *The Electric Kool-Aid Acid Test*.[1]

The sight of the psychedelic bus was a big shock to Jack, who had returned home to live with his mother (whom he called Mémère) and had become a has-been drowned in whisky. The driver of the mythical bus was the equally mythical Neal Cassady, hero of *On the Road*.[2] According to some, Neal was but a shadow of his former self, high on amphetamines, hardened, vacant; but according to others, including Tom Wolfe, he was never in better form! He had spent two years in Alcatraz (1958-1960) after he was caught with two grams of marijuana. Partly thanks to Kesey and his Merry Pranksters, Neal Cassady once again became a living symbol, the incarnation of a whole new generation. William Plummer wrote in his biography devoted to Cassady, *The Holy Goof*: "With Kerouac and Ginsberg, Cassady was an enfant terrible; with Kesey and Co., he was a monstre sacré."[3]

In 1963 the psychedelic journey across the USA from West to East by Kesey, Neal and the Pranksters was the exact repetition, but in the opposite direction, of the trip Kerouac and Neal had made from East to West, related in *On the Road*. The travellers in the bus "Further" must have been conscious of this symbolic dimension to their trip—homage, re-enactment and renewal of the myth. Plummer wrote: "In most every aspect the latent content of Kerouac and Cassady's comparatively modest picaresque fantasy was made manifest, turned inside out, and projected onto a larger screen."[4]

Now the bus had stopped outside Kerouac's home in Northport. On board were: Neal—a ghost from his past, and Allen—the spokesman of a new generation for which Jack felt no affinity. Nevertheless, he went to the elegant apartment on Park Avenue on the Upper East Side where Ken Kesey and the Merry Pranksters led a hellish ball. Kesey—the dazzled reader of *On the Road* and author of *One Flew Over the Cuckoo's Nest*, published in 1962 and later adapted for the cinema by Milos Forman. On their arrival, the disorder was indescribable. Music at full blast, gear and cables everywhere. Shit and acid.[5]

So many legends were reunited—Kerouac, Cassady, Ginsberg and Kesey. Although each of them was expecting fireworks at this meeting, there was nothing! Kerouac and Kesey didn't click at all and scarcely spoke a word to each other. Tom Wolfe wrote: "Here was Kerouac, and here was Kesey and here was Cassady in between them."[6] It was as if

Upper left: Cassady and his two passions: a car and a girl, 1960. Center: Kesey in bus Furthur, 1998.

the passing of the baton between Kerouac and Kesey had happened before, indefinably in the past. Neal was the only one of the two primitive Beat legends to be reborn like a phoenix to incarnate a generation "wilder and weirder out on the road."[7] Kerouac had no desire to undergo this transformation. He refused the drugs offered him, limited himself to a glass of red wine from time to time and was outraged when one of the Pranksters tied an American flag around his neck. The sofa was also covered with the national flag, so Jack was not keen to sit on it and folded it up before taking a seat. This earned him gibes from the Pranksters, and Kesey, in vain, tried to smooth things over with flattery: "Jack, your place in history is secure. —I know," retorted Jack icily.[8]

In *The Electric Kool-Aid Acid Test* Tom Wolfe concluded from this evening that: "It was like hail and farewell. Kerouac was the old star. Kesey was the wild new comet from the West heading Christ knew where."[9] Ginsberg also talked gloomily of the night: "History was even out of Jack's hands now, he'd already written it 15 years before, he could only watch hopelessly one of his more magically colored prophecy shows."[10]

Was this really the fulfillment of one of Kerouac's most colorful prophecies? Maybe, on the contrary, the misunderstanding was complete and there was neither link nor continuity between his perspective and the counterculture of the '60s. In "The Origins of the Beat Generation," an article which *Playboy* commissioned from him in 1959, Kerouac clearly stated that it was not his intention to speak and write "against," but to speak and write "for." "I want to speak for things, for the crucifix I speak out, for the Star of Israel I speak out, for the divinest man who ever lived who was a German (Bach) I speak out . . . ."[11] His best books—*On the Road, The Dharma Bums, The Subterraneans* and *Visions of Cody*—are all stamped with a wild and pure petulance; a sincerity and a kind of positive wonder towards life; a confident support for a certain natural order which seduced his first readers. It is uncertain whether Kerouac ever wanted to challenge the established order. Any nostalgia he had was not for a future utopia, but for a utopia well and truly past—and for tradition. His quest was for origins (the first ecstasy, sensations, powers, rhythms and musicality of language—American and French—a quest for his Breton ancestors: he liked to sign his letters Jean Lebris de Kerouac).

He repeated his sole and greatest expectation many times, even in front of television cameras when he could not make himself understood by his interviewers. In both life and writing, this expectation was to approach "the face of God." As the years passed and he lost his first interest in Buddhism, the term *beat* in his mind was gradually associated more with the beatitudes of Catholicism that had never left him. This was one of the reasons he immediately liked Timothy Leary—Leary, with Ginsberg, introduced him to psilocybine in January, 1961. Leary, like Kerouac, had been brought up a good Catholic in Massachusetts and both were distinguished athletes in high school. Ginsberg and Leary wanted to include Kerouac in their messianic hopes. The experience did not go well. Leary had his first bad trip and Kerouac disappointed his companions' expectations with this disenchanted remark: "Walking on water wasn't made in a day."

However, Jack did try the psychedelic experience again at the end of that year, 1961, shortly after completing *Big Sur*, which he wrote in ten days on Benzedrine. Not content with celebrating the achievement with a case of cognac, he took a dozen psilocybin mexicana mushrooms, supplied by Leary, in a single afternoon. In a state of euphoria he took Leary with him to a snow-covered Lower East Side, before sinking into depression and a disheartening certainty that whatever drug you take, life is decidedly pointless. What good is this mad race that makes us believe that there is still further to go after we have crossed the finishing line? This was vastly different to the hopes of the Beat and hippie generation. And when

Leary again asked his permission to publish the account from the first experience—which Jack had promised—he had no success. Jack refused, arguing that it was merely communist brainwashing techniques.[12]

Nine years later in 1969, one month before his death, Kerouac published an article in the *Chicago Tribune Magazine* entitled "What Am I Thinking About" which the editorial staff changed to "After me, the Deluge." In it, he described his disenchantment with a movement whose origin was still attributed to him, in which he saw only illiteracy: "Really, so What's New if they would like to see to it that under Timothy Leary's guiding proselytization no one in America could address a simple envelope or keep a household budget or a checkbook balanced or for that matter legible."[13] If Thoreau commended civil disobedience, it didn't prevent him leading a very strict life in *Walden*, and keeping the most detailed accounts. It is easy to imagine Kerouac prone to a similar rigor, faced with a movement that disoriented him with its excesses and an anarchy of which he disapproved.

Already back in 1958, Kerouac believed the authentic Beat spirit belonged to a bygone era, limited to the second half of the '40s and the beginning of the '50s. He wrote in a magazine: "In actuality there was only a handful of real hip swinging cats and what there was vanished mighty swiftly during the Korean War [1950-1953] when (and after) a sinister new kind of efficiency appeared in America."[14] According to him, the rest (the postponed publication of *Howl*, *On the Road* and *Naked Lunch* published years later) was nothing more than literature. He added that ". . . the beat characters after 1950 vanished into jails and madhouses, or were shamed into silent conformity; the generation itself was short-lived and small in number."

What remained of all this in 1958? Was it merely a fashion statement or something more closely linked to the Beat movement? Maybe the dawn of the rock generation looked to the original Beat movement (clothes, look, etc.) only to gain

William Burroughs and Kerouac locked in mortal combat, 1953.

from it an extra mythical basis—a need for a basis in the literary field to find equivalents to the icons in film and music. Perhaps it is significant that several of Kerouac's manuscripts which had been kicking around various agents and publishers since 1951 (*On the Road, The Subterraneans, Dr Sax, Mexico City Blues, Maggie Cassidy* and *Visions of Cody*) were suddenly published from September 1957 onwards. This was two years after the success of the film *Blackboard Jungle* and Bill Haley's song "Rock around the Clock." It was the time when the rock wave was reaching its height (Jerry Lee Lewis, another apostle of spontaneity, burst on to the stage and stood on his piano wailing "Whole Lotta Shakin' Goin' On"). It was the time when the whole baby boom generation woke up and gave full rein to its aspirations for new freedoms. In 1961 Bob Dylan was the first artist of the new generation to seal the link, loudly affirming his attachment to the Beats, explicit in the choice of song titles like "Subterranean Homesick Blues," "Desolation Row," and "Visions of Johanna." He was touched by the poetry of *Mexico City Blues* (and by Presley's music: on his death in 1977, Dylan didn't speak for a week).

Back from the Navy and now studying at the university, the still unknown Thomas Pynchon, future author of *Gravity's Rainbow* noted in *Slow Learner* that "We were at a transition point, a strange post-Beat passage of cultural time, with our loyalties divided. As bop and rock'n'roll were to swing music and postwar pop, so was this new writing to the more established modernist tradition we were being exposed to then in college. . . . It looked as if the attitude of some literary folks toward the Beat generation was the same as that of certain officers on my ship toward Elvis Presley."[15]

Although these books had been written several years before James Dean and Elvis Presley exploded on to the scene, Kerouac only became famous in September 1957 with the publication of *On the Road*. The social scene had finally caught up with Beat literature, a few years belatedly. At this time all Kerouac's dormant texts in publishing houses were at last published—he completed one of his best books, *The Dharma Bums*—and he started to decline. Joyce Johnson, his girlfriend at the time, tells in *Minor Characters* about when he saw the review of *On the Road* in the *New York Times* that would make him famous the next day. She thought it bizarre that he showed none of the joy that she had expected; in fact he appeared troubled.[16]

Several months later when considering this belated recognition, he gave a retrospective account of the whole phenomenon in an article published in *Esquire* entitled "The Philosophy of the Beat Generation." He commented on the strange germination of a Beat generation whose impact up until then had been dead and buried: "by some miracle of metamorphosis, suddenly the Korean postwar youth emerged cool and beat, had picked up the gestures and the

Cover from one of the pocketbook editions of *On the Road.*

style: soon it was everywhere, the new look, the "twisted" slouchy look; finally it began to appear even in movies (James Dean) and on television . . . the bop visions became common property of the commercial, popular, cultural world . . . and even the clothes style of the beat hipsters carried over to the new rock'n'roll youth via Montgomery Clift (leather jacket), Marlon Brando (T-shirt) and Elvis Presley (long sideburns), and the Beat Generation, though dead, was resurrected and justified."[17]

In June 1959 in the famous article in *Playboy* he expressed the same opinion: "'Beat Generation'" has simply become the slogan or label for a revolution of manners in America. . . . People began to call themselves beatniks, beats, jazzniks, bopniks, bugniks and finally I was called the 'avatar' of all this. . . . And so now they have beatnik routines on TV, starting with satires about girls in black and fellows in jeans with snapknives and sweatshirts and swastikas tattooed under their armpits . . . ."[18]

For Kerouac the dregs must have been hard to swallow at times. He was snubbed by those who embodied the era and who had inherited and adopted the Beat spirit. This was the case with Marlon Brando. At first Brando was interested in filming *On the Road* (Paramount was ready to buy the rights in 1957), but he then decided that the plot was too loose. Kerouac's admiration for him did not weaken. At the end of 1960 when he was depressed and disillusioned with his writing career, Jack haunted the Actor's Studio thinking of starting a career as an actor (he gave up on the idea very quickly). One of his friends had to dissuade him from asking Brando for an autograph. When the two finally did meet, Kerouac told Brando how much he had liked him in *On the Waterfront* and invited him for a drink—Brando declined.[19]

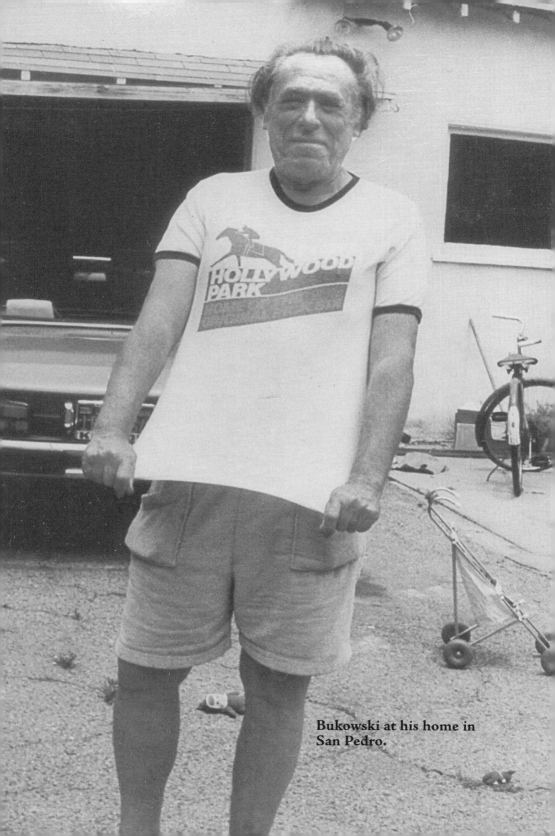

Bukowski at his home in
San Pedro.

BUK GOES DOWN IN LEGEND WITH THE BEATS

The text—in which Bukowski ironically depicts Ginsberg, Burroughs and Genet as sorcerer's apprentices, completely and comically overwhelmed by events at the Convention in Chicago of 1968, despite their conspiratorial OOOOOOOMMMMM OOOOOMMM—was resumed in the first edition of *Notes of a Dirty Old Man* in 1969 and in the second in 1973 published by City Lights, the publishing house founded by Lawrence Ferlinghetti, one of the poets at the origin of the poetic renaissance in San Francisco in the '50s. Ferlinghetti is also the editor par excellence of the Beat generation, who inflamed the country when he published Ginsberg's *Howl* in 1956.

It was Ferlinghetti (Lorenzo who lends his cabin to Kerouac in *Big Sur*) who welcomed Bukowski on to the City Lights' catalogue. A French translator of Bukowski's works writes in a recent postscript to *Notes*: "A happy time when taste did not allow itself to be reduced to defending a clan!"[1] Because, in this collection, Bukowski also laid in to William Burroughs: "the only junky who can make it is William Burroughs, who owns the Burroughs Co., almost, and who can play it tough while all along being a sissy fat wart-sucking hog inside." His work is cut down to size in a single sentence:

"Burroughs is a very dull writer and without the insistence of knowledgeable pop in his literary background, he would be almost nothing."[2]

This is revelatory of Buk's feeling of exclusion—the world of pop-literature is a world of relationships, as opposed to his own. As mentioned before, his only relationships were the drunken brawls in the backyards of bars that Barbet Schroeder directed in the film *Barfly* (based on Bukowski's script).

At the time Bukowski jeered at the Beats, he had no idea that he, too, would soon have to face the bright lights of fame, swagger in the public eye and play the role expected of him. Ironically in autumn 1974 he even went on a tour of readings with some of the most famous Beats. He wrote about it to a correspondent:"Been on the reading kick . . . the old survival suck . . . Detroit, Riverside, Santa Cruz . . . Ginsberg, Ferlinghetti, Snyder at S.C. drew 1,600 at 3 bucks a head."[3] As it was the first time he had met Ginsberg, Buk could not resist recording a few impressions of him, all the

City Lights, the publishing house founded by Lawrence Ferlinghetti.

more so as an incident allowed him to emphasize the portrait: "There was a bomb threat and old Allen's ears jumped. He got on stage and improvised a poem about the situation. . . . Next day we hung around town testing the bars. . . . Ginsberg was all right, he seemed a good sort."

From the end of the '60s two important things happened to Bukowski. First, the interest shown by Lawrence Ferlinghetti. It is clear that the attention that Ferlinghetti gave Buk could only flatter him, even if "he stated categorically that he did not feel a part of the underground."[4]

Ferlinghetti had read some of Buk's poems and short stories published in small private magazines. From 1964 onwards Buk was published in *Ole*, founded by Douglas Blazek, a young poet from Illinois who was attracted by the distance Bukowski put between himself and the Beat generation. "I could identify with Bukowski from working in the foundries. . . . Bukowski opened up an aperture to explore from another point of view."[5]

"Making poetry dangerous" was Blazek's aim, a sentiment with which Buk would have agreed wholeheartedly. The young editor was so pleased with Buk's first and sensational contribution that he quoted him in the first issue: "Poetry is dying on the vine like a whore on the end stool on a Monday night." His intention, all the same, was to disprove this provocative statement. Blazek commented: "*Ole* is hoping to prove Mr. Buk wrong."[6] Buk was delighted to find his own poems in his post box, badly printed on a cheap mimeo, unpolished and crude—how true! It is interesting to note that at that time he was already 44, but via *Ole*, the dirty old man touched the young generation who saw itself in its rejections and dislikes, in the mix of tenderness, hardness, madness and the grotesque in his poetry and prose.

Ole also featured the poet Harold Norse, another of the underground greats and friend of Ginsberg, Burroughs and Michaux. In 1967, when Norse was in London, Nicos

Stangos (responsible for poetry at Penguin) proposed devoting a book to his work. Norse was amazed. He wrote to Stangos: "I thought only T. S. Eliot, W. H. Auden and Ezra Pound got single volumes from publishing houses like Penguin!"[7] Norse chose two other poets to accompany his work in the "Penguin Modern Poets" series—the Beat surrealist Philip Lamantia, and Charles Bukowski: "I chose him and Lamantia, also little known then, solely because each of us had an individual style that was unique and forceful and deserved to be better known. Stangos was astonished at first that I didn't accept a solo book. Then he saw the power of the book containing the three of us and agreed enthusiastically to it. The Penguin anthology brought us international attention."[8]

This was the second determining event for Bukowski that helped him to believe more in himself. On hearing that he would appear in the Penguin catalogue, Buk wrote to Carl

Harold Norse. Bukowski referred to him as the "Prince of Poetry."

Weissner: " . . . it appears Norse and myself and one other, maybe Lamantia, will possibly appear in their next poet's series of 3-in-a-book. which would feel very strange to me."[9] We can appreciate this feeling when reading Norse's *Memoirs of a Bastard Angel* that appeared twenty years later: "Charles Bukowski, whom nobody had ever heard of . . ."[10]

When Norse decided on his companion from *Ole*, he had never actually met Bukowski. Their meeting took place in January 1969. Norse wrote in his *Memoirs*: "From his first drunken letters, I knew that a wild Falstaffian ruffian had come to shake things up with more fiction than fact, more fantasy than truth." He painted one of the most striking pictures of Buk ever created: "Bukowski was misshapen—a big hunchback with a ravaged, pock-marked face, decayed nicotine-stained teeth, and pain-filled green eyes. Flat brown hair seemed pasted to an oversized skull—hips broader than shoulders, hands grotesquely small and soft. A beer gut sagged over his belt. He wore a white shirt, baggy pants, an ill-fitting suit, the kind convicts receive when released from prison. He looked like one, down and out."[11]

Bukowski had a wild attack of nerves at the thought of meeting someone he considered to be among the greatest.

He also knew what he owed to Norse. "Buk admits this in the letters [he wrote to me]. He got his first big fame through me."[12] If until then "he was jealous and envious of Burroughs and Ginsberg—he was unknown when they became famous," he could now let those kinds of feelings of rejection fade away. Fortunately, a mutual admiration grew between the two men through their letters. Norse wrote: "His were explosive with pain and humor, an amazing amalgam of wordplay, ripe, earthy, vulgar; his language leapt from the page like a Van Gogh, galvanic, whirling, immediate, full of raw violence, color and light; he was an American Dylan Thomas but bolder, cruder, meaner, more daring, not stuck in tradition."[13] When they spoke on the phone, Norse was also aware of the suffering apparent in Buk's voice, "a slow weary drawl, not hysterical, but measured, controlled, unutterably sad."[14]

Even though Buk styled Norse "Prince Hal, the prince of poetry," Norse did not find it easy to tolerate his friend's competitive streak, apparent when he was drunk—which was frequently the case after five o' clock in the afternoon. Norse said: "I believe his hurt eyes got their color from envy and jealousy. He'd shout "I'm Charles Bukowski. Watch my steam, baby. I'm the king, I'm the greatest."[15] When he had sobered up again the next morning Buk was "a lamb, literally sheepish with shame and guilt."

Success came to Buk in 1972 after the City Lights' publication of *Erections, Ejaculations, Exhibitions and General Tales of Ordinary Madness*. Ferlinghetti confessed to Norse during the summer of 1971 that while he had missed out on Bukowski's poetry, he planned to publish all his available prose, six or seven hundred pages, convinced that he would be one of the greatest names of literature in the future.[16]

Something else clicked in to place when Buk was invited to San Francisco for a reading. He stayed, with his companion, Linda King (not to be confused with Linda Lee Beighle who became Mrs. Bukowski in 1985), at Ferlinghetti's, a small three-bedroom apartment above City Lights. At first he was nervous. Cherkovski notes: "Only when he met Ferlinghetti, an easy-going man with soft blue eyes and a kindly disposition, was he able to relax. He enjoyed the treatment he received as a peer of a world-famous poet, a man widely read and translated since the mid-fifties."[17]

The reading itself "was more a sports event than a poetry reading."[18] In front of a white-hot audience Buk, extravagant and drunk, indulged in a show of obscenities and antics. He declared many times afterwards that this kind of event made him sick, literally and figuratively—frequently he threw up in the hours beforehand. But from that evening onwards Bukowski was aware of his showman and quasi-rock star qualities. Joe Wolberg, the organizer, noted: "I think when he saw the people packed into this huge gym he really understood how big an impact he was making on his readers. He had never been lionized like this before, and I think it really unnerved him, although he would never admit to it."[19]

Buk really got into his stride at this kind of performance on November 25, 1974 during the aforementioned 2nd annual Santa Cruz Poetry Festival, held at the coffee shop the Catalyst, and thereafter. He felt that he had caught up with the Beats, if not surpassed them, with regard to fame. So much so that he no longer harbored the slightest inferiority complex in relation to them (if he ever had one). In the presence of Ginsberg or Gary Snyder, for example, he gave

Bob Kaufman, Gregory Corso, Hal Norse, Neeli Cherkovski.

Lawrence Ferlinghetti, Allen Ginsberg, Hal Norse, and others.

full rein to his extravagant behavior, no longer hesitating to occupy front stage.

Linda King, his girlfriend at the time, who was one of the guest poets (along with Jack Micheline, Ferlinghetti, etc.) clearly recalls the wild party after the reading in a house near the ocean: "Bukowski hardly knew Ginsberg. In fact I think he met him for the first time that night and he was drunk out of his mind, forcing drinks into Ginsberg's hand. He was insulting him, but it wasn't serious and Ginsberg knew it. It was more like he was teasing and testing him. He was being 'drunk Bukowski.' He was pretty wild that night . . . They were San Francisco, he was Los Angeles."[20]

The *Berkeley Barb* of December 6-12, 1974 gave a memorable account of the event, giving the leading role to Bukowski who "unlike most poets was accessible." Ric Reynolds writes: "He didn't stand in a corner watching others with sad or cold poetic eyes. He pushed on you and covered you with drunken hands. While everyone watched Bukowski make an ass of himself, his mind was churning up the scene . . . When Allen Ginsberg arrived at the party, Bukowski latched on to him and buried him under his shoulder. 'Ladies and gentlemen,' Bukowski shouted, 'we've got Allen Ginsberg as guest of honor tonight. Can you believe it? Allen Ginsberg!'" The praise was both sincere and tinged with jealousy. A kind of internal suffering drove Buk to literally drown Ginsberg under lavish compliments, killing him with exaggeration. He drew Ginsberg up tighter: "'A man of genius, the first poet to cut through light and consciousness for two thousand years . . . Have a drink, Allen.'" Ginsberg was sensitive and slightly defensive in the face of such a demonstrative approach: "Bukowski hugged Ginsberg closer and he rubbed Bukowski's back: 'That feels good Allen, real good. No lie.' Ginsberg had been taken in by all the flattery, but when he saw that Bukowski was going to force some booze down his throat he slumped into a fake drunken brawl and said that he had been drinking all night." Buk immediately made the parallel between this small deception and the deception that he believed characterized Allen's work from then on: "'God, it's good to see you Allen really. I don't care if you are a fake. Did you hear that folks? Washed up. Everybody knows that after *Howl* you never wrote anything worth a shit. How about that folks, a vote? Has Allen written anything worth a shit since *Howl* and *Kay'dish?*'"

Even though Ginsberg himself was provocative, a political agitator, he was far too civilized to produce an adequate riposte to this kind of attack (a real blow to the stomach). He was on a completely different wavelength and gave a mechanical response:

"'Kah'dish,' Ginsberg said, correcting Bukowski."

This type of cultural, academic response could obviously only intensify Buk's barbs and irony. "Allen, you're tearing me apart. You're a barracuda, Allen. Eating me up with your tongue.'" Yet Buk, ambivalent as ever, also sought to calm the confrontation and keep it under control by suggesting, as usual, the magic cure-all, alcohol: "'Hey, why don't you have another drink?'" And Reynolds reports, "Bukowski ripped a drink out of someone's hand, drank half of it, stuck it in Ginsberg's hand. Ginsberg took a sip of the Jack Daniels straight and nearly vomited, thinking it was wine. As Bukowski turned he dashed for it, slipping away through the crowd."

This is all typical Bukowski and we must also admire the way Reynolds depicts this whole scene, with all the comical humor required, perfectly in tune with the atmosphere that Bukowski's presence conferred to the party, that's to say a kind of apocalyptic touch: "Bukowski was finally talked into leaving after he tried to smash one of the swinging light fixtures, and the floor was covered with broken glass and your feet stuck to the linoleum because of all the drinks he had dropped." It was around 3 a.m.

Barb

Partying with the Poets

—Charles Bukowski

Apparently, Ginsberg did not hold these outbursts against Hank. In *Whitman's Wild Children*, Cherkovski relates an episode that took place thirteen years later when he was celebrating Halloween with Ginsberg and the Italian journalist Fernanda Pivano, the Beats' good friend and translator.[21] The conversation came round to Buk, and Pivano, who met him in 1980, suggested calling him. Cherkovski did so and after exchanging a few words with Buk passed the phone to Fernanda, who then passed it onto Ginsberg. If Ginsberg was not overly enthusiastic about speaking with the Dirty Old Man, he did not show it. What did they say to one another? Although it seemed like just a few banal sentences, it was significant as that was all that was needed for them to know where they stood with each other again. They casually stated starkly different and antagonistic attitudes towards their philosophy of literary work. Banal in appearance, this brief conversation was in fact a fresh heated exchange between Buk and one of the most eminent Beat representatives.

Cover of *Laughing with the Gods*—Pivano's interview.

Allen immediately set the conversation on an objective and professional terrain, thereby avoiding any great emotional or human stakes. However, unwittingly or not, he could not prevent himself from provoking Buk. He told Buk right away that he had engaged an agent to manage his work. Buk displayed surprise and shock—how could a poet take an agent! Buk found this completely incompatible with poetic requirements, quite incongruous! (We, his readers, witness here something of Buk's firmly held belief that the only things that a poet needed were a typewriter and a wall to sit in front of.) However, Ginsberg gave an astute response about the role of literary agents: "No, they do the business for you!" Why not off-load subsidiary tasks onto those whose job it is to deal with them? Surely this frees up more time for poetry? Unburdened of pointless concerns, the poet can devote himself completely to his work . . . Buk was not ready to parry this blow. Driven back against the ropes as in a boxing match, caught on the hop, he merely replied flatly: "It wouldn't work for me." He was shutting his eyes to his own situation since his editor, John Martin, spared him the trouble of anything of a commercial nature, leaving him entirely free to devote himself to writing.

Later during that evening, in order to redress the balance against these outbursts and to reassure Allen that they did not necessarily mar a deeper admiration, Cherkovski told a visibly flattered Ginsberg something that he had never previously heard. Around 1965, in the mimeographed magazine *Ole*, Bukowski paid him a compliment that appeared to come from the heart! Cherkovski quoted Buk to Ginsberg who was in seventh heaven: "I believe I'm high enough now to say that Ginsberg has been the most awakening force in American poetry since Walt W."22

The expression "I'm high enough . . ." indicates (as well as an advanced state of alcoholism) how exceptional, indeed unique, this praise was. There would never be praise on such a level again. This is symptomatic of one of Bukowski's traits of which he was relatively aware. His mood swings and shifts of character frequently made him unpredictable and regularly baffled those who came close to him. Harold Norse clearly depicted this Bukowskian phenomenon in the preface to his forthcoming book of correspondence with Buk: "If he put you on a pedestal he'd also knock it over. It was a bumpy ride on a roller-coaster. Though his admiration was genuine, ups and downs were the norm in his relationships."23

Showered with praise by some, subjected to public criticism or ignored by others (the literary establishment for starters), Buk's renown corresponded exactly to the demands of his temperament. In December 1974, he said to *London Magazine* that he didn't care whether his work was praised to the skies or shot down in flames, he just wanted readers to be touched: "I want reactions to my work, whether they be good or bad; but I like an ad-mixture [*sic*]. I don't want to be totally revered or looked upon as a holy man or a miracle worker. I want a certain amount of attack, because it makes it more human, more like where I've been living all my life. I've always been attacked in one fashion or another, and it's grown on me. A little rejection is good for the soul; but total attack, total rejection is utterly destructive. So I want a good balance: praise, attack, the whole stewpot full of everything."[24]

Buk had gone down in legend with Burroughs, Ginsberg and Genet. However, it was still difficult to imagine him participating in demonstrations or sit-ins . . . Participation would assume a share in utopia, the dream of its possible realization, a political will that he did not possess. It was impossible for him to speak on behalf of others, on behalf of the people, because he was a man of the crowd, "a man made of all men and who is worth all of them and what is anyone worth," as Sartre said in *Words*.

Buk preferred Bach's music to Bob Dylan and Joan Baez's protest songs. His social commitment was virtually zero. "I don't want to get as holy about being active and involved with mankind as Camus did . . . ."[25] Undoubtedly, Buk had never heard of Cioran (his *Tears and Saints* was not published in the USA until 1995, although we can read an article by him in *Evergreen* No. 6, Autumn, 1958) but in many ways he, more than Sartre or Camus, was cut out to be Buk's speaker among French writers of that time. There are certain aphorisms in *Notes* that Cioran, with his ironic nihilism, would definitely have agreed with: "each of our joys is a bargain with the devil," "the well balanced individual is insane," "a brave man lacks imagination. Cowardice is usually caused by lack of proper diet," "almost everybody is born a genius and buried an idiot."

Buk's view that the possible destruction of the human race did not bother him in the slightest, as told to the Italian journalist Fernanda Pivano in 1980, should be taken at face value.[26] Pivano concluded that the source of this statement was a fundamental nihilism (if this is the case, Buk is poles apart from the Beats and Kerouac who wrote in 1958: "I prophesy that the Beat Generation which is supposed to be nutty nihilism in the guise of new hipness, is going to be the most sensitive generation in the history of America and therefore it can't help but do good").[27] In fact, despite the apparent realism and harshness of his texts, their rough and crude aspect, there was a side to Bukowski close to the romantic complaint that he could never rid himself of (even though he claimed to loathe romanticism, which prevented him from fully admiring Hemingway). Just as the so-called nihilist Cioran stated quite correctly that he could never shake off his "Russian Byronism."

Buk was afraid, above all, of deluding himself. He was a million miles away from the great hopes cherished by the Beats, and then by the hippie generation: nothing less than changing the world! Changing the way we look at things! Buk fostered no such pretension. Quite simply he intended to share a common experience lucidly—and that was more than enough.

It would be equally incorrect to make him a punk icon—though some have been tempted to do so. *No Future*, after all, is an expression of a message, but Buk rejected any message, even that one. His was just an attempt to explain our daily labors and failures—at dusk in front of his typewriter, a pack of beer or a glass of wine within reach, and the words of poetry to ward off this defeat a little, to confront it to the best of his ability: *You get so alone at times that it just makes sense.*

His refusal to give in to any illusion led him, at the end of his life, to look more closely at Buddhism—which is perhaps his last link with the Beats. At Bukowski's funeral on March 14, 1994 in San Pedro, one of his friends, Gerald Locklin, was struck that three Buddhist monks led the ceremony. It was a personal initiative of Buk's wife Linda, but she also said that Hank had become very interested in Buddhism towards the end of his life and that he even meditated.[28]

The funeral also made one feel that the media figure, the perpetually drunk dirty old man, disguised an unknown Buk. This was indicated by the fact that alongside his family and friends—his editor John Martin, the actor Sean Penn, his translator Carl Weissner—there were a number of the local people, small corner-shopkeepers and notably one young girl in tears during the reception at Hank and Linda's house which followed the burial. Gerald Locklin asked Linda: "Is she a relative?" She replied: "No, she lives across the street. Hank loved her and she adored him. She may be taking his death the hardest of any of us."[29]

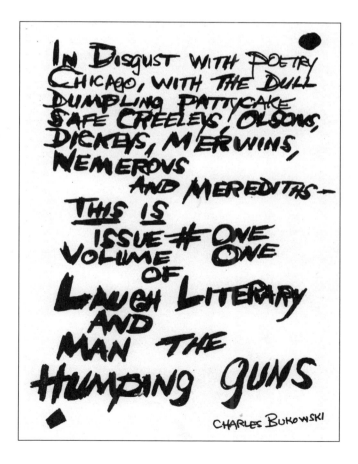

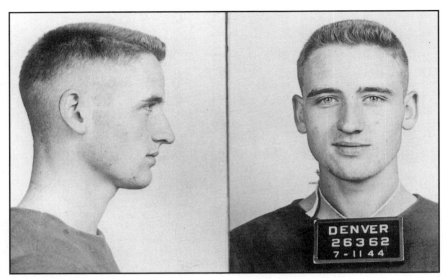

Neal Cassady, 1944, mugshot from the Denver Police Department
after his third arrest for car theft.

Solitude gets sweeter and
sweeter.

Once knew a guy who did
time. They threw him in the
hole.

When they asked him, "Do you
want to come out now?" He
said, "No."

So they pulled him out anyhow.
They thought he was crazy.

He was one of the sanest
men I ever met.

Yes, yes,

A person, when he drinks, likes the other person to drink with him.

—Charles Bukowski

BUK AND NEAL CASSADY

Ann Charters, leading specialist of Kerouac and the Beats, included one of Bukowski's texts in her anthology *The Portable Beat Reader*, doubtless aware that it would be a mistake to omit him. The anthology includes about fifty names—Huncke, Corso, Ferlinghetti, McClure, Snyder, Whalen, Lamantia etc. Bukowski opens the fifth section (of six) entitled "Tales of Beatnik Glory" where he rubs shoulders with Carolyn Cassady, William Burroughs Jr., Diane DiPrima, Brion Gysin, Ken Kesey, Jan Kerouac . . . Mocking a little, Charters notes in her introduction: "Bukowski was so bowled over by Cassady's performance behind the wheel of a car that he made Cassady the center of his piece (in his chronicles for *Open City*) instead of his customary self-presentation."[1]

It is true that she would have been wrong to omit this choice piece from her anthology. In the Beat perspective this text is almost unmissable, because on close reading Bukowski claims nothing less than to have written the last chapter of *On the Road*!

It is worth relating this episode in detail, particularly because according to Harold Norse "Bukowski spoke highly only of Neal Cassady."[2] It is one of the first episodes in *Notes*;

it seems as if Buk did not want to delay mentioning his contribution to the Beat legend. His tale starts abruptly, right to the point, as usual: "I met Kerouac's boy Neal C. shortly before he went down to lay along those Mexican railroad tracks to die." The description of Cassady is striking, Bukowski at his best in prose: "his eyes were sticking out like on ye old toothpicks and he had his head in the speaker, jogging, bouncing, ogling . . . ." A contrast to Buk's attitude: "I sat down with my beer and watched him."[3]

The meeting took place in the offices of *Open City* in San Francisco at the beginning of 1968. Bryan, the chief editor, was handing out work and film to two young photographers getting ready to go out on an assignment. Buk ended up alone opposite the guy who was the hero (Dean Moriarty) in Kerouac's *On the Road*. A living legend, a myth. Bukowski never travelled without a couple of six-packs and offered Neal a beer, who needed no persuasion and emptied it straight-away.

He then accepted another. After this brief introduction through beer, sizing each other up, a bit like two stray dogs that start off by sniffing each other, Buk forged an allegiance after seeing the speed with which Neal downed the beer. "I thought I was good on the beer," he said to him. Then the comment soon entered the realm of literature. In response to Buk's veiled compliment on his qualities as a great drinker in front of the Eternal, Neal retorted: "I'm the tough young jail kid. I've read your stuff.

—read your stuff too, replied Buk. that bit about climbing out the bathroom window and hiding in the bushes naked. good stuff.

—oh yeah."

This episode is found in the famous letter to Joan Anderson, which will be discussed later.

After this well-mannered exchange, Bukowski continues with his portrait of Neal Cassady (no Beat writer worthy of the name has evaded this obligatory topic): "he never sat down. he kept moving around the floor. he was a little punchy with the action, the eternal light, but there wasn't any hatred in him, you liked him even though you didn't want to because Kerouac had set him up for the sucker punch and Neal had bit, kept biting. but you know Neal was o.k. and another way of looking at it, Jack had only written the book, he wasn't Neal's mother. just his destructor, deliberate or otherwise."

Buk did not lack nerve! On the basis of only a few minutes drinking beer with Cassady, he claimed to understand the man better than Kerouac himself, who had misrepresented Neal in *On the Road*. Factually this might be correct. Carolyn Cassady, Neal's second wife, has told that Neal's tragedy was that all the character traits that enraptured readers of *On the Road* were precisely those that he hated and hoped to rid in himself. Joyce Johnson reported that after reading one of the first copies of *On the Road*, Cassady gave Kerouac a fairly cool reception.[4] However, Kerouac himself was so dissatisfied with his portrayal of Neal in *On the Road* that he immediately wanted to perfect it in his next book, *Visions of Cody*. For Kerouac, Neal Cassady instantly represented much more than an ordinary man—he was almost a mythical figure.

A vision of Jack and Neal, by Rick Bleier, *Rolling Stone*.

William Plummer notes that for Jack, Cassady had taken on the dimension of a character as huge and complex as the whale Moby Dick for Melville.[5] Jack was as obsessed with Neal as Achab was with his giant whale. Except that for him, Neal embodied the soul and spirit of his ideal America. The road and the car were to Kerouac's America what the sea and ships were to Melville, the prairie to Fenimore Cooper and the Mississippi to Mark Twain.

Neal baptized this mythical image, which Kerouac had created from him, "Keroassady" during a recording with The

Grateful Dead.[6] For him this was the most suitable name for the hybrid creature born from his meeting with Jack. Even taking into account Bukowski's inherent humor, this is the image that he seriously claimed to retouch. With the blessing of the archetypal Beat hero (Cassady), he would try to surpass the "master" himself, Jack Kerouac.

Rarely has such good use been made of two packs of beer and a single evening. Buk leaped on the opportunity to exercise his competitive spirit, to spar with the Beat writers on their own territory.

Bryan, who had finished with the two photographers, noticed what was at stake and shouted over: "you want to try him, Bukowski?"

"—yeah, ya wanta go, baby?" Neal asked.

Bukowski noted that it was said without hatred, just going with the game (as if Neal seized and accepted the stakes). Buk declined: "no, thanks. I'll be forty-eight in August. I've taken my last beating."

After this parrying, Buk immediately turned the subject to Kerouac. He asked Neal when he had seen Kerouac for the last time. Neal gave a vague reply that it had been a long time back. Bukowski noted that the umbilical cord had broken entirely between Neal and Jack. This gave him all the more scope to write the last chapter in question, and deal with the "Cassady topic" in his own way.

Bukowski does not explicitly make the connection—it is not even certain that he was actually conscious of it—but "the last chapter" of On the Road does effectively take place on the road. Bryan invited the two men to dinner at his place. Contrary to expectation it was Neal who took the wheel. Car driving was to Cassady what bullfighting was to Hemingway—to the extent that Ken Kesey and the Merry Pranksters nicknamed him Speed Limit. All that mattered to him were cars and women. Driving affairs. When Timothy Leary met Neal Cassady for the second time (the first was when Cassady came to him for psilocybine) he put his finger on the link, the woman/car confusion perpetually in Cassady's mind, one constantly becoming the metaphor for the other, and vice versa.

Leary's second meeting with Neal happened as follows: Leary turned up at the apartment where Neal had been staying for a few days. A girl in jeans and T-shirt opened the door for him. Leary asked where Neal was and the girl—called Salinas, like Steinbeck's small town of bums—gestured towards an open door: "He's in there balling Patty-Belle. Go in and tell them that you're here."[7] Leary went towards the bedroom and found two naked bodies violently banging together doggy-style on a narrow bed. Leary noted that the girl was blonde and had a pretty face, all shaken up but well in rhythm. She smiled at him and even waved a hand in greeting. Cassady was on his knees, shafting her. He also greeted him cheerfully. Leary was embarrassed, rooted to the spot. "I was forty years old and this was the first time I'd ever watched two people copulate."

"Hello Timothy," gasped Cassady breathlessly. "Please . . . ah . . . please excuse us for a moment. This . . . is . . . Patty-Belle and if she doesn't get her juicy streamline chassis overhauled every day, you understand, she gets . . . pouty." He closed his eyes to narrate: "So I gotta grind her sweet soft valves, lubricate her tubes, fire up her spark plugs, you understand, lay down some tire tracks across her rumble seat, oil her transmission, grease her gearbox, you understand, tune up her soft li'l cylinders, and jam her throttle to the floor."

To return to Buk—did he suspect what was going to happen? Had the two swiftly-downed packs of beer make him lose all well-informed perception? ". . . a bit high I didn't realize what was going to happen." He got into the car—unaware that Cassady was going to inflict on him something similar to his treatment of Patty-Belle. The same pleasure in driving, the same joy, the same control, the same skill of delicate negotiation, the same art of taking your breath away without any respite, the same technique of controlled

Timothy Leary visiting Neal Cassady who drove Prankster Bus to
Millbrook Psychedelic Research Center, Election year 1964. Allen Ginsberg

acceleration and skidding—Neal Cassady was in his element in both cars and women.

When they went out, the road was luminous and slippery because of the fine rain that was falling. Bryan got into the front passenger seat, Bukowski into the back. Bukowski, clearly inspired, spoke of a ride ("and the ride began"). A ride along the slippery streets, unaware if Neal would take the left or right at the crossroads, always deciding at the last second, like in a Charlie Parker improvisation, surprising everyone. Their lives sometimes hanging by a thread, the thin thread that separated them from the white line. Each time they escaped as if by a miracle, and Bukowski would shout: "well, suck my dick!" unaware how accurate his metaphor was. Neal remained in a state of concentration, impassive and engrossed in his driving.

The climax came when the drizzle worsened, hampering his vision, and Neal decided to leave Sunset to head north towards Carlton, calculating his move with the speed of a chess champion preparing to checkmate. When he turned left, there was a car in front of him and the two were head on. Logically, Neal should have slowed down and let it pass— Buk reckoned that this would have been possible, but Neal would have lost his movement, broken the rhythm, the trajectory, shattered the harmony, the time, interrupted the sentence or coitus, call it what you will. Bukowski then felt lost, done for, wiped out, fucked, blown away, powerless; he felt that nothing mattered, nothing was important anymore, he was out of himself, overtaken by the event. In a state of ecstasy he saw the two cars heading straight at each other; the other car was "so close that its headlights completely flooded [my] back seat." The other driver must have braked, allowing them the hair's-breadth that Neal must have known he would give them. He skimmed the car as if he were dancing, pushed, accelerated ("Patty-Belle, I gotta jam her throttle to the floor, you understand, Tim? . . ."). But the ride was not over yet. There was the second car that bolted from

Hollywood Boulevard and blocked the bend on Carlton, the car was so close that Bukowski would never forget its color—an old badly-dented gray-blue coupé, "hard," said Buk, "like a rolling steel brick thing." Neal swung to the left as if, Buk commented, he wanted to ram the other car through the middle. It is unclear how the head-on path of the two vehicles and Neal's sudden swerve to the left coincided so perfectly that the whole thing ended happily, to the mutual, then ecstatic relief of both parties. Several minutes later Bryan's girlfriend Joan gave them their dinner.

Bukowski had not finished his portrait. He took his turn at cranking up the speed, now that they were no longer on the road. Taking the initiative, he settled his account of the Beat era in four or five sentences that finished his tale. Neal had just devoured his plate of food and half of Buk's, washed down with a little wine.

At the end of this single and unique evening that he spent with Cassady, Buk said to him: "Kerouac has written all your other chapters. I've already written your last one."—"go ahead, write it," said Cassady.

Several days later Bryan called Buk:

"Neal's dead. Neal died."—"oh shit, no."

All those crazy rides, all those girls, all Kerouac's pages, ended up by a Mexican railway line, alone under an icy moon. This was perhaps the end of Neal's path, the perfect movement that Neal was looking for. One grace—that which left him lying there, abandoned by that Mexican railway line.

Tom Wolfe also mentioned this grace in *The Electric Kool-Aid Acid Test*, when he tells of the memorable crossing of the States by Kesey and the Merry Pranksters with Cassady at the wheel. He writes: "Coming up over the Blue Ridge Mountain everybody was stoned on acid, Cassady included, and it was at that moment that he decided to make it all the way down the steepest, awfulest windingest mountain highway in the history of the world without using the brake."[8] The description that follows is as hallucinating as Bukowski's. Wolfe depicts Kesey on top of the bus, completely in sync with Cassady. Their emotions are synchronized, and all feeling of panic is suppressed: "It was as if, if he were panicked, Cassady would be panicked, panic would rush through the bus like an energy. And yet he never felt panic. It was an abstract thought. He had total faith in Cassady, but it was more than faith. It was as if Cassady, at the wheel, was in a state of satori, as totally into this very moment, Now, as a being can get, and for that moment they all shared it."

It was about much more than just driving a car. Some have noted that one of Cassady's most fascinating characteristics was his extraordinary rapport with time, which enabled him to be completely in tune with the moment and to hold, for example, several conversations at once, integrated in the same flow. Neal was as famous on the West coast for his rap style flow of speech as for his rapid seduction of women and speed on the road. According to William Plummer, speed was a kind of regulator for Neal. Speed enabled him mentally to disperse painful visions from the near or distant past, and to intensify the good vibrations of the present.[9] If Proust was Cassady's favorite author, maybe it is precisely because *Remembrance of Things Past* links time and sensations in a similar way.

OM PH ! But Yes

NEAL AT VANISHING POINT

Neal Cassady's character was multifaceted. The most interesting facet is the one presented by his wife Carolyn in *Off the Road: My Years with Cassady, Kerouac and Ginsberg,* which was published in 1990. Fascinating memories— Carolyn loved Cassady, who was loved by Ginsberg, who was loved by Burroughs and Orlovsky, and the icing on the cake, Carolyn, Neal and Jack Kerouac had a real ménage à trois for a while, before Jack slept with LuAnne, Cassady's first wife, a ravishing teenager, aged 15 at the time of the marriage. Every situation and relationship which seemed to reverberate on the romantic, sexual and incestuous level, appears in Kerouac's direction of the Beat heroes in his novels where the characters are intertwined: one moment Cassady is on centre stage, then it's Ginsberg, Gary Snyder, Whalen . . . Kerouac admired Balzac's *The Comédie Humaine* and Proust's *Remembrance of Things Past,* and his ultimate ambition was to restore unity to his work. Unfortunately, compliance with the demands of different editors led to compromise—different character names in each book refer to the same person in real life. Neal is Dean Moriarty and Cody Pomeroy; Ginsberg is Irwin

Carolyn Cassady (nee Robinson), 1940. She held the affections of both Neal and Jack.

Garden, Adam Moorad and Alvah Goldbook; and Kerouac himself is Sal Paradise, Jack Duluoz, Ray Smith and Leo Percepied, etc. If he had had the chance, he would have assigned each person his or her real name and the whole of his work would have been entitled "The Duluoz Legend."

Carolyn's Neal Cassady (who she fell in love with in 1947) is not Timothy Leary's Neal, nor Ginsberg's, nor Kerouac's, nor J. C. Holmes' (Hart Kennedy in Go), nor Ken Kesey's (who wrote of the moment he learned of Neal's death in "The Day After Superman Died"), nor Tom Wolfe's, nor Bukowski's, nor Cassady's himself (as he reveals himself via his letters and in The First Third, his incomplete autobiography).

Carolyn met Neal in March 1947, when she was 24. Bill Thomson, her student friend and unlucky suitor, introduced them. In an attempt to impress her, Bill would tell Carolyn of the exploits of his friend who hung around Columbia University, New York with a footballer called Kerouac and a poet called Ginsberg. Thomson brought this phenomenon to Carolyn; Neal had just gotten off the Greyhound to spend a few days in his hometown Denver. Neal had scarcely entered her room, aged 21, wearing a white T-shirt and sporting a short, square-naped haircut, and said to the young woman: "Bill tells me you have an unusually large collection of Lester Young records."—"Lester who?" said Carolyn, astounded.[1] Neal was like a film star to her, with his intense blue eyes and charismatic aura. She thought that in describing Neal's exploits Bill had perhaps toned down the reality. Neal spoke to her in a fast delivery in his usual rap style, without pausing, not letting her catch her breath. With the result that she found herself putting on her coat, and being taken off for the afternoon. Neal gave her one of his poems to read, and then took her and Thomson to leave his suitcase in a small hotel room where Carolyn noticed straight-away, and not without a twinge of sorrow, signs of a woman's presence— clothes, make-up, etc. She was not yet aware that Neal

Cassady was married to sixteen-year-old LuAnne—a relationship which was heading towards a very temporary end (LuAnne is Marylou in *On the Road*). Nor did she know that at the same time, Cassady—"in an act of compassion and gratitude more than desire" according to his biographer William Plummer—was having an affair with the young Allen Ginsberg.

However, after he met Carolyn, the tone and the content of Neal's letters to Ginsberg, who was desperately in love with him, changed. "I have met a wonderful girl. Her chief quality, I suspect, lies in the same sort of awareness or intuitive sense of understanding which is our (yours and mine) chief forte. . . . She is just a bit too straight for my temperament [sic]; however, that is the challenge, just as that is the challenge in our affair. Her basic inhibitions are subtle psychological ones tied up indirectly with conventions, mannerisms and taste. . . . Somehow, my respect for her seems unimportant; I feel the only reason, really, that she affects me so is the sense of peace which she produces in me when we are together."[2]

Things got complicated when Ginsberg arrived in Denver. The three of them spent the night in the same room and Neal chose that moment to deflower Carolyn. This was the brutal revelation of Mr. Hyde. "I wanted some buildup, some preliminaries—why, Neal had never even touched me except for a few hugs or to kiss or hold my hand. . . . My emotions refused to fall into the proper groove for surrendering to passion, so acutely was I aware of Allen not two feet from my feet. How often I'd visualized our initial blending—but not like this!"[3]

She remembers what followed as a particularly painful experience, Neal showing none of the attributes of the attentive lover that she had expected. (At the age of nine he had let himself be dragged into the gang rape of a young girl with boys of his age). Instead of the expected tenderness there was pain and suffering. She felt as if she had been handed over to a wild beast, and she held back her tears and cries, and remained completely stiff and frigid. Paradoxically this was the man that Carolyn—always naively hoping that next time would be better—married and had three children with.

The reasons for the detail here are that Carolyn relates it very well in *Off the Road* and that the Beats' wives and girlfriends have been in the shade of their men for too long. Yet it is thanks to Edie Parker (who introduced Lucien Carr and Kerouac in 1944) that all the Beats gradually met up, and it was at her house that they got together. Carolyn Cassady is indissociable from the Cassady-Kerouac relationship. Joan Vollmer, who married William Burroughs despite his homosexuality, had a deciding influence on the dawn of his writing. He himself said that without her and without her dramatic death he would never have written, never even started *Junky*. There are many more examples.

It is fortunate that the Beat revival now reveals a whole series of women writers: Carolyn Cassady's *Off the Road*; Joyce Johnson's *Minor Characters*; Jan Kerouac's *Baby Driver* and *Trainsong*; her mother Joan; the poetess Elise Cowen (Ginsberg's unfortunate lover); Hettie Jones, the wife of LeRoi Jones (Amiri Baraka), and many others. A number of these unpublished works were compiled in 1996 in *Women of the Beat Generation*.[4]

The post-war Beat women, like their male partners, opened up a gap in the rigidity of moral standards and covertly prepared the sexual revolution of the '60s. It was in the USA that Vadim's film *And God Created Woman* first had huge success; the young Brigitte Bardot danced on a table, possessed and wild with desire. We also remember William Reich's theories and his conviction of "liberation through orgasm."

Despite his Catholic inhibitions, Kerouac associated the processes of love-making with those of writing (and not

The Beat Women: Carolyn Cassady (top left), Diane DiPrima (top right), Hettie Jones (center left), Anne Waldman (center), Joyce Johnson (center right), Joan Haverty (lower left), Jan Kerouac (lower right).

Heart Beat
My Life with Jack and Neal
Carolyn Cassady
The intimate portrait of Kerouac and Cassady, fathers of the Beat Generation
—by a woman who loved both intimately

driving). In 1957, in the *Black Mountain Review*, he sets out the requirements of his "Essentials of Spontaneous Prose" and he recommends that you always ". . . write excitedly, swiftly, with writing-or-typing cramps, in accordance (as from center to periphery) with laws of orgasms, Reich's 'beclouding of consciousness.'" "*Come* from within, out—to relaxed and said," urged Kerouac.[5]

Kerouac was a real writer and Neal Cassady was simply a reference figure in the legend; the Perceval of the Beat generation. It is scarcely a metaphor: Ginsberg and Kerouac really saw Neal as a kind of saint, and Plummer entitled his biography of Neal *The Holy Goof*.

However, Cassady also hoped to become a writer. One of his motives in going to New York in 1946 to meet Kerouac was that he wanted his advice about writing. He soon became aware of his limitations and wrote to Jack: "Yet, perhaps, words are not the way for me. . . . I am not too sure that the roots of the impulse to write go deep enough. . . ."[6]

But what a paradox! Without him, Kerouac's work would probably have never seen the light of day, just as *Moby Dick* would never have done if Melville hadn't gone to sea. The relationship between Neal and Jack was a bit like the one between Huckleberry Finn and Tom Sawyer. Cassady, under Jack's admiring gaze, broke all the rules, shattered taboos and did everything that wasn't "right." In the end, the role that fell to him was of a legendary character, in which he often felt imprisoned and unhappy. In 1948 he wrote to Ginsberg: "Everything I do is not great. I've never done anything great. I see no greatness in myself. . . . I'm a simple-minded, child-like, insipid sort of moronic and kind of awkward feeling adolescent."[7]

Jack and Neal were fascinated with each other, two complementary characters. A famous photograph taken by Carolyn shows them arm in arm, as if they were one person. When *On the Road* came out, the public inevitably got them mixed up believing Dean Moriarty (Neal Cassady) was Kerouac. Yet they were not duplicates, still less, inter-changeable characters.

Carolyn Cassady's clear portraits in *Off the Road* show this distinctly. In 1947 Jack also arrived in Denver from New York to visit Neal and Allen. He met Carolyn. One evening when they were in a tavern and Neal would not dance with her, Carolyn accepted Jack's offer. She instantly felt something of the sensual charm that was so lacking in Cassady. "Dancing

Tom Sawyer and Huck Finn, Neal and Jack, the inseparable duo, San Fransisco, 1952.

with Jack was the only time I felt the slightest doubt about my dedication to Neal, for here was the warm physical attraction Neal lacked."[8] Jack also noticed what had happened between them and whispered to her: "It's too bad, but that's how it is—Neal saw you first." But this was not the end of the story—even though Jack would have to overcome his shyness (with Carolyn's help).

This happened five years later in 1952 in San Francisco when Neal, who was working for the Southern Railway Pacific, had to go away for three weeks leaving Carolyn and Jack alone together. When Neal left, as if a last thought had sprung to mind, he said: "You know what they say: My best pal, and my best gal" and he left them with this sibylline recommendation: "Just don't do anything I wouldn't do—okay kids?"[9] An order as enigmatic as it was threatening.

Kerouac hardly dared to leave his bedroom in the attic, and when he did it was to creep outside, avoiding Carolyn, who on the floor below was worrying and wondering what Neal had meant. Three weeks of (sweet?) torture, at the end of which Neal came back to a faithful wife and friend—although virtually lovers through thinking about it.

One or two evenings later Carolyn seized the opportunity of one of Neal's absences to invite Jack down from his den to share a pizza that she had made. While she waited for him, she set the table, lit a candle, tuned in to "KJAZ," his favorite jazz program, made herself up without going over the top (she couldn't wear anything but her usual jeans and white T-shirt or else Jack, already nervous, would have been

Jack and Carolyn with the Cassady Children, 1952.

completely unnerved—so she just put on a bit of make-up and did her hair). Lastly she had a sip of wine to give her courage.

By candlelight, the wine made them more talkative. We can imagine Carolyn's charm by the content of her secret thoughts:"When we had finished eating, I knew I had to keep Jack downstairs until I'd finished what I'd started; I'd never be able to repeat it. I poured more wine and walked to the couch we kept opened out to double bed-size. As I sat down on its edge, I held out Jack's glass to him. He followed me, accepted the wine and lay back upon the couch, balancing the glass on his chest."[10] "My Funny Valentine" was playing on the radio, Carolyn paused a moment, and then said:"Do you remember when we danced together in Denver?" Of course he remembered. And then it happened just like in the movies:". . . we both put down our glasses at the same time, not unlocking our eyes or looking at the table but making perfect contact."

From that evening onwards Carolyn, Neal and Jack lived together—each perfectly happy with the arrangement. The young woman felt integrated like never before in the relationship between the two men: "Now, I was part of all they did; I felt like the sun of their solar system, all revolved around me. . . . How lucky could a girl get?" The best moments were the evenings in the kitchen, when she was cooking and Kerouac and Neal talked interminably about Spengler, Proust and Shakespeare, or about riffs and musical arrangements.[11]

This is Beat Romanticism without a doubt. It is difficult to picture Bukowski using such a setting to create a love scene, to evoke, as Carolyn did, some new metamorphosis of Guinevere and Lancelot's love. Buk was hardly duped by the Western mythology of courtly love; he was closer to the modern theories of chaos and randomness. In 1974 he said to *London Magazine*: "You've got to be lucky with women, because the way you meet them is mostly through accident. If you turn right at a corner you meet this one; if you turn left, you meet another one. Love is a form of accident. The population bounces together, and two people meet somehow. You can say that you love a certain woman, but there's a woman you never met you might have loved a hell of a lot more. That's why I say you have to be lucky."[12]

Linda Lee Bukowski.

Love didn't really happen for him like it did in King Arthur's court or in Hollywood, even if he could count himself among the lucky ones. In *Women* this is how he recounts his first night with Linda Beighle whom he met in 1976, married in 1985 and stayed with until his death. Linda had approached him at one of his readings, and several days later Buk decided to go and see her at the health-food restaurant she ran. They ended up in her apartment. On the way, she had probably talked to him about Meher Baba, her Indian guru who died in 1971 "claiming to be God" said Bukowski, and whose pictures, to his surprise, seemed to invade Linda's life literally, on the walls of her restaurant, the inside of the VW camper . . .[13]

They downed several bottles of wine at her place—Linda (who appears in *Women* with the pseudonym Sara) kept up remarkably well. So well, that Buk felt drunk and confessed that he was incapable of driving home. Linda/Sara offered: "Oh, you can sleep in my bed, but no sex."—"Why?" said Buk, surprised.

—"One doesn't have sex without marriage" she clarified, "Drayer Baba doesn't believe in it." A fairly comical scene follows (reminiscent of Boccaccio?) with the two in bed; the narrator casually declines any temptation to be romantic and resorts to grotesque hard porn to create the situation: "Sara held my cock in her hand, petting it, rubbing it. Then she pressed it against her cunt. She rubbed it up and down, up and down against her cunt. She was obeying her God, Drayer Baba. I didn't play with her cunt because I felt that would offend Drayer. We just kissed . . . . And then I turned, rolled over and put my back against her. Drayer Baby, I thought, you've got one helluva believer in this bed."

A refusal to adorn the scene with the slightest magic cure-all, to dress it up in the delicate lace of fantasy and illusion, Buk prefers to let something else shine through, with humor and the crude aspect of the description—something like tenderness. All the same, Romanticism is present—hard porn defused here with humor—"I felt that would offend Drayer" is instantly tinged with an unconfessed affection.

Behind the scenes, things are already happening on a more emotional than carnal level. The gestures and the bodies only play a restrained and eventually puritanical part in the action. Exhibitionism in Bukowski is probably just the flip side of a core of modesty and puritanism.

Buk felt much closer to Boccaccio than to Henry Miller. He said that nothing had delighted him more than reading *Decameron*. He wrote in one of his tales: ". . . sex is obviously the tragico-comedy. I don't write about it as an instrument of obsession. I write about it as a stage play laugh where you have to cry about it, a bit, between acts. Giovanni Boccaccio wrote about it much better. he had the distance and the style. I am still too near the target to effect total grace. people simply think I'm dirty. if you haven't read Boccaccio, do. you might begin with *The Decameron*."[14]

This is something that the French writer Philippe Djian (author of *Betty Blue*, from which Jean-Jacques Beineix made a film with the same title in 1986, and an admirer of Bukowski's work) was very aware of: "For a writer," he stated, "sex scenes are the ordeal by fire. It is in such scenes that one can see immediately if this is a real artist or not. It is here that a writer reveals himself: if he has any flaws they will be visible at once." According to Djian, Buk fell into this category, as did Henry Miller but for different reasons: "Some make too much of it and others not enough. With Miller, everything to do with sex appears absolutely natural, intrinsically part of life, which is admirable. With Bukowski, it is something else. He had an unbelievable modesty that made him endearing. He appears brutal. He used the crudest words and called a spade a spade, but he treated sex essentially as a tragedy, because it was not the sex that interested him when he wrote this type of scene. Rather, it was what he would discover on the emotional level from the relationship between a man and a woman. I see Bukowski as someone who had huge respect for women and who was totally the opposite of the image that has often been portrayed."[15]

ON STYLE

It could be said that Cassady inseminated the whole movement, even including the area of style, via Kerouac (Ginsberg himself confessed that his poetry came from Kerouac, "who was the best of all of us").

Ann Charters and others have noted that although Kerouac and Ginsberg encouraged Cassady to write, Cassady had a greater effect on Kerouac, than Kerouac did on Cassady! (Neal did begin to write *The First Third*, the first third of his autobiography, shortly after his meeting with Kerouac and Ginsberg, which was published by City Lights in 1971, three years after his death.) Kerouac read some chapters from Cassady's *The First Third* and these inspired his *Visions of Neal*, which he started just after *On the Road*—this was published in 1972 entitled *Visions of Cody*.

Cassady's letters (from 1947 onwards) filled Kerouac with enthusiasm. Cassady's letters were something else! It was through the letters that Neal sent from a reformatory in Denver to Hal Chase, one of his friends who was studying at Columbia University, New York that (unbeknown to him) he was introduced to the group of Beats that hung around Times Square circa

LuAnne Henderson /Marylou from *On the Road*, Neal's teenage bride.

1945. Chase showed Neal's letters to Kerouac, Burroughs, Ginsberg, Herbert Huncke and the rest. In 1946 when Cassady left Denver for New York on the Greyhound, accompanied by his young wife LuAnne (this is the first episode recounted at the beginning of *On the Road*), his reputation had preceded him and he was already known for his style of writing. To a certain degree, he was the messiah that the Beats had been waiting for.

It was Neal's completely uninhibited writing (akin to his attitude towards sex) that struck and captivated Kerouac. The letter Cassady wrote while getting drunk in a bar and sent to Kerouac on March 7, 1947 from Kansas City, was labeled the "Great Sex Letter" by Kerouac. It told of Neal's seduction of two girls on a bus, one called Pat, the other a virgin of unknown name. At that time Kerouac was finishing *The Town and the City*, his first novel which was published in 1950. Cassady's letter challenged his whole work and he was suddenly aware of its conventionality. He recounted this in a biographical note for *The New American Poetry*: "The discovery of a style of my own based on spontaneous get-with-it, came after reading the marvellous free narrative letters of Neal Cassady, a great writer who happens also to be the Dean Moriarty of *On the Road*."[1]

He was instantly aware of the huge contradiction between *The Town and the City* and what Cassady repeated in his letters: "I have always held that when one writes, one should forget all rules, literary styles and other such pretensions as large words, lordly clauses and other phrases as such— rolling the words around in the mouth as one would wine, and, proper or not, putting them down as they sound so good. Rather, I think, one should write, as nearly as possible, as if he were the first person on earth and was humbly and sincerely putting on paper that which he saw and experienced and loved and lost."[2]

In December 1950 it was Neal's famous letter posted from Denver—known from then on as the "Joan Anderson's letter"—

that released Kerouac from writer's block while creating *On the Road* (published in 1957). In April 1951 Kerouac wrote his masterpiece in three weeks in an uninterrupted flow on a single roll of teleprinter paper, so that he didn't have to break his train of thought by putting fresh pieces of paper in the machine.

This determining letter (believed to be dated December 17, 1950) told of Neal's visit to his friend Joan, hospitalized after a suicide attempt, and of Neal's escape through a bathroom window to avoid being caught after making love to one of his girlfriends "Cherry Mary" while she was baby-sitting.[3]

Kerouac wrote to him at the beginning of 1951: "Just a word, now, about your wonderful 13,000 word letter about Joan Anderson and Cherry Mary. I thought it ranked among the best things ever written in America . . . . You gather together all the best styles of Joyce, Céline, Dusty & Proust and utilize them in the muscular rush of your own narrative style and excitement." And further on: "You and I will be the most two important writers in America in 20 years at the least. Think that."[4]

At the end Jack makes this recommendation for Neal's benefit: "Don't undervalue your poolhall musings, your excruciating details about streets, appointment times, hotel rooms, bar locations, window measurements, smells, heights of trees. I wait for you to send me the entire thing in disorderly chronological order anytime you say and anytime it comes . . . If that ain't life nothing ain't."

Bukowski, twenty-five years later, spontaneously followed this advice. This is clear in the last few lines of his novel *Women*. After 320 pages of female peripeteia, Buk finishes the book by briefly describing a cat that turned up at his door and followed him inside. "I walked back inside and he followed me. I opened him up a can of Star-Kist solid white tuna. Packed in spring water. Net wt. 7 oz."

HE TOOK A GOOD HIT, LOOKED INTO THE MIRROR AND STUCK HIS TONGUE OUT AT HIMSELF.

Full stop and that's it, finished.

"If that ain't life nothing ain't."

Buk's perspective is clear: like the Beats "the point he hoped to make, was that a writer must create his art from the world around him, not from others' voices."[5]   It is breathtaking to picture him spending so many hours of his life devouring books in public library reading rooms, to reject them all in the end. If Crumb were to give the picture concrete expression it would be a drastic image. He swallowed everything from Boccaccio to John Fante and from Shakespeare to Artaud. But it only made sense to him if afterwards he could make a clean sweep of everything that had gone before, to return from it to the expression of a raw and uncut experience. It was a return to square one. An aesthetic demand reflected, for example, in Buk's systematic return—in particular after a full stop—to lower case where you would expect upper case: an apparent casualness of style, neglect of a major rule of punctuation, scorn of convention. A way for him to lay claim—like an honor—to "lower-case letters."[6] Yet it had all filtered down from a great literary (and musical) culture. Philippe Garnier notes in a preface to a French translation of *Post Office*: "His poems in particular, under their false simplicity, conceal a skill of imagery and compression comparable to that of Japanese poets."[7] Each of his words has its own weight, carefully calculated, decided. "You get so alone at times that it just makes sense." The line is as dazzling as a haiku, phrased in such a way that it creates vertigo.

Neeli Cherkovski, who associates Bukowski with the Beats in his *Whitman's Wild Children*, also put it well when he wrote: ". . . The Beat poets, from Allen Ginsberg to Gregory Corso, often weighed their work with traditional, literary devices and language." This is certainly not the case with Bukowski: "There was a tough edge to the poems I had never seen before," continues Cherkovski, who discovered Buk's poetry when he was fifteen years old. "When I read him, it was as if he had pulled me over to his side from the rotting hulk of school and everything else that oppressed me. It wasn't so much what he said, but his attitude that crept up on me slowly. Unlike the Beat poets, his declamations were subtle."[8] Rough and subtle! This is also Bukowski's magic tone.

Returning now to Kerouac. In his preface to *Good Blonde and Others*, Robert Creeley, poet and publisher, explains what was different in Kerouac's writing after *The Town and the City*: ". . . there was such a clear difference between a novel like Saul Bellow's *The Adventures of Augie Marsh* with its potted plot and persons as 'examples,' or else the later 'adult' 'children's book,' *Catcher in the Rye*. Jack's was another story entirely."[9]

The difference was that his spontaneous prose strove to have the same effect on literature as an improvisation by Lester Young or Dexter Gordon on jazz. Writing had to be in complete balance with the feeling of the moment. Kerouac was not like the writers who write "about" something, and who manipulate language with subject and themes right before the eyes to create an external point of view (as Flaubert did). He wanted to be inside the flow of language itself, to be perfectly in tune with it, like a jazzman running through improvisations. He believed that this was the only way to achieve the beat in writing. The particular state which reflects the completeness of being, unveiling the face of God.

He kept to the maxim "First Thought, Best Thought." He did not revise his work, except to correct the occasional aberrant detail, a purely factual error, a date, a place, name spelling. He was convinced that the truth, in the text and man, comes in the first flow. This is always richer because it still harbors in its purity (and even in its possible impurities) the initial ecstasy, the trance with which the text flows (he said that writing should only be done in a trance), and everything that the artist would be wrong to silence and conceal. In a letter in 1955 he neatly describes himself as a "Running Proust," and considered his work as a single huge dream, which was only lost and regained time in his own life, which he hoped would one day be entitled "The Duluoz Legend." He saw the art of spontaneous prose like a fragment torn from the constant movement of a storm—"and the uproar, like uproar of *Finnegan's Wake*, has no beginning and no end . . ."[10] It is easy to see from this that the necessity of a plot was the least of his worries.

Steve Turner sums it up well in his book *Angelheaded Hipster*: "Jack made writing sound exciting."[11]

In a short piece entitled "Written Address to the Italian Judge" published in *Evergreen Review* in October/November 1963, Kerouac tried to explain his process to the judge responsible for banning *The Subterraneans*, which Feltrinelli had just published in translation in Italy. He wrote: "Once a storyteller has told his tale he has no right to go back and delete what the hand hath written." To explain himself better to his Italian censors, presumably Catholic like himself, he added: "This decision, rather, this vow I made with regard to the practice of my narrative art frankly, Gentlemen, has its roots in my experience inside the confessionals of a Catholic childhood. It was my belief then that to withhold any reasonably and decently explainable detail from the Father was a sin."[12]

This is one of the reasons that Kerouac's works—apart from *The Town and the City*—are not fiction, and perhaps not novels. In December 1950 he wrote to Cassady: "I hereby renounce all fiction."[13] His girlfriend Joyce Glassman (now Johnson) became a bit jealous after reading *The Subterraneans*—she was aware of the passion in the book which united Leo (Jack) and Mardou (a black woman with whom he had spent several wild days)—and asked Jack if this had all really happened. He replied: "I don't write novels, I only write books. BOOOGS. That's what I call' em."[14] This freed him from limiting himself to a worn-out and traditional genre that at the same time in France there were attempts to revive under the term Nouveau Roman.

All the Beat writers are autobiographical by nature. And it is clear that Bukowski's prose texts and poems, even when he presents Henry Chinaski, do not escape this rule. It's the same whether the narrators call themselves Duluoz (Kerouac), Chinaski (Bukowski) or Mr. Miller (Henry Miller in *Sexus*). The events and the gestures of the characters/narrators are the same as the authors' (while the link between Proust and the narrator in *Remembrance*—Cassady and Kerouac's favorite work—is an entirely different matter). In an interview, Anne Waldman said: "All these people were on the same wavelength, acting in the same interesting period of

Anne Waldman.

95

time, so culturally informed by the same kind of impulses . . . Bukowski was not linked to that community, he was not hanging around with Cassady and William Burroughs and so on, but he is kind of informed by, and, in terms of what is going on culturally, artistically, psychologically, he is very much on the same kind of wavelength. There were always these amazing intersections between the psychedelic exploration of freedom, religion, politics, these worlds were really . . . I mean, there were many things going on simultaneously that, as I said, were informed by the same kind of impulses. What was going on in our culture, in the world at large, in terms of people's individual experience and gravitating to certain places on the map, whether it was Paris or . . . I mean, when you look at the parallels in jazz, in films, in music, the political, they are all connected, even though they are in these different time cycles and intersecting at moments, very powerful moments . . ."[15]

However, there are gaps between Bukowski and, let's say Kerouac, that would be impossible to fill. For Philippe Djian, sometimes called "the most American of French novelists," there is something in the style of Kerouac that is not to be found in Bukowski: "In Kerouac, there is a breath, an unbelievable rhythm. It is so much like music that when reading it you want to tap your foot. This is something that is not found in Bukowski. I consider him more like a poet."[16] Comparing Bukowski and Kerouac, Anne Waldman also said: "I don't think he has got the same sort of delicacy or beauty if you will in his writing. It's a different kind of writing, it's more stripped bare, but he has really got a definite voice . . . His poetry has this amazing directness that you don't see anywhere else, he is able to say anything with that edgy sarcasm nihilism. He is not exploratory in the way Kerouac is. They are just different minds. Bukowski is more earthy, more earth bound, more interested . . . there is a funny story: when I ran the St. Mark's Poetry Project in New York, in 1970, I invited him to come on and read. And my assistant was taking him round the city. And they were standing in front of this very famous three-sided building on Fifth Avenue and 23rd Street—Bukowski was just looking at these sides around New York—and he looked up at the building and said: 'I wonder how many toilets are in that building?'"[17]

"What set the characters in Bukowski's work apart from Kerouac's is that although both have in common a feeling and an experience of rejection, the former do not seek to compensate that rejection by recourse to a spiritual philosophy; both feet, as well as their backsides, are on the ground."[18] As James Campbell puts it, it is a question of two radically different worldviews and, while on this subject, their respective success can be considered. The Beat ideal was elevated, carried by angels, but those angels ultimately fell from grace: "The image of the Beat writer as a Zen monk and twentieth century Daniel Boone rolled into one was an image which they themselves were foolish enough to believe in . . . There was a quest behind Kerouac's running around . . . But it appears evidently to have been a blind quest; a quest without a Grail . . . The Beat's quest—via confused religions and near-sighted visions led them not along the road to an identity, but up the blind alley of an image. They substituted image for identity."[19]

This kind of misadventure could never have befallen Bukowski. In a 1962 letter to Sheri Martinelli, the editor of the *Anagogic & Paideumic Review*, he wrote: "The language must be a *basic* language that does not change. Your Kerwhoreac had an idea of this when he began but he found it too easy and he now beats on it like a drum, and as a consequence, he writes very badly. Basic language does not mean easiness."[20] Bukowski kept his feet on the ground, so how could he have fallen? His writings are as autobiographical as those by the Beats, but there is a subtle and deep distinction: "By choosing to write about himself, from the very bottom and with nothing whatever to hide, Bukowski is enabled to make a confession which bears witness to his identity; the confession which is the key to truth." In other words, Campbell argues, "Bukowski is really beat," the only real beat writer . . .

NEW YORK A 95 CENTS LA JOURNÉE

ANGELS AND THE GARGOYLE

It could be interesting to draw up a list of features that Kerouac, the Beats, and Bukowski have in common, to highlight a close sensitivity—the same profound interest in Dostoevsky (Kerouac's *The Subterraneans* makes explicit reference to Dostoevsky's *Notes from Underground*). Bukowski enjoyed classical music above all, Haydn and particularly Bach. Kerouac, so great a believer that there was a link between Beat literature and jazz, also readily referred to Bach—for reasons which are perhaps not too far removed from Bukowski's, even if for Jack the reasons were tinged with mysticism. When Kerouac summed up the Four Noble Truths of Buddhism in "Last Words" (1959) he considered that it could be said of the fourth: "you might as well say it is just as explicit in Bach's *Goldberg Variations*."[1] Bach—a Beat musician, Buddhist and Bukowskian without even knowing it!

Their dreams of literary glory also took the same path on occasion. In 1963, in a letter to Jon and Louise Webb, the editors of *Outsider*, a paper which was almost entirely devoted to Bukowski, Buk wrote: "I remember when I was very young, Hem used to work out in the ring, you know, and I always dreamed that I would volunteer to sit in the opposite corner, and in my dream, of course, I kayoed HEMINGWAY, and therefore I was a great writer, I was a greater everything. Which is pure shit . . ."[2] In 1968 in *Vanity of Duluoz*, Kerouac wrote: "I went into the parlor and sat down in my father's old deep easy chair and fell into the wildest daydream of my life." Two pages of fantasy follow, which culminate in the evocation of a world heavyweight boxing championship against Joe Louis: "I train idly in the Catskills, come down on a June night, face big tall Joe as the referee gives us instructions, and then when the bell rings I rush out real fast and just pepper him real fast and so hard that he actually goes back bouncing over the ropes and into the third row and lays there knocked out. I'm the world's heavyweight boxing champion, the greatest writer . . ."[3] The great Hemingway myth still hovered over both Jack and Buk. Even though neither wanted to give in to it. Kerouac: "I woke up from this daydream suddenly realizing that all I had to do was go back on the porch and look at the stars again, which I did, and still they just stared at me blankly. In other words I suddenly realized that all my ambitions, no matter how they came out . . . it wouldn't matter anyway in the intervening space between human breathings and the 'sigh of the happy stars' so to speak, to quote Thoreau again."

This awareness of the vanity of success was retrospective in Kerouac's case. He was already famous when he wrote those lines in 1968. However, for Buk it was premonitory. He was still completely unknown in 1963. But when public recognition did come and had to be faced, they both had similar reactions. In February 1968 Bukowski wrote to Carl Weissner: "rumors on town hall reading of Bukowski, Corso, Micheline . . . impossible, didn't you know I have made it known for years that I don't read publicly? . . . I've never read in public, don't intend to . . . have turned down fees of from $200 to $700 and told them to go screw . . . I am not an actor, I am a creator."[4] Of course he did go on to play the actor, and was considerably successful at it. However, as previously

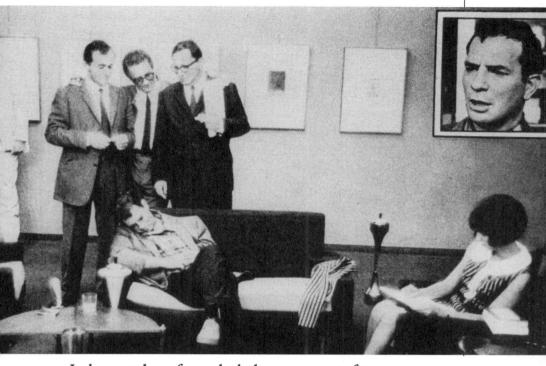

Jack, passed out from alcohol, at a press conference to promote the Italian version of *Big Sur* (Milan, 1966).

mentioned, he experienced queasiness and vomited before each reading.

Kerouac was the same. After the success of *On the Road*, he ignored Ginsberg's warnings, and in need of money he agreed to read parts of *Mexico City Blues* and some of Corso's and Ginsberg's poems in Vanguard Village in New York. He was drunk, timid and uncomfortable in his jacket and tie; he was ignored. Each evening he got drunker, more pathetic and more reluctant to get up on the stage. Max Gordon, the club owner, found him bathed in sweat, crouched in a corridor running a rosary through his fingers to pluck up courage.[5] In 1965 when Kerouac went to Paris and Brittany in an attempt to trace his family tree, an experience he related in *Satori in Paris*, he was thrown out of Gallimard, his French publisher, for being drunk. This precedes Bukowski's misadventures on the program *Apostrophes* on French television by thirteen years. A photo in the Italian magazine *Gente* on October 12, 1966 shows Kerouac overcome by alcohol, sleeping during a press conference. He is pictured snoring on a sofa surrounded by four or five journalists who seem most unconcerned, in true Italian fashion.[6]

Kerouac did not do well in interviews; he was too trusting and let himself be manipulated by journalists, he didn't know how to protect himself or to keep the required distance. On the other hand, he was in his way a skilled interviewer. In *Visions of Cody*, considered by many to be his real masterpiece, he used conversations, recorded on tape recorder, between Cassady and himself. Use of this new machine began to spread. Why not introduce it and use it as a literary technique? Kerouac mischievously followed this section of the book with a chapter entitled "Imitation of the Tape," stunning in its subtlety, worthy of James Joyce in the parodic multiplicity of the voices that he presents.

Bukowski, however, excelled at the interview. Here too, he was aware of the weight of words, even in this kind of verbal exchange. The spirit of repartee was like a match or a fight. An interview with Buk was like a game of table tennis: landing the balls, landing his words. Not that he had to search hard for them. Words always seemed to flow from the source. But he was careful to let them clear a path. In interviews (he gave them much less frequently from 1980 onwards: "quote my books"), he spoke in a slow voice, as if to give each word its own necessary time to reach its goal, in the fullness of its meaning. In 1980 when the Italian journalist Fernanda Pivano interviewed him, he said that several days earlier he had enjoyed reading an interview with Moravia (a writer that he did not know; at first he struggled for the name . . . Maromia? . . . Pivano corrected: Moravia!). Buk said that Moravia's work would probably not interest him but "the answers he gave to the questions were good," that "this way of answering questions had really pleased him." In particular he quoted to Pivano one of Moravia's retorts, which he remembered as well as if it had been one of his own: "This question is not very important to me, and questions which are important to me have no importance."[7]

There remains one big difference between Kerouac, the Beats and Bukowski. The Beats believed themselves bards of a new reality. Kerouac had his face constantly turned towards God, towards an assumed paradise. He believed in the celestial nature of his hobos and bums—the angelic generation is another name he gave the Beat generation during a conversation with J. C. Holmes in 1948.[8] Behind everything, he discovered the flip side of the Void, i.e. potential fullness. A palpitation, a kind of joy, a kind of grace runs through his writing. Bukowski considered himself a painter of hell and the grotesque. A gargoyle like a distant descendent of Jerome Bosch.

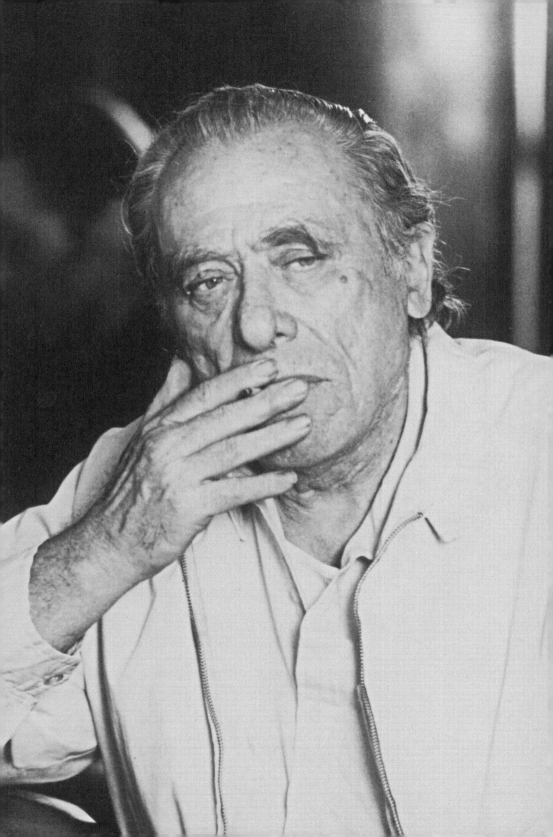

THE COUNTERPUNCHER

Violence occupies a significant place in Charles Bukowski's imagery. It is seen in the harshness of human relationships and of a life which, for most, leaves no other choice but a daily battle for survival. It is also evident in drunken brawls in the backyards of seedy bars, in filthy hotels and in unmade beds where couples appear knotted together in a fight to the death in which both are losers. Sex itself evokes combat (some of Crumb's illustrations depict

"THEY ROLLED OVER AND OVER ON THE RUG, BREATHING HEAVILY, ALL LEGS AND ARMS AND BODIES IN A DESPERATE JUXTAPOSITION....."

Crumb drawing.

this perfectly). There is no victor in this kind of violence; there is only defeat.

It should be understood that, for Bukowski, it is reality itself that is violent, in its sordid truth that permits no way out to illusion. The very fact of existence is violent. Everything that follows is just a progressive extension of this ontological violence: in love, in sex, in relations with others, oneself, work . . . So much so that the different manifestations of violence are endless in Bukowski's work. When violence is not physical, material or psychological, when it isn't bouncing off the repellent walls of a shabby room or the darkness of depressions, it is conveyed in word, becomes verbal and is concentrated in insults and fight scenes. Bukowski's terminology—his choice of the most raw, crude and simple words—is itself the expression of a violence created with language, stripped back to its most elementary forms of expression, considered to be "more real." Because Buk was perfectly aware that the "simplicity" of his style was a rhetorical effect: "Writing is painting and the sooner people realize this the less dull crap will dull the market . . . A good style comes primarily from lack of pretentiousness."[1] Buk attacked polished turns of phrase, conventional style and words rolled around the mouth like a good wine. Literary language is deceptive; an intolerable veil thrown over reality that should be torn up and reduced to rags. "If it's decaying, if it's violent, then my writing will be decaying and violent. I don't want it to be that way. But if it is, there is nothing else I can call it," he said in our interview.

To coin a term from the world of boxing, Charles Bukowski was a counterpuncher. He responded blow by blow with words, the writer's weapons, to the knocks that reality inflicted on him. In this ring, which was his battleground, he was knocked down less frequently than in scenes from Schroeder's film *Barfly*, for which Bukowski wrote the screenplay. The brutality of reality is matched by the brutality of words. His blows are precise and tight. As

Roddy Doyle commented with regard to *Post Office*: "Bukowski's writing was inarticulate, but deliberately so. Each word clung tight to the next; there was no room for any more. It was a tight choreographed clumsiness. And it was great."[2]

Bukowski's genius lies in this use of language. Something like poetry erupts through the rawest words from this stripping of language, from this violence that bursts open the straightjacket. Poetry as pure and rich in human density as it is lacking in all vain artifice. As the French newspaper *Le Monde* put it once, "it is beautiful vomit. Vomit with a whiff of beauty, or the sublime thrown into the gutter."[3]

His use of linguistic violence makes Bukowski an innovator somewhat like Beckett, for example, who used language to deny language. Harold Norse gets it right again in establishing a parallel between Bukowski's tormented prose and the violence that pours from Van Gogh's paintings ("his language leapt from the page like a Van Gogh, galvanic, whirling, immediate, full of raw violence").[4] It is impossible to miss the role of creative violence in this work, above and beyond the destructive violence that it seems to present. This distinction between creative and destructive violence also explains Bukowski's willingly provocative attitude. The act of provocation indicates a desire to shake up the normal order of things; it is a call to react. The boxer's stance was, therefore, a dialectical position for Bukowski. In this posture there was no desire to crush, annihilate or humiliate the opponent. Destructive violence played no part. Bukowski considered it to be another kind of violence that in destroying all artifice, re-establishing an original scene from chaos and stripping to the essentials, attempts to create new forms from this chaos. Forms that he asserted are truer and closer to the human experience. "Picasso does with paint what I would like to do with words," he said.[5] Regarding Buk's style, James Campbell makes another interesting comparison when he says that "reading his work can provide the same exhilaration as listening to the playing of certain jazz musicians. Like Thelonious Monk he seems to hit all the wrong notes, but in the right places."[6]

This requires strength and courage. "Humor, guts and courage," as he said, since it is more difficult to manhandle language than to stroke it the right way.

In both life and writing it is a question of attitude and style. In *Hollywood*, when the director Joe Pinchot (a pseudonym for Barbet Schroeder, the director of *Barfly*) is seen briefly depressed by filming difficulties, Hank remarked ruefully: "I didn't like to see Jon lose his bravado." According to Hank, the right attitude is to swagger a little, not so much in front of other people but in the face of life and adversity: "We all played at being brave. I did too," he wrote in *Hollywood*.[7]

It is for this reason that when Schroeder alias Pinchot asks him if the scene he has just filmed reflects the reality of a backyard brawl between drunks, Hank recalls the most sordid and pathetic times of his past and objects that it is "not quite right."

"Why?

—Well, in our fights, the gladiators were more like clowns, they played to the crowd. One guy would land and almost blast the other guy off his feet, then turn to the crowd and say, 'Hey, how'd you like that one?'

—They hammed it up?

—Yes . . ."[8]

In life, as in his writing, Bukowski observed the same rule. He overdid things a little in order to both endow them with more expressive strength and to accentuate their grotesque element. With regard to this caricatured, and thus comic, element (certainly one of the reasons he admired Boccaccio and his *Decameron*), no one—I believe—has commented on the remarkable parallel that can be established between Charlie Chaplin and Charles Bukowski. There is even the happy coincidence of almost identical first names: when

Hank chose a first name that would sound good from the literary point of view, it is as if he let his subconscious decide for him: Charles Chaplin . . . Charles Baudelaire . . . He was indeed in good company with his choice.

Examining this parallel a little closer, it is evident that the tramp in *Modern Times* and the antisocial character in *Post Office* and *Factotum* have more than one trait in common. There is the swaggering element (Chaplin also adopts the boxer's stance) and also nagging destitution. Both are tramps, bums that are found each dawn struggling awake on a public bench, drop-outs trying the most diverse jobs, misfit playthings of circumstance. In short, they are outcasts by definition. Recall the scene in *The Gold Rush* where Chaplin looks forlornly through the window of a bar from the outside at the wild New Year's party that is in full swing. For those who have seen this, it is impossible not to link it with the scene in *Ham on Rye* where Hank watches the end of year ball at his school through a window. All the students from his class are dancing, unaware that they are being watched, twirling a thousand light years away from his silent suffering.

There are indeed many similarities between these two odd figures. They knew how to roll with the punches, how to face up to an unfavorable fate. Chaplin found support in his walking stick, Buk on a six-pack of beer. Both managed to make a stand through derision, laughter and humor. They generated grace and poetry from a sordid world. It is for this reason that they are like grains of sand in the system, which jam and incapacitate the machine of modern times.

This is perhaps what Buk would have liked Pinchot/Schroeder to have put across in his film. This is also perhaps the reason that, knowing the response could only be negative (as merited as it was), he set to writing the novel *Hollywood* that would replace the cinematographic endeavor in his own perspective:

"What are you going to do now?" Sarah asked.

. . .

—Oh, hell, I'll write a novel about writing the screenplay and making the movie.

. . .

—What are you going to call it?
—*Hollywood.*
—*Hollywood?*
—Yes . . .
And this is it."

And this is it. Fantastic ellipsis! *Hollywood* does not end with the celebration or success story that the achievement of the film *Barfly* represents but rather with that superior accomplishment that is the book in the reader's hands. This is certainly not unintentional. Hank distrusted the cinema, an art of illusion by definition, which he could only challenge. In *Hollywood*, he lets fly like small left and right hooks an endless list of cutting remarks at this specifically American art form, linked more than any other to the American way of life. The disabused blows that Buk inflicted on the world of cinema were in a way meant for the American dream in its entirety; the aim of his whole work is to denounce illusions, to tear up the veil that the world would have thrown over reality. There is, therefore, a certain irony in the first pages of *Hollywood* when a producer approaches Hank, who is leaning on the bar at Musso's, and says to him:

". . . I want to finance your screenplay. . . . I've read your work: very filmatic!"[9]

And as the conversation continues, the producer (renamed by Buk as Harold Pheasant) tells Hank what he has been involved in recently:

"Just finished producing a film about the life of Mack Derouac.

—Yeah? What's it called?
—*The Heart's Song.*"

The allusion is clear for anyone familiar with the Beat legend. *The Heart's Song* can only be *Heart Beat*, the film with Nick Nolte and Sissy Spacek in 1979 based on *Heart Beat*,

Carolyn Cassady's first book, and the draft of what in 1990 would become *Off the Road*. In *Heart Beat*, Carolyn tells of her marriage with Neal, her idyll with Jack and their temporary ménage à trois. The character Harold Pheasant provides the opportunity for Hank to cross paths with the Beats once again. In the exchange of words that follows, the kind of confusions that awaited him in *Hollywood* are evident.

"Hey wait a minute! You're joking! You're not going to call it *The Heart's Song*?

—Oh yes, that's what it's going to be called."

Hank could not believe his ears.

"You can't fool me, Pheasant. You're a real joker! *The Heart's Song*! Jesus Christ!"

What's worse, Pheasant was supposed to be producing Hank's future screenplay! When Sarah/Linda rejoined him a few minutes later at the bar he told her about it:

"Pheasant came over and he told me about this movie he produced. It's about a writer who couldn't write but who got famous because he looked like a rodeo rider.

—Who?

—Mack Derouac."

Kerouac fans will certainly not appreciate this Bukowskian portrait of their hero. "A writer who couldn't write!" Fortunately, Linda has that remarkable quality of being able to sort out people's relationships, including those that Hank had with long-dead writers. She, too, is a counterpuncher, diffusing the most delicate situations with a light tone. She retorted to Buk:

"You just wanted his movie to be about *you*.

—*That's it!* Hank exclaimed. I'll write a screenplay about myself!"

Ironically, we perhaps owe *Barfly* to the making of a film on Kerouac, to Buk's sensitivity, more affected than real, when a film about "The King of the Beats" is mentioned in front of him.

It was Jack's matinee idol looks that irritated Hank primarily. "He was even better looking than Marlon Brando," Joyce Johnson, one of his girlfriends, said of him.[10] As a good-looking rodeo rider and actor, Jack was too handsome to be "real," authentic in the Bukowskian perspective (which was ever tinged with humor). Jack was lacking in ugliness that, according to Bukowski, allows a truer contact with the reality of the world more than beauty; ugliness is a safe-conduct for hell and, as such, is infinitely closer to the truth. In fact, beauty is not even real to Buk's eyes, beauty doesn't make sense at all. As he said to Sean Penn, "there is no such thing as beauty . . . it's kind of a mirage of generalizations."[11] In Buk's opinion, Kerouac seemed like a cheap Roy Rogers whose work gets lost in a swirl of glitter and illusions where the word "wonderful" crops up every three sentences. Jack went wrong in trying to go with "heart's songs" and the illusions attached: hope of salvation on the road, faith in an idealized America, poetically fantasized, escape into an uncertain mysticism, oscillating between Buddhism and Catholicism. This was not Buk's cup of tea at all.

Neither was cinema. He did not understand at all "this great interest in a medium that relentlessly and consistently failed, time after time after time, to produce anything at all. People became so used to seeing shit on film that they no longer realized it was shit."[12] He believed even less in the cinema when it was a question of conveying his own work by this art of illusion. He had always known it was incapable of expressing his universe.

Maybe the art of comic strips was more successful at that. It should be underlined here that Buk came to represent an icon, chiefly for the underground but also a wider public, almost to the same extent as Tarzan, Felix the cat, Marilyn Monroe, James Dean and Charlie Chaplin. A character that incarnates a *type*, whether or not this type corresponds to its underlying reality. In popular imagery, Bukowski became the classic poet-bum figure, the unconventional and unrepentant drinker, the blind drunk dirty old man more or less obsessed with sex. This is undoubtedly the reason that Buk was the only writer that comic strips picked up on, from Crumb to Schultheiss, not only to illustrate some of his short stories but also to depict Buk's actual features in these short stories. One can hardly imagine Kerouac or Ginsberg as comic strip heroes! Nor Thomas Wolfe, Faulkner or even Hemingway. Hem clearly lacked the important attributes necessary to truly succeed in the comic strip realm, which relies greatly on humor, the grotesque, exaggeration, derision, caricature and extravagance—all elements that Bukowski had sole rights to. Buk had the face he had for a reason and he seduced the postmodernist cartoonists. His world opened up for them an inexhaustible source of iconographic inspiration, bursting with richness and garrulity, encouraging them to defy all the taboos as well. As Robert Crumb, who met him twice at the beginning of the seventies, said: "I like drawing Bukowski. He was an ugly bastard . . . I can identify with anyone who's ugly and alienated . . . I guess I like him because he's an alienated ugly man and 'makes no bones about it' and says what he had to say in as few well-chosen words as possible."[13] It is also clear that, more so than in the realm of cinema, Bukowski met in Crumb someone who was capable of completely identifying with him on an existential level: "Both times I met Bukowski he was fairly drunk. I don't think he was a great guy to socialize with. He didn't like people 'in-the-flesh' very much. To say he lacked social grace would be an understatement."

To return to the cinema, one man, however, succeeded in conveying some of the raw violence of Buk's work. Jean-Luc Godard, the French filmmaker who at the start of the '60s made *A bout de souffle*, the seminal film of the New Wave (a movie in which the actor Jean-Paul Belmondo, very much a Neal Cassady type, played the role of a young car thief . . .). This was an avant-garde movement that in some respects was akin to the Beat aesthetic. The New Wave also renounced all preliminary production and composition in favor of spontaneity, freedom and invention throughout filming. At

Jean-Luc Godard.

the end of the 1970s Godard wanted to use a scene from one of Bukowski's novels when he was preparing the film *Every Man for Himself*, which would mark his return to centre stage after several quieter years. This wish led to him being—without knowing it— integrated into *Hollywood* as a mini-guest star under the name of Jean-Luc Modard, "the French filmmaker," staying in suite 530 of the Beverly Hills Cheshire.

It will surprise no one that the meeting between Hank and Jean-Luc Modard was as doomed to failure as his meetings with William Burroughs and Jean-Paul Sartre. Great minds never met when Bukowski was involved. A first "meeting," which is not mentioned in *Hollywood*, took place between the two men at Hank's house in San Pedro. Linda Lee Bukowski recalls it: "Godard came first to our place with Barbet Schroeder, to spend the afternoon with a few friends and assistants, setting up cameras. Barbet was making the tapes. Sunny time, very hot. Godard didn't say a word, he just smiled, he went and sat in a corner, he asked his assistants to find food and sodas. They met, but no dialogue at all. Later we went to his hotel, and it was just as in his book *Hollywood* . . ."[14]

In the novel, Pinchot, Sarah, Henri-Léon Sanrahi, Jean-Luc Modard and Hank met one afternoon in suite 530 (which cost them nothing as the well-renowned Frances Ford Lopalla was paying, convinced that this gesture was the least necessary to welcome three or four geniuses brimming with screenplay ideas). Buk weighed up Jean-Luc Modard perfectly: "He stood very still, said nothing. You got the idea that he was posing, being a genius. He was small, dark, looked like he was shaved badly with a cheap electric razor."[15] Whoever met Godard would recognize the striking truth of this brief portrait that Buk completed by adding: "Jean-Luc Modard turned and walked to a dark corner, placed himself there and watched us." In short, Godard/Modard spontaneously took up his position in the other corner of the ring. Buk records the whole scene as if he were pacing about and reveling in a boxing ring.

Several bottles of red wine were opened. Modard was heard to cough slightly in his corner from which he eventually emerged to come closer to the small group and get a glass of wine. It was, of course, Buk who served him.

"I've read your shit, Modard said. Best thing about it, it's so simple. You have a case of brain damage, no?"

Buk was not at all bothered by the comment, agreed that the question was quite justified and went so far as to support it! The match had begun. Over a few glasses of wine this was how the scene was decided which would earn Bukowski an appearance in the credits of Godard's next film, one of his best. In Suite 530, Modard explained his plan to Hank:

". . . I have a scene I want to use from one of your stories, where the man gets a blow job under the desk and just goes about his business, answering the telephone and all that crap. Is it a deal?

—It's a deal, I said."

Now that the ice had apparently been broken between the two men, the chairs were pulled closer, they sat down and Modard started to talk without pause, pouring out on Buk an uninterrupted flow of words which soon wearied him despite their potential interest. So many words from the mouth of a genius and all irreparably lost, Hank thought. But what matter? At school they had bored him to tears with even greater geniuses such as Shakespeare, Tolstoy and others. So Buk let himself politely sink into one of his "pathetic cut-off periods" that he explained neatly: "Trying to be kind to others I often get my soul shredded into a kind of spiritual pasta."

The aforementioned scene—the man getting a blow job under his desk while carrying on with his business—would appear as planned in Godard's film. It is the most striking scene of *Every Man for Himself*, the one that is remembered when all the others have been forgotten. Visually it is the strongest, most shocking and violent. With this single scene, Godard gave due recognition to Bukowski's world by denouncing the absurd and grotesque mechanics of human relationships when they are regulated solely by money, sex and power, by dialectics of master and slave, by primary urges and total lack of sentiment.

Incidentally, the same criticism of the dehumanization of relationships is made by Raymond Carver in his poem "You Don't Know What Love Is (An Evening With Charles Bukowski)."[16]   A poem in which, using the first person singular, he parodies Buk in a manner that is both tender and full of humor tinged with mocking sarcasm:

> But you don't know what love is
> You don't know because you've never
> been in love it's that simple
> I got this young broad see she's beautiful
> She calls me Bukowski
> Bukowski she says in this little voice
> and I say What
> But you don't know what love is
> I'm telling you what it is
> but you aren't listening
> There isn't one of you in this room
> would recognize love if it stepped up
> and buggered you in the ass . . .

As a matter of interest, the real meeting between Bukowski and Godard followed the same pattern as those with Burroughs and Jean-Paul Sartre: it proved to be as impossible as bringing the two poles together. If Godard and

Buk did meet it was on screen in this single scene. Asked twenty years later if he had seen his portrait by Buk in *Hollywood*, Godard answered with a totally indifferent "No," saying he didn't even know about it and never read the book.[17]

The abortive meeting with Sartre was similar in that it did not take place in real life and yet on a certain level it did occur. Bukowski, like the Beats, had always been interested in French existentialism and such figures as Sartre and Camus. To a certain extent the Beat movement, born just after the war, had its counterpart in France—the mania for existentialist life: Sartre, Greco, Vian and Saint-Germain-des-Prés. Kerouac wrote about it in *Esquire* in March 1958: "The same thing was almost going on in the postwar France of Sartre and Genet and what's more we knew about it."[18] It was the same in New York and Paris—bohemia was born from the war in reaction against bourgeois order and propriety. They had more or less the same questions—What paths of freedom should we follow? There are many links. Genet, for example, was a friend of Sartre, Ginsberg and Burroughs. And Bukowski had passionately read Sartre's *Saint Genet, Comédien et Martyr* in 1964.

It looks all the more bizarre that Bukowski, as legend has it, refused to meet Jean-Paul Sartre when he was in Paris, in 1978.

It all started with an article in *Rolling Stone* in June 1976, which had it that Jean Genet and Sartre claimed that in their opinion Bukowski was "the greatest American poet alive today." No one knows where the magazine got this statement—possibly from Carl Weissner, Bukowski's German translator, who tried to create some publicity for him in his country. In his biography *Charles Bukowski: Locked in the Arms of a Crazy Life*, Howard Sounes, after taking the advice of several Anglo-Saxon philosophy specialists and a French poet, believed it highly improbable that such praise could ever have come from Sartre or Genet. It appeared that neither was familiar with Hank's work.[19]

Whatever, there is an element of truth in this legend. Hank and Sartre seemed destined to meet. Firstly, Buk's fans wanted public recognition, and if possible the greatest recognition possible, of their favorite author. A meeting between the American poet most disdained by the American literary establishment with one of the most important philosophers of the century could only enhance the profile of the former and increase his notoriety. A more significant reason is the close relationship in the underground imagination between these two striking figures. Sartre and Bukowski shared an external ugliness that transformed both to Socratic Sileni. Sartre's ugliness was due to his divergent squint while Buk owed his to his nose, which is marvelously described by Steve Richmond: "His nose, though, is unforgettable. It took over my vision for the first ten seconds or so . . . Veined, huge, red long drinker's, sot fellow's nose. It said immediately to me I have been there and you haven't."[20] Moreover, in both men this surface ugliness was contradicted and wiped out by a formidable creative power, a presence and power of seduction that ensured them a good deal of success with women (mostly after the age of 50 for Hank). In some respects Sartre and Buk were brothers in ugliness. Physically they incarnate rejection of beauty and the classical aesthetic. They embody the most radical challenges to the established order and its bourgeois values.

What could be more logical than to imagine a meeting between the two men when the opportunity arose? Although he was by this time almost blind, Sartre was still an accessible man, open to any meeting and still as curious about everything. He had written a whole book about Genet, and Hank's character couldn't but interest him. If he hadn't read him himself, there were in his entourage journalists, editors and all kinds of people who were familiar with Buk's work . . .

But first, are the reports that Sartre really requested to meet Bukowski true? Was such a proposition actually made? Linda Lee Bukowski is adamant: "Definitely, Sartre wanted to meet Hank! I guess it became known that Hank was in Paris . . ."[21]

If so, why did Hank refuse?

Of course, they differed in many areas. Firstly over the question of political and social commitment. One can no more imagine Buk by Ginsberg's side than one can picture him climbing on a barrel with Sartre to harangue the workers at the gates of the Renault factories. On the other hand, from the Sartrian perspective, Buk's lack of social and public commitment cannot be held against him. Bukowski's books, which reached a wide audience even if he did not write them with this intention, are perhaps the best evidence that despite himself Hank acted as a revolutionary factor for social change. The notion that Buk was a Sartrian character can even be defended. As a barfly, his situation was frequently comparable to that of the characters in Sartre's play *No Exit*, where "hell is other people." Buk was a man forced to put up with reality and get his hands dirty. A nonconformist who throughout his life tried to choose freedom and come to terms with his contradictions and darkness. In short, a man who, to use Sartre's terminology, couldn't be classified among the "bastards." However, the notion of Buk as a Sartrian figure should not be taken too far. Philosophically, they were poles apart. Sartre systematically deluded himself, particularly on the political level: Marxism is the impassable philosophy of our time, he maintained. Despite all his good intentions he was always fooled. Being taken in was what Buk wanted to avoid at all costs.

Was Bukowski unfavorably prejudiced against Sartre? Or, as legend has it, did he view the French philosopher as the incarnation of the whole intelligentsia of the time and want to send it packing? Even though Sartre himself had had the nerve to refuse the Nobel Prize for Literature in 1960.

In fact, the reason Sartre and Bukowski didn't meet was much more simple: the proposition came at the wrong time. Linda Lee Bukowski remembers it: "The second night in Paris, we had been out all night long, gathering and drinking at parties . . . We slept two hours. And then there was a big interview downstairs at the hotel with all kinds of people, French publishers . . . The message came that Sartre wanted to meet him. But Hank was so fucking over. He was done. Sartre may be a good guy or not. Hank couldn't do it. He refused it. It's not that he didn't like Sartre, but . . . He was also intimidated a little bit, maybe."[22] In other words, Buk didn't refuse to meet Sartre. He just couldn't meet him because he was drunk.

It was indeed a lost opportunity. Yet not as much as could be thought if it is acknowledged that books exist precisely to join souls, hearts and spirits.

For there is an epilogue to this story.

Years later at the end of the '80s and when Sartre had been dead for nearly ten years, there was a moment of communion between them in quite a strange and wonderful way. Whether it was conscious or not, Linda Lee—Buk's habitual guardian angel—instigated it. When Hank was going through a difficult period she gave him a book by Jean-Paul Sartre. "After he got tuberculosis," she recalls, "Hank couldn't go to the racetrack. He was depressed, very weak during that time. I gave him one of Sartre's old books. I can't remember which one . . . Concentration was difficult at that time and I gave him short stories . . ."[23] As Sartre published only one book of short stories, it is quite safe to say that the book she gave him was *The Wall*. Linda confirms this: "Yes, *The Wall*. He was blown away!"

Of the five short stories in *The Wall*, the one that particularly struck Hank was probably the one that gave its title to the collection, the one that appears first and is perhaps the most well-known. *The Wall* takes place during the Spanish Civil War and describes the last night of three men imprisoned in a cell, alone with their thoughts and panic. At dawn they are dragged blindfolded in front of a wall to be shot. In the hours before the execution Sartre lets the reader share the prisoners' different states of mind. He depicts the grey tinge of their skin, the feverish sweat that soaks their faces and clothes and their incontinence. They are so afraid that they are not even aware of the physical symptoms. Hank could identify with this type of situation only too well, the type of situation that puts a person in front of a "wall" to face his own ability to confront the inescapable. It could even be considered that his last novel, *Pulp*, where he plays a game of hide-and-seek with Death, was conceived from the knowledge, sharpened by illness, of this kind of ultimate confrontation.

The Wall poses the only question Buk considered important: how does a person make a stand whatever the given conditions? What fascinated him in this short story was the terrible and very real challenge posed by a situation that forces a man to draw on his internal resources in order to make a stand. Hank was at that time striving to make his own stand against tuberculosis. He didn't meet Sartre, but he was, at that time, just like one of his characters: "He said: 'I should have read him before, I should have met him in Paris . . . But it was too late.' Then he regretted it," says Linda.[24] A meeting regretted in this way is perhaps not completely lost . . .

BUK AT THE END: BEYOND THE MYTH

As said previously, before the release and success of Barbet Schroeder's film *Barfly* in 1987, only a narrow circle of poetry lovers was aware of Buk's work and they surprised their friends when they asked: "Didn't you know that Bukowski is a star in Europe?"

With Mickey Rourke and Faye Dunaway in the leading roles, Bukowski suddenly became a well-known name to a lot of people who had never read any of his work. At the film's première, the rich and famous crowded in and discovered him. According to Linda Lee Bukowski: "I really think that exposed him to a more general public. Definitely."[1] However, the misunderstanding about the author and his work was not dispelled. Hank was clearly unhappy with the result of the film, for which he had written the screenplay years earlier, on the request of his friend Barbet Schroeder, who worked very hard for seven years producing it; successive revisions of the script, financial difficulties, etc. Buk recounts all these events in detail in *Hollywood*.

Barfly confirmed a number of clichés about him. Rourke, who played Buk, conformed to the whole popular mythology of the "drunken poet." According to Linda, the actor went over the top: "Mickey Rourke made a choice to make Hank be a certain way, which Hank was not . . . He was neat, and Mickey just didn't pick up on that, he took this total opposite sort of image and portrayed him like the slob, this sort of disgusting and dishevelled bum."[2]

Obviously this could have been one of the producer's liberties. A film does not have to respect a literary work to the letter; but at least it should not betray its whole world. Linda continued: "Hank really was not happy with the film. He didn't think that the actors really expressed those people whom he had known, I mean, they were really living people in his life! And he didn't feel that Faye Dunaway was at all what he would have liked to have seen portraying Jane, this person who was somebody real to him. Faye Dunaway was trying to make it back in her career. She was getting older and she wanted to do something a little bit different. She was doing this character as if it were herself, becoming what she would be like if all this had happened to her. She thought that might help, which really did. It brought her back. But she is not experiencing the character whom Hank was writing about . . . She wasn't crazy enough, she just didn't let herself loose enough. She never really hit it. She didn't find the emotional confusion of this woman."

Far from the character that the film projects, Buk was never the tramp or the bum that has often been imagined. He was never slovenly, hirsute and neglected, sprawled out in the squalid mire of a filthy apartment with dirty, greasy hair, like Rourke in the film (it is a fact that Hank washed his hair every day). In order to live very frugally, in cramped rooms, he owned two sets of clothing. While he wore one of them, he washed the other and dried it by the window at night. Who would have believed that Hank had a clean shirt every day! Clean. Well turned out. More exactly: simplicity.

Perhaps the misunderstanding originates from the fact that his external appearance did not reflect his internal confusion at that time. The public got an impression of Buk from his writing, which expressed this "madness," supported by his physical ugliness and was fostered by the media, but that did not correspond to the reality.

By way of example, there is a photograph with Buk pictured next to a woman known as Georgia (she graced the cover of the Italian edition of *Tales of Ordinary Madness*, published in 1979 by Feltrinelli, entitled *Compagno di Sbronze*). Hank, evidently in a good mood, a bottle in his hand, a big drinker's paunch hanging out from his T-shirt, has his arm around the woman's shoulders. She was about forty with an odd appearance, dressed bizarrely, and the distracted look of a drunk just two steps away from madness, distress painted on a lived-in face, like it had been beaten up by life. Whoever came across this photo would imagine Hank with one of his flat-broke, shady girlfriends. This is not the case at all. Georgia was only a passing, casual affair to him—a local woman, a gypsy hooked on speed, who half an hour earlier that morning had a few troubles with the police. She turned up at Buk's place, disturbed, looking for shelter, help, comfort, a few moments of warmth. That day Hank was expecting Joan Levine Gannij, a freelance photographer who jumped at the opportunity to immortalize Georgia next to Hank for a future book titled: *Frigid:Air*. This photo perpetuates the legend . . .[3]

Georgia and Hank.

But it is not necessarily an unfaithful image. Buk thought a lot of that photograph, a real "icon" he would say. The above does not aim to detract from its surprising trueness to reality.

It expresses a poor woman's distress and helplessness very authentically. The fact that Hank is by her side is revealing in itself, symbolic. It says something, too, about his work.

Linda said: "Hank might have been dishevelled in his head, inside himself, but externally, even though he had nothing, he didn't look like a tramp or a bum. He had this wild image early on, like getting into fights, and drinking and all this stuff, but somehow he had a decorum about himself in spite of all that. Even in those terrible times, those crazy times, that was still there."[4]

Despite all the Hollywood compromises that Schroeder had to comply with, *Barfly* is not a bad film. Linda commented accurately: "It became like a cartoon, like a comic book . . . I mean, I think that's like a comic book version of the story that Hank wrote." Sean Penn did not get to play the leading role and he would perhaps have lent more credibility to the character, especially as he was a friend of Hank and Linda's ("like a surrogate son, like a little son to us"). Sean said: "I'll do it for one dollar, but you've got to have Dennis [Hopper] director." Buk, true to his word to Barbet Schroeder, could only reply: "Sorry man."

The only way to discover the real Buk is to reread his work, including his poems, of which a small amount is translated into French, German, Italian, etc. Between the projected image of Buk, the perpetually drunk poet, the agitator, bum, tramp sprawled in a pile of beer bottles, between lays, vomiting and insults, there is another Bukowski, less immediately visible, with a more discreet presence. But this Buk is more real, more human, one that we never knew or wanted to know because we had not read him properly. A Buk hiding great sensitivity to human pain under the appearance of Quasimodo: kindness, beauty and paradoxical sensitivity, that only an Esmeralda could see. A striking contrast. Not the beauty and the beast. But the beast and poetry: ugliness and beauty curiously joined in a single being. Quasimodo indeed: the monstrous bells he rang violently and demonically with full force from the top of Notre-Dame are like Bukowski's shouts and madness. The chords that this gargoyle plucks in us are born from the same sensitivity to despair. The same deformed and grotesque fury masks the same pain. Bukowski also had intelligence and humor. All this along with the distance he kept, enabled him to create works of art. Perhaps Bukowski was a Victor Hugo kind of character with the same excessiveness that only the virtues of poetry could ease. Buk's life and work never lacked humor and a sense of the comical. If there are elements of Boccaccio, there are also elements of Gargantua in Hank, and some Poe, the sense of the grotesque and bizarre, occasionally macabre.

Buk was undoubtedly under pressure from the public and success and he projected the image that was expected of him. Playing on his rock star status, he was surprised himself by the popularity that his unexpected showy performances brought him, which he discovered at the beginning of the '70s. Yet at the same time he did not merge with this character. On the contrary, he distanced himself from it, not to take a step backwards, but to go forwards, towards himself.

The Hank of the '80s and '90s was no longer the Hank of the '60s and '70s. Linda said: "In the early days indeed it was not an exaggeration, those stories people told about him. But of course, just like anything else that is alive, it evolves. He evolved, and he didn't retain that image. He seemed just to grow into another part of himself, another aspect of himself. And then he wasn't that image anymore. Not to say he didn't act up sometimes, meaning getting a little bit crazy and become that again on different occasions. Indeed at one point, he was like that. But in general he just evolved, he grew up. He just did other things and acted maybe not so frivolously. It wasn't something that he tried to do, that was just a natural evolution of himself. He became more of himself, I think, he explored more of who he was, within himself."[5]

One of the aspects of Hank that has thus never really been highlighted is his authentic naivete with a real friendly disposition towards people that was evident to all those who met him. Linda commented: "He was not a malicious man. He was very naive. Or it would be easier to say he was innocent." He had two faces of innocence peculiar to childhood: "He was childlike and sometimes childish— which are two different things. Childlike is somebody who takes things, experiences in wonderment. Childish is somebody who reacts to life in a very immature emotional way. He did both. But, I think, as he got older, his simplicity, his natural naivete came through all of the emotional sort of hanging on to unfortunate experiences that he had in his life. And so he eliminated them eventually to a point where he could explore different possibilities within himself."

Gradually through experiences, difficulties, and hardships, everything became clear, and he came to a point where he found himself more in tune with himself; in other words, with a new field of exploration before him. "He could respond differently, not necessarily violently or negatively. He became more responsible in a sense . . . Not to react but just to experience it and not have a bad time with himself, and not hurting himself so much."[6]

Quite surprisingly, towards the end of his life, he became friends with Buddha (which leads us to the Beats . . .). Five or six months after the leukemia was diagnosed, in 1993, Buk had a period of remission during which he set himself to studying transcendental meditation with Linda in the direction of Santa Monica. Twice a day, Hank sat in his armchair in the house in San Pedro, and he meditated for twenty minutes, reciting a mantra (while a family of possums sometimes came onto the veranda to eat the food left there for them). Hank was very calm. "He accepted." Tuberculosis (in 1988), death's approach, writing *Pulp,* and leukemia surely change a man.

He practiced this kind of meditation until the end, even when he had to go to chemotherapy sessions and stay in the hospital again. He and Linda were in the white room. Linda said to a nurse that she and Hank would like to pray for a moment—it was a Catholic hospital—and the nurse left them alone. Linda closed the door, she sat next to the bed and they meditated together. When he was alone Hank would meditate again sometimes, right until his death.

Buddha really was a friend of his, but Hank had no intellectual interest in him. Not the slightest inclination to undertake the slightest study, to read up on the subject, to go into it deeply. "He didn't study Buddha, he didn't read, he didn't even practice necessarily. He just liked him."[7] Not the least temptation for hazy philosophy or shallow religiosity. Quite simply it was the guy that interested him. A guy with guts, Buddha. Better still, a guy that had understood fairly

early on what Buk had also realized, perhaps at the same age: you have to know how to keep your distance in everything. This is the only way to respond to the hand destiny deals you. The only way to take up the gauntlet.

Although he had no philosophical interest in Buddha, Buk had sympathy for him, a completely intuitive sympathy. Buddha's attitude and posture seemed to Buk to be deeply and correctly founded. Linda said: "He never put him down, he never had a bad thing to say about Buddha. That itself was pretty good for me. He seemed to have an inner calm, quiet presence all the time within himself, even when he was very upset or very filled with anxiety or negativity."[8]

The feature perhaps runs deeper in Charles Bukowski than it seemed to and it gives us a good insight into him. As the years passed, a fundamental element that had always been present in the dirty old man's heart, this same element that had undoubtedly enabled him to write, became more clear. A kind of deep interior calm that inhabited him despite all the external manifestations of his "madness" and that always enabled him to reconsider the "accidents" of his own life by relativising them.

A part of him remained in the eye of the cyclone. This part stayed intact while all the rest: fury, despair, disappointments, human and inhuman comedies whirled both outside and inside him. For the readers of his poems, the matter suddenly appears clear: internal detachment was already there touching everything in life from the most banal to the maddest.

Buk had attained a kind of calm presence—right down to the delivery of his slow voice that seemed to put the world we live in in its correct place. He had succeeded in being like a boxer who kept all the incidents at the correct distance by his simple and calm speech. He never seemed to lose this internal calm, even in the final agony. In spite of the distress of imminent death, and understandable anxiety, this zone of deep calm remained at the deepest part inside him. Linda confided: "I think that somehow he was just in tune with his inner self." It is precisely in this that his attitude runs parallel with Buddha's. Even though, as Linda said, "he wouldn't put a category on his internal attitude."[9]

Hank's internal attitude was very similar to that of the Beats, Kerouac, Ginsberg and Snyder who were sensitive very early on to this form of mental attitude. It could even be said that his work itself, from the outset, contained the seeds of an essential feature of Buddhist philosophy. James Campbell had already highlighted this in *Bananas* in 1981: "Out of a face-to-face confrontation with constant failure and grief, Bukowski has learned compassion; it is the hallmark of his writing. For all his aggressiveness, its anger and its sour impatience with people and places, Bukowski's work is made with compassion."[10]

His gravestone, number 875 I at Green Hills Memorial Park in Palos Verdes a few miles away from San Pedro, bears the epitaph "Don't try." Some of his fans concluded that it meant: don't try to move my gravestone. In fact, "Don't try" was Hank's response to a questionnaire for the development of a Who's Who In America (the kind of questionnaire to which Beckett when he was asked why he wrote, responded: "Bon qu'à ça," which means "It's the only thing I'm good at"). The Who's Who asked nothing less than a definition of his "personal philosophy of life." "Don't try," Buk replied. What did he mean by this? The answer remained for a long time sort of a mystery. Linda was not wrong when she said it could mean: "Don't try, be it! do it! at the exact moment." In *Reach for the Sun*, the third volume of his letters, published in 1999, Hank explains: "Well, it means if the stuff doesn't jump on you and make you do it, forget it, in writing and in everything else."[11]

How should the pair of boxing gloves engraved on the gravestone be understood? Buk was a man of combat, a "counterpuncher" as the Americans say. A guy who retaliates with a punch to the punches thrown at him. It was true of his skill in writing as of his conversation. This internal attitude, this boxer's stance was natural to him. But it did not end by winning the slightest fight. Neither life nor death can ever be conquered. It was simply a behavior. Show courage, stand up. Don't try. Do what you have to do (kind of the same idea is found in Hemingway, except that Hem, says Buk, "had no humor at all" and lacked this important thing: "the laugh through the flame"). Fight because it is the only worthy attitude, the only one that is acceptable when life wants to break you.

It was in the same frame of mind that Hank would sit down in front of his typewriter, or later his Mac, to write. He tuned into classical music, drank a mouthful of beer or wine, lit up a cigarette and started to type, without giving it any prior thought. A completely physical, natural activity without any involvement in or deliberate appeal to the intellect or tradition, without anything romantic, visionary, affected, forced or inspired. Being the most natural possible; this should come from inside oneself. His poetry, with its defects and faults, flowed from the source.

AN EVENING
AT BUK'S PLACE

BUK

A good story is a good story. It is immortal.
                                        —*Charles Bukowski*

AN EVENING AT BUK'S PLACE

The meeting took place on a Monday evening. Several weeks earlier, on the other side of the Atlantic, I had received a card from Buk with the simple typewritten message: *Interview o.k. Skim over Hades.* The card was accompanied by a small funny drawing, as was Buk's custom. On the Sunday evening, I called from my hotel—the post-modern Westin Bonaventure, which Jean Baudrillard describes so well in *America*—to make sure our meeting was still on for the next day at 2 p.m. Linda, his wife, answered the phone. Hank thought it would be better for me to come at 8 p.m. Okay. The next evening outside the hotel, night was already falling—it was in February— and an inactive limousine chauffeur offered me his vehicle, which was as long as three cadillacs and had the full works—bar, saloon and TV—for the price of a normal cab. So I arrived in style in San Pedro at the house hidden by greenery where Charles Bukowski and Linda had lived for several years. A path lined with pantagruelian rosebushes with worrying thorns led to the front door. I knocked.

How long did we spend in the candlelit living room? Buk and me on the sofa; Linda, young, slim and beautiful, sitting on the floor; the coffee table in front of us bearing the red bottle and large glasses. Was it three, four hours? Everything else around was quiet, only the occasional sound of a cat knocking into something. We saw the large trees outside rustle. The evening remains unforgettable.

Linda and Hank.

JEAN-FRANÇOIS DUVAL: Hey, there is just this tiny candlelight on the table . . . You prefer the dark?

LINDA LEE BUKOWSKI: Oh! You don't like it?

DUVAL: Well, I really don't mind.

LINDA: You see, Hank ordinarily prefers the light out, or less light . . .

CHARLES BUKOWSKI: That's just when I'm drinking.

DUVAL: Yesterday, on the phone, you told me you preferred me to come at 8 p.m. rather than at 2 p.m, as we first arranged. Is there any meaning in this?

BUKOWSKI: Oh yes, there is. I'm not at all alive in the daytime. I just walk around like a dead thing. I was always like that as a child, till the sun went down, I was dark, I didn't lighten up. My mother always used to say: what is it with you? . . . nothing happens till it gets dark and then you start doing things . . . So I relate to night. Night to me is more lively, more romantic, more real than the day. Daytime makes me dizzy. So it's better you come at night. If you

were here in the daytime, I would just sit here and say: yeah . . . okay
. . . Maybe I'm doing it now . . . (laughs)

DUVAL: And no night without wine? You prefer it to beer now?

BUKOWSKI: The blood of the gods. You can drink a lot of it and stay
relatively sane. I used to drink an awful lot of beer. But wine is the
best for creation. You can write three or four hours . . . You drink
whisky, there is trouble . . . So I don't want to drink any whisky
around you. Because then I think I'm tough. Then I got to prove it.

DUVAL: (laughs) Do you still have to prove it, sometimes?

BUKOWSKI: (roars) Oh, only when necessary. But it was always like
that.

DUVAL: (laughs, a little uneasily) Huuh! But what do you mean by
"only when necessary"?

BUKOWSKI: When I feel like it, it's necessary. It may not be just . . .
But it's needed. Hey man, don't take us too seriously, Linda and me.

DUVAL: Is life a fight, from the beginning to the end?

BUKOWSKI: It appears that way. However, I think the secret is pace.
Fight a little, rest a little. Fight again, rest. Pace is the secret. That
means stopping, starting, going at a certain rate. A rhythm of doing
things.

DUVAL: But we do need to fight?

BUKOWSKI: That's what they tell us. They also tell us we need pain.
Who are these people who tell us these things? All I want is
happiness. I'll take it twenty-four hours a day if I get it. But I can't
seem to get it. Any other questions? This is it?

DUVAL: (laughs) Of course not, it's just the beginning of it! . . . So
you're not happy now?

BUKOWSKI: Oh, I'm just like you. I'm happy some time, other times I'm very depressed. And most of the time I'm just in the middle—a little happy, a little unhappy, a little content . . . I'm generally contented.

DUVAL: Whom am I talking to tonight? Henry Chinaski or Charles Bukowski?

BUKOWSKI: Well, the few people I know call me Hank. My first name is Henry, you see. Hank is slang for Henry. And when I first started writing, I said it can't be Henry Bukowski, because nobody would ever publish it. Because Henry and Bukowski were too much alike. You see, they both have this curve of sound: Henry, Bukowski . . . Up and down. You put Charles Bukowski, that's a straight line. That sounds like a writer. Also my father always called me Henry. So I thought I would get rid of Henry for a while. Linda has heard all of this . . .

LINDA: Yeah, ha, ha.

BUKOWSKI: So I'm really Hank, but I write as Charles Bukowski. The last name is the same: Bukowski.

DUVAL: You are also Chinaski in some of your short stories.

BUKOWSKI: Chinaski, yes, and Bukowski a very few times.

DUVAL: So who is who?

BUKOWSKI: Mostly I'm Chinaski (laughs). I'm Hank Chinaski. He is the more interesting one, you see. Generally he has done the interesting things, or the painful things. And I only write about the interesting things—I think they are interesting.

DUVAL: Do you mean he is some sort of a fictitious character? Or a double of yourself?

BUKOWSKI: No. He is me. The same.

DUVAL: *(bringing out one of Hank's books)*. Look, I've got one of your books here with me. The French editor put "novel" under the title . . . But it's not!

BUKOWSKI: What is that book?

DUVAL: The French title is *Souvenirs d'un pas grand-chose*. The book where Chinaski tells about his childhood. Your story in fact.

LINDA: When he first was a young boy? Oh, *Ham on Rye* . . .

BUKOWSKI: Oh, *Ham on Rye*. You see, ham on rye is an American sandwich. So they couldn't use it in French, no one would understand.

LINDA: *(going to the bookcase and coming back)* You see, this is the American version.

DUVAL: Mmm, okay, yes.

BUKOWSKI: So you were going to say it doesn't appear to be a novel?

DUVAL: I wanted to know if everything in it was completely true, or if there was some part of fiction.

BUKOWSKI: Well, it's 94 percent true. The rest is just polishing. It's really all true except parts I left out that shouldn't be in . . . Let's say it's a hundred percent true, okay? I haven't read it in a while, so it's difficult for me to know what I've written. I write so damn much. When people ask me something, I have to think . . . I write too much.

DUVAL: Did you write today?

BUKOWSKI: No, I was at the track. Race track. I probably would have written tonight. But see, you're here, so . . .

DUVAL: Sorry.

BUKOWSKI: *(laughs)* So you spoiled my night.

DUVAL: But did you write last night?

BUKOWSKI: No. Just the night before.

DUVAL: And what are you writing now?

BUKOWSKI: Just poems. I'm on a poem kick, and I hope it will end soon, and I'll get to short stories. But right now, it's all poetry. It just keeps coming out, poetry. I don't know why, and I don't question it, I go with it. So I never plan anything. Whatever comes out, comes out. So . . . right now, it's all poetry. Perhaps because my next book is going to be all poetry, and I'm giving him—my editor—this now so we have a good choice, I hope.

DUVAL: I think you are best known in the U.S. as a poet, whereas in Europe, we don't know much about your poetry. We read mainly your short stories or novels.

BUKOWSKI: Yeah, I think you're right. I don't know why. But here in the United States, poets seem a romantic kind of people. A man as a poet, he is supposed to be more exceptional, have more soul, or something . . . I don't agree with this. But they tend, here in America, to make a poet out of a man if they possibly can, because it's more romantic in their eyes for a man to be a poet than a novelist. What the hell is a novelist? He takes two or three years to write something! A poet is always on fire! Shit, he is typing every other night. So if I'm known as a poet, that probably has something to do with a more romantic aspect of looking at a person. That's all I know . . . Is it over now?

DUVAL: (laughs) No!

BUKOWSKI: No?

DUVAL: Well, that's just the beginning of it, I told you.

BUKOWSKI: All right.

DUVAL: I've plenty of questions as you see.

Hank at the entrance to his childhood home on Longwood Avenue in Los Angeles.

BUKOWSKI: *(as if apologizing)* Oh, I was just worried: when I run out of wine, I stop talking. You see, we have two bottles . . .

LINDA: No, we have three!

BUKOWSKI: Three? Well, that should do. One for him, two for me, okay. Or two for him, and one for me.

DUVAL: *(laughs)* A drinking contest? You used to do drinking contests, I think.

BUKOWSKI: Yeah, I remember that. *(Filling the glasses)* The drinking contests? Yeah, I often won them.

DUVAL: Did you ever lose?

BUKOWSKI: Not that many. But at the time I was very good. I could drink a lot, and I could outdrink about everybody. I think I've always had a taste for it, you know. It's pleasant. It feels good. And during these contests, all the drinks were free, you know. It was very nice. And to get paid for drinking.

DUVAL: Alcohol, wine, are they a kind of veil of illusion you throw upon reality? Or is it a way to see things more clearly?

BUKOWSKI: Well, to me, it gets me out of the normal person that I am. Like I don't have to face this person day after day, year after year . . . The guy that brushes his teeth, he goes to the bathroom, he drives on the freeway, he stays sober forever. He only has one life, you see. Drinking is a form of suicide where you're allowed to return to life and begin all over the next day. It's like killing yourself, and then you're reborn. I guess I've lived about ten or fifteen thousand lives now. But a man who drinks, he can become this other person. He has a whole new life. He is different when he is drinking. I'm not saying he is better or worse. But he is different. And this gives a man

141

two lives. And that's usually in my other life, my drinking life, that I do my writing. So, since I've been lucky with the writing, I've decided drink is very good for me. Does that answer your question a little?

DUVAL: So you drink to write?

BUKOWSKI: Yes, it helps my writing.

DUVAL: Preferably wine, as you said.

BUKOWSKI: Wine helps keep things normal. I used to drink beer and scotch together. And write. But you can only write for maybe an hour or an hour and a half that way. Then, it's too much. But with wine, as I said, you can write three or four hours.

DUVAL: And with beer?

BUKOWSKI: Beer, well . . . you have to go to the bathroom every ten minutes. It breaks your concentration. So the wine is the best for creation. The blood of the gods.

DUVAL: Does all that make you feel near to such poets as Verlaine or Rimbaud, all this tradition? Though, I think, you don't seem to like Rimbaud . . .

BUKOWSKI: Their lives are sometimes interesting, but their work isn't. I always had problems with the poets. Frankly, they just bore me. They don't do anything for me. And also the prose writers. All my life I've had problems finding something to read. And I guess this is why I write the way I do. In a fashion that I think can be read by somebody else. It's very difficult for me to enjoy a book. Like *War and Peace* . . . Tolstoy, Shakespeare . . . I can see why the children in literature class are bored. The stuff is bad.

DUVAL: *(laughs)* Diogenes was looking for a man. So, you're looking for a book?

BUKOWSKI: Oh, I see. He didn't find his man, did he? I haven't found my book . . . Oh, there are maybe six or eight books I've enjoyed. But nothing that really makes me say: this is so exceptional! So I'm just not built to read literature. I'm not made right to appreciate literature. What I enjoy reading, I think, are the daily newspapers. I can start at the beginning, and find little things here and there. It's much more interesting than a great novel, the daily newspaper. And sometimes, you know, I get a short story out of it, a short story idea of something I read in there, what people do . . . And what does a newspaper cost? Twenty-five cents . . . A book costs money.

DUVAL: And which are those six or eight books you like?

BUKOWSKI: Well, I have to think about that . . . Dostoyevsky. All of him. All his books. And then there is Celine's one book. I never get the title . . . *Journey to the End of Night?* . . . *Time! Journey to the End of Time* . . . or *of Night?* I never get it right! Okay. Anyhow, I really enjoyed that. When I went to bed, I read it cover to cover. Shaking with laughter in bed. It was so good, it made me laugh out aloud. Strange what it did. And I said: Here is a man that can write better than I can. There was no jealousy. I loved the fact that somebody could write better than I could . . . Then, let me think . . .

DUVAL: But Celine wrote out of hate, of a horrible hate . . . Is this also the case with you?

BUKOWSKI: No, I don't write out of hatred. If I write from anything, it's from two things: one is disgust, and the other is joy. If we have to name something. It's very difficult to name what makes you write. Then I would say those two things. Disgust and joy. I don't have them at the same time. But that's my minefield.

DUVAL: Where does your disgust come from? And your joy?

BUKOWSKI: You see, if I analyze that, it might go away. If I found out where joy came from, maybe I would never have joy again. I don't play with things like that. I let them be. That's for the philosophers to play with. Whoever wants to.

DUVAL: And style? What is style to you?

BUKOWSKI: Style is just doing the best you can under any given conditions. That's all it is. And when people don't do the best they can, under any given conditions, they don't have style.

DUVAL: I meant style in writing.

BUKOWSKI: Oh, I thought you meant in living.

DUVAL: Maybe it's the same.

BUKOWSKI: Well, again, writing . . . I can't tell you about my own writing. Because that's a gangue, you break the egg to see what's inside, you don't get the chicken. So that question I don't quite understand it—what is style in writing.

DUVAL: But the fact that you never found the book you wanted in libraries, is it not a question of style? Was it not the style that disappointed you in all those books?

BUKOWSKI: Oh, yes. They took too long to say too little. And they said it in an uninteresting fashion. They wasted a lot of pages. That's all. It's disappointing.

DUVAL: But who are "they"?

BUKOWSKI: Name anybody!

DUVAL: Norman Mailer . . . Shakespeare!

BUKOWSKI: Shakespeare! you can put him at the bottom of the list.

LINDA: Oh!

DUVAL: But wasn't he good in his time?

BUKOWSKI: Yeah, I realize there is a change of language there that makes it difficult. But even with the language changes! He says things now and then. I can take a sentence or two, you know, a phrase that's very nice. But it's tied in with kings and ghosts and all that crap, you know . . . It's too fucking fancy for me. Even though at

144

"I'd rather read the newspaper."

times you get awful good shots here and there, it's not worth it to me. I'd rather read the newspaper.

DUVAL: You prefer what your friend Becker wrote, which you tell about in *South of No North* and *Ham on Rye* . . .

BUKOWSKI: It wasn't his real name.

DUVAL: He was just an unknown guy, whose talent was promising. You say, it was full of emotion and at the same time very contained. But he could have become a great writer . . .

BUKOWSKI: I think in the book, I have him sitting in a bar and he is going to the war, and he says: suppose some stupid son of a bitch points a machine gun at me, and squeezes the trigger . . . That's what happened. He caught I don't know how many bullets, and he didn't make it. Who knows if he would have been a good writer or a bad writer . . . but he was good at the time.

DUVAL: But what did you like about his writing? His ability to express emotions?

BUKOWSKI: Yeah, he was a good writer, but he was careful. Too careful. He didn't gamble enough with his words. And if you don't gamble, you're not gonna go anywhere.

DUVAL: Do you think that in their life people are, in general, too careful? That they live too restrained a life?

BUKOWSKI: Well, in our society, they are almost given no choice. Either do your eight hour job, or you starve to death. So the restraint is laid upon them by society and their fear keeps them that way. How many can break out of that? What can they do? Some people can't paint, some people can't put on boxing gloves, I mean you have to have some exceptional thing to get you out of this eight hour day,

145

and the restraint is their choice: should I die in the street, or should I go to my job everyday, which I hate? It's not so much restraint. There is no choice for them.

DUVAL: Did you feel that you had choice yourself?

BUKOWSKI: No, I always figured that I would be at the eight hour job forever, and the only thing I could figure out was: the only way to save a little of yourself there, was to keep changing jobs all the time, no matter how bad the jobs were. And to travel, from city to city. At least you get some variety. It's not the same place everyday, back and forth. So that's all I could see, my only way out was to change jobs, work as little as possible, and change cities, which I did for many many years. Then I got lucky, and now I just sit by the typewriter, I go to the race track, and give interviews . . .

DUVAL: You felt rejected from society from the beginning. You mentioned your father just before. You dedicate *Ham On Rye* "to all the fathers," adding later on in the book that "fathers aren't much." That's hard.

BUKOWSKI: Yeah. I'm hoping all the fathers read that. So maybe they will be better fathers to their sons. The fathers aren't much, so when I say "to all the fathers," it's kind of a joke. Care of you, to all of you, who act this way . . . I didn't feel rejected. I just felt as if I were in the wrong place, being a child with those parents. Like when I went to sleep at night . . . I'm sure many children have this feeling. You lay in bed in the dark and you say: those aren't my parents in the other room, that's somebody else. That's the feeling you get. It's more lost, confusion, because you really don't want them, because they don't act right, you understand? You can't be rejected by somebody you don't care too much for. So, it's more confusion of being where you don't feel like you should be. And then you go to school: it's the same thing. The teachers are just like your parents. And then you get a job, and your boss is like your parents. And you get married and ha, ha, ha . . . No, no, that's a joke. (*To Linda*) We make little jokes, don't we?

146

Hank and his daughter, Marina.

LINDA: Mmm.

BUKOWSKI: All right.

DUVAL: You felt as if you had been adopted by your parents?

BUKOWSKI: Yeah. I've read many other children have that feeling. That's a normal feeling. You probably had that, right? You just say, my parents wouldn't treat me like that.

DUVAL: At that time, the air seemed to you completely white . . .

BUKOWSKI: Milk white. You got it, the air was always white. It was not right. Everything was wrong: the air, the people and there was no smog either.

DUVAL: You felt a kind of cruelty, especially from the other children at school.

BUKOWSKI: Children certainly tend to get together and gang up on anybody who is a little bit different. Adults do too. But children are very good at it. And I was one of the victims of the schoolyard gang. When I was small, I was what they call the "sissy." Because my father never let me go outside to play with the other children. So I didn't know how to catch a ball, swing a baseball bat. I didn't get in the games. So suddenly I am at school! I'm put in a game, somebody throws a ball at me, and I didn't know, I couldn't care, I dropped it, cause I had no practice *(with a childlike mocking voice)*: "Hey! Henry can't catch a ball! Whoa! Henry can't catch . . ." They had been practicing for, you know, all their life. So this was my father . . . *(with the voice of his father, trying to make him feel ashamed)*: "Henry, you can't play with those children." See, all this helped make a writer out of me, my father was a good man . . . Anyhow, in school, this continued, but I did get some practice, you see, finally, and gradually, from being the sissy, I turned it all around, and I became the leader, the tough guy. They came to me. Well, this took six, eight, ten years . . . Till I got into high school, or junior high . . . They started following me around, kind of a leader, in high school, and then in college, I was the

148

guy, in class and out of class. So from being the sissy, I turned all around into, I don't mean the leader, but the mean and the vicious. I transformed it all around, which is interesting, I don't know how many do that . . . And now I don't know even what I am . . . That's all.

DUVAL: Was it so important to become the tough guy?

BUKOWSKI: Well, it's wearing to be picked on, it is not nice to be followed home by eight or ten people threatening to beat you up. And for your own survival, you must do something about this or you keep taking the beatings. So I started beating people up. And I found it wasn't bad. Better to beat than to be beaten. It feels better.

DUVAL: It all happened in the schoolyard?

BUKOWSKI: Not too often. Because they knew that I wasn't a true sissy. They knew there was something very dangerous about me. They used to follow two of us home, me and my friend Wencho. And they'd circle us, and they'd finally close in on Wencho, and start beating him on the ground, hitting him. And they would circle me, and I would just wait . . . but they never closed in on me. They felt there was something dangerous there. And I felt it too. I said if they come in on me, I'm gonna do something . . .

DUVAL: You say somewhere that you felt the other children always knew something you didn't know.

BUKOWSKI: I said this? No, no, I always had the opposite feeling . . . Oh, you mean when I was very very young? . . . The schoolyards are very confusing . . . The most terrible places . . . They always knew what to do. They played games, they played little balls, ran around in a circle. And I would stay watching them and saying: What are they doing? Why do they do that? Why do they run in a circle like that, back and turn this way? But in another sense I said: This is stupid. I said: They know something, at the same time they don't know.

DUVAL: How did you feel about girls at school?

BUKOWSKI: Well, I feel about girls now, just like I did then. That the calling part on the part of the male entails a lot of bullshit and falseness that I had rather not go through. Like dating and talking and making all the jeers and going through all these movements, making little jokes and cleaning yourself, standing in front of the mirror, all this bullshit, I didn't want to bother with that. I think that's why I went directly to the whore. I said, hey, have a drink, you know, and that was it. We just dispense with one other. Courtship? Nonsense! Because there is a lot of lying in that. A lot of untruth. A lot of game playing, what I don't come to do.

DUVAL: People who don't suffer lack something? All that suffering helped you create?

BUKOWSKI: I guess it did. But . . . you know, that's an old theory, an old formula, that you have to suffer in order to write. It might be true . . . but I dislike it. I'd prefer never to suffer, and never to write. I'd rather be happy, and never write, you understand? Writing is not that important. It is to me now, because they have me all fucked up, and I have to do it.

DUVAL: Who?

BUKOWSKI: You, them (laughs) . . . You know, a long time ago, I used to fight against happiness, I'd say: Anybody who is happy, there is something wrong with him, they are not thinking right . . . I don't do that anymore, and I say: If I can be happy, I'll take it, and if it's unsophisticated, I'll be unsophisticated. And I'll take all the happiness I can get. So you see, I have changed in certain ways . . . And I've often written what I think is my best stuff when I'm feeling very good. So no, I don't entirely agree with that theory. I think happiness can create great works of art. You take Bach's music, he is very joyful. He believed in God. I don't. But believing in God made him very elated. His music doesn't come from pain. And Haydn, his music is very joyful. Great poetry comes from happiness, from unhappiness, from disgust, joy, boredom, it comes from everywhere.

So I guess that's an old formula. Everything creates poetry. And very little poetry is created. Does that answer some of it?

DUVAL: But each time you are celebrated, invited to give some lecture, you destroy the party—as if you didn't want people to love you . . .

BUKOWSKI: I gave readings for money. To get the rent. To eat. For a drink. But I didn't like the people at my readings. And I didn't like to read. I don't think writing has anything to do with getting up and reading your writings in front of a crowd. I think that's a form of vanity. That's acting. Nothing to do with creation. So I only read because I needed the money. And I disliked it, and I disliked the crowd, and I disliked the whole thing. So all I did was get drunk, read my poems and insult the audience, collect my money and leave. Because it was just another job.

DUVAL: That's what happened in Paris, at the famous TV broadcast *Apostrophes,* which everybody remembers . . . You left in the middle, completely drunk . . .

BUKOWSKI: Ha! ha! ha! Yes, I keep getting into trouble. Well, that was a snob bit there. It was just too much for me. It was too much literary snobbishness. I can't stand it. I should have known. I thought maybe the language barrier would make it easier for me, but . . . I couldn't handle that. I couldn't handle that crap. It was stiff, the questions were literary and refined, there wasn't any air, you couldn't breath, there wasn't any oxygen, you couldn't feel any goodness. Just these people around talking about their books! It was horrible. So I went crazy.

LINDA: I was there. It was even worse than on TV.

BUKOWSKI: (laughs) Linda told me more what happened later.

LINDA: They got him drunk, before he went on. They gave him wine . . .

BUKOWSKI: Oh, that's all right, that has nothing to do with it.

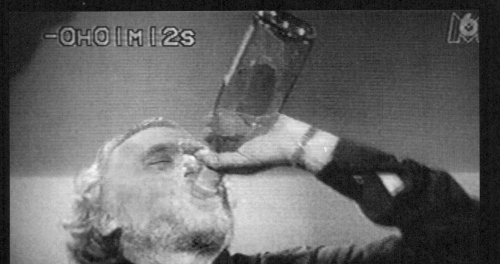

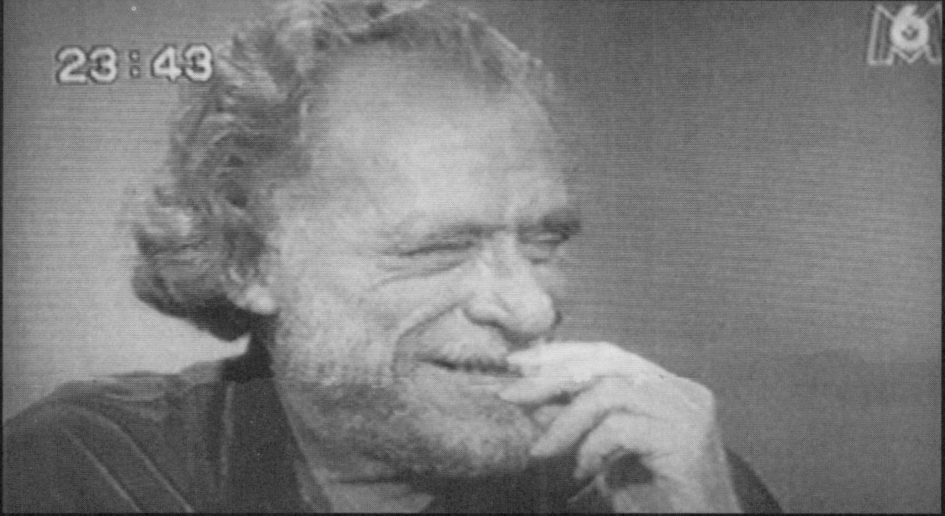
23:43

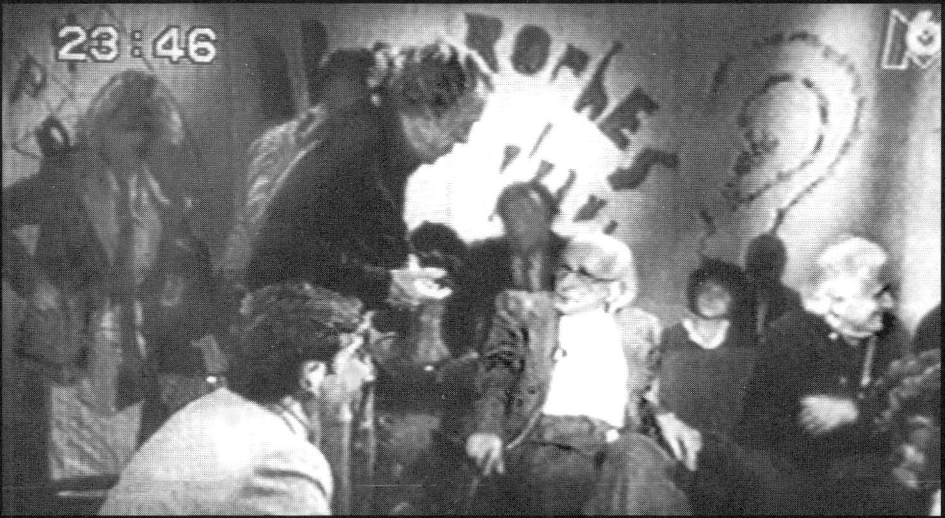
23:46

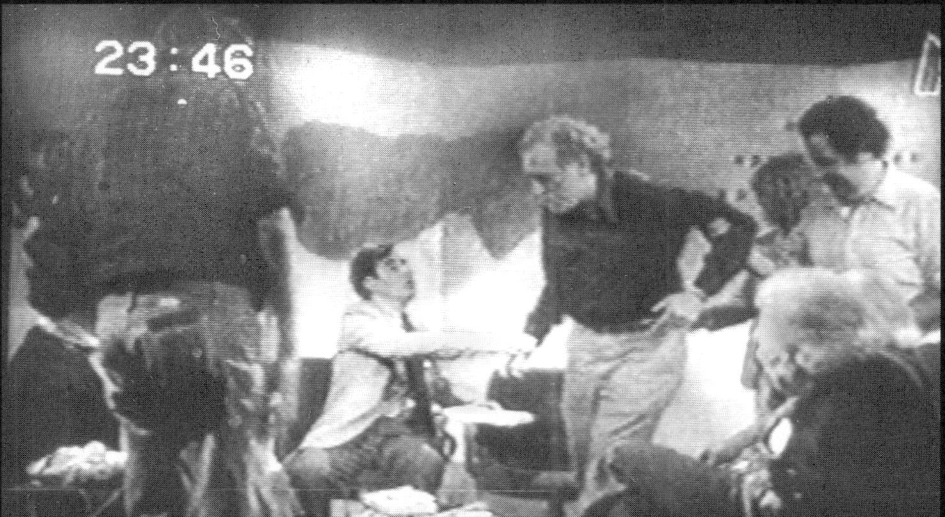
23:46

LINDA: But what the hell did they expect, you know what I mean?

BUKOWSKI: Yeah . . . Linda said I pulled my knife on the guards.

LINDA: *(laughs)* He caused a riot when he left. Because French television, at the doors, they have guards, with guns, from the military I suppose; it's national television. And so he came down there—there were about twelve people in the entourage. And then, of all a sudden, Hank has got his blade which he carries around all the time. And with this big blade, he is going on to one of these guards . . . !

BUKOWSKI: I was just playing. I am very tenderhearted.

LINDA: THEY were serious guys, I mean these were military guys, they did not think it was funny. So they took him, and they THRREEEW him out! . . .

BUKOWSKI: And as we went out in the street, all these lights came, there were a thousand motorcycles coming down the street . . .

LINDA: Ten thousand! They have this every year . . . They go through Paris . . .

BUKOWSKI: That was a crazy night. We had to cross the street, didn't we?

LINDA: Yes, and we waited . . . *(laughs)*.

DUVAL: Motorcycles?

BUKOWSKI: *(laughs)* They were all readers of Bukowski! . . . They also wanted me to meet Jean-Paul Sartre in Paris.

DUVAL: Did you meet him?

BUKOWSKI: No, I refused . . .

DUVAL: But why!

BUKOWSKI: Well, you know . . . You think I should have? Anyhow, that was a curious night. But I usually seem to get into these

154

problems, these troubles. I can't go anywhere: to a wedding party, or any place at all I'm invited to, someone's birthday party . . . These movie stars are around, once there was one fellow there that had got very obnoxious—when I first knew him, he was a very nice bashful boy, and now he had become a sophisticated dumb pig of a man, I walked up behind him and I told him, and then I walked around to other people, you know, what was wrong with them? . . . And so I should never be invited anywhere. I should just stay here, and drink my wine.

DUVAL: And stay on the sidelines . . . There is this deeply moving passage in *Ham and Rye* when you describe the graduation ball at your high school. The girls and the boys dancing . . . And you are outside, looking through the window. It's quite symbolic for all your life, isn't?

BUKOWSKI: And the guard came up at me and asked me what I was doing there . . . I see you've read all my life . . .

DUVAL:. You always stayed on the sidelines . . .

BUKOWSKI: Well, I was strange, you see . . . I hadn't had a normal upbringing, you know: taught to dance, and meet children, and . . . I was a freak, you know. Girls, dancing, this was beyond me . . . So this gave me another view of things, I didn't choose it, it chose me.

DUVAL: That ball, was it some sort of illusion? A kind of midsummer night's dream? And the dancers were not conscious of that illusion . . . ?

BUKOWSKI: They didn't know it was an illusion, no. Their lives were ahead of them. But that's all right. That was their night not to think. It would come and get them later (*laughs sadly*).

DUVAL: There is also this moment of grace in your childhood when you discover you can write. You had to write for the school something on the arrival of President Hoover in your town. And you had great success. It was read in front of the class. And you had great success—for the first time in your life.

BUKOWSKI: Yes, this was the best piece. And I wasn't even there! She read it to everybody, and I sat and I said: Say, that's pretty good *(laughs)* . . . Pretty good bullshit! I described everything, I wasn't even there: the secret service men, and the crowd . . . I wasn't even there . . . So, everybody started looking at me, even the little girls *(imitating their little voices)*: "Henry? Really?" That was so strange. That was probably the first inkling that I was a writer. And another one was when I was in College. We had a class we were supposed to submit one article every two weeks, or as many as we wanted to do. So the teacher, at midterm, she read, well some of you haven't been doing very well . . . now these articles, Smith's: one, Daily: two, Mac Alvy: four, that's good, Bukowski: seventy two! The class went: OOOOH! And she said: And they are all good! So that gave me a strange feeling, you know, like you're loaded with something, loaded with something strange. So then I went out, and I was a laborer for forty, fifty years . . . *(laughs)* after that. So you can't tell . . .

DUVAL: About that piece on Hoover's coming, you said: I had success, and I was celebrated, and I was recognized, but I lied . . . Did you lie, or was it a first step into fiction?

BUKOWSKI: That was one of the few times that I lied, maybe the first time. In a sense, that could have been my way of writing fiction: not being there, I fictionalized it. But I did lie. I wasn't there, and I said I was there. You've got me. I have sinned . . . Good wine.

DUVAL: Excellent. Where does it come from?

LINDA: It's domestic. In northern California, there is very good wine.

BUKOWSKI: Hey baby, so do you do this very often, interviews?

DUVAL: Well, from time to time.

BUKOWSKI: You know, the strangest thing I find about meeting famous people—I've met quite a few lately—I find that they are not very much. It's discouraging. So, I hope you have some luck *(laughs)*.

DUVAL: *(laughs)* I'm sure. Though you write in a very crude way, there is much poetry emanating from this crudity, and despair . . .

BUKOWSKI: I prefer the term simple. I always try to write clearly, so people know what I am saying. And so that I know what I'm saying. So I try not to use large words. I try to use the easiest, smallest word possible to say anything. I don't use the dictionary, and I like it raw, easy and simple. That way, I don't lie to myself. Because what I'd read first, the classical literature, is not raw, easy, and simple. It's confusing, contrived, cloudy and devious. I want to get rid of these things.

DUVAL: But why do we need simplicity so badly, just now?

BUKOWSKI: Well, I need it anyhow. Maybe as we get closer to the end, we bullshit less. This could be our last night together as we are talking here now, you're aware of that?

DUVAL: Well . . . I don't . . .

BUKOWSKI: You think we're gonna make it then? for five or six thousand years?

DUVAL: *(laughs)* I don't know. But this is surely not our last night . . .

BUKOWSKI: But it is not a good time to bullshit, with the bomb hanging over your head, right? It's time to start saying things. It's time for the end of bullshit. So I try to keep it simple and clear. That's all I can do.

DUVAL: You respond to the violence and decaying of society with the violence of your writing . . .

BUKOWSKI: I only photograph society. If it's decaying, if it's violent, then my writing will be decaying and violent. I don't want it to be that way. But if it is, there is nothing else I can call it.

DUVAL: Where is hope? And hope in your work?

BUKOWSKI: The hope is a touch of graceful humor, no matter what's occurring. The ability to laugh, the ability to see the ridiculous, the ability not to tense up too much when things become impossible, just to face them anyhow. A touch of humor in the fire. Let's say laughter through the flame. Or, guts. Courage . . . Humor, guts, and courage, no matter the odds. We can always face it . . .

DUVAL: How did you meet, Linda and you?

BUKOWSKI: Well, I think Linda will tell it better than I could.

Linda laughs.

BUKOWSKI: I shift the load.

LINDA: I knew about him before he knew about me. I had read all the books that had been printed of his. And he would give poetry readings a lot, in those days—this is about twelve years ago. And I would go to the ones that were within a hundred miles or so. And so finally I went to one in Hollywood and—that was during an intermission—he came out to the bar and was sitting at the table, and he was very drunk, and there were about fifteen women around him . . .

BUKOWSKI: Oh, life is glorious.

LINDA: All types of sizes and shapes and forms, and so I said it's about time I introduce myself to this gentleman. And so I said something after everybody had left, and *(turning to Hank)* I gave you a note with my telephone number.

BUKOWSKI: Oh, Oh!

EARLY 1978

LINDA: And he gave me a note with HIS telephone number on it and a little picture of a little man with a bottle *(laughs)*. And he called me two days later . . . And a few days after that he drove down to see me, I used to have a little natural food restaurant, called the Dew Drop Inn, at Redondo Beach, and he came there. And—that was in September 1976.

BUKOWSKI: Oh, God!

LINDA: And that was it. Because he was doing research . . .

BUKOWSKI: Hum . . . I ate a sandwich.

LINDA: He was doing research at the time on a novel called *Women*. And so he was stuffed with experience researching women. *(Hank laughs with some embarrassment)*. And so I found that I was part of that in the beginning. And then finally, the women would sort of dwindle away, and then this one would be gone, and that one, and finally they are all gone. But me. I am the only one to have the guts, the courage and the humor to stay. ha! ha! ha!

BUKOWSKI: There, she took my words!

LINDA: And then we got married last August. *(Showing a photograph)* This is me, with my wedding gown.

BUKOWSKI: Just like that . . . after eight or nine years, right?

LINDA: We believe in long courtship. It's good to wait a long time, as long as possible.

BUKOWSKI: Yeah.

DUVAL: So that the decision will be more meaningful?

LINDA: So you more or less know what you're gonna put up both with—with one another.

160

BUKOWSKI: For you never do know *(laughs)*. But you can guess a little bit. You worked me out that much anyway, didn't you, Linda? *(laughs)*

DUVAL: So you do believe in love, after all?

BUKOWSKI: You're asking me? Love is a word . . . I really mistrust it, cause everybody uses it so much. I wish we had another word for love. It's a very abused word. It spoils the sound of the word. So when you say do you believe in love, I can't answer that at all. But if you ask me: Do you believe that treating another person as nicely as possible and being around and continually, do you believe that makes you feel very good, do you think that's a valuable feeling, I would say yes.

DUVAL: And friendship? Was it difficult for you to make friends?

BUKOWSKI: With anybody. Man or woman. I had problems. I don't have the same interests. I guess I would call a friend someone who drank with me, ha! ha! ha!

DUVAL: That's the illusion of friendship . . .

BUKOWSKI: Nothing wrong with illusions as long as they work . . . and continue to work . . . Good wine, hey?

DUVAL: Yeah . . . Regarding illusions, what about the movie Marco Ferreri shot from your *Tales of Ordinary Madness* ?

BUKOWSKI: A piece of shit. I was in the theater at the opening, and I screamed from my seat. I told them what it was. I think my comments were more interesting than the movie. I didn't help the picture at all, in fact. I was screaming about it, and some guy said: Bukowski, why don't you keep quiet? I said: This god damned movie is about me, I have got every right in the world to dislike it.—Shut up! . . . And I went on. It was terrible.

DUVAL: It really has not much to do with your writing.

BUKOWSKI: It hasn't to do with me at all *(laughs)*. One of the worst parts was at the end, when he is grabbing this girl's legs down by the ocean, and he is reciting a poem about the atom bomb, and he is grabbing this girl's ass, in the way they were coming in . . . I mean, my God, this is the world I wanna see blowing up. This type of thing. No, it was terrible.

DUVAL: And this guy is supposed to be you . . .

BUKOWSKI: Yeah, I mean, he is a very relaxed, self-satisfied, happy guy—he has no ulcers, he sleeps all night, he feels good, he came back from a poetry reading, he walked down the hall, and some black maid said: Oh so good to see you. When I came back, nobody ever said anything, you know, I just went in and went layed down . . . I wasn't popular, you know . . . Raaw, it was awful . . . So I met Ben Gazzara, before the movie. We drank together. I kept emptying mine, he held his glass of wine there, and he'd take a little sip, and look around . . . One day they interviewed him in a magazine. He said: I OUTDRANK Bukowski. Ha! ha! Anyhow, that's all. He drinks like he acts. Not very well.

DUVAL: And Marco Ferreri?

BUKOWSKI: I liked him, as a person. He seems like a nice little round fellow. We had a little drinking contest. He put his foot up on the table, and I put up my foot on the table . . . We drank together. He was likeable. But he turned out a piece of shit.

DUVAL: Maybe the movie helped you sell more books in Europe . . .

BUKOWSKI: Or maybe less! You know: I don't want to read this guy.

DUVAL: What does money mean to you?

BUKOWSKI: Money means nothing, except getting by without having people crashing your doors down, or wanting to take you away somewhere. To have enough money to live quietly without anybody bothering you, so you can do the few things that you wanna do before you die. But a lot of money is not needed. Enough money is needed so they don't fuck with you. So you can do your thing. That's all. You get a flat tire, you can get a new tire on your car . . . Or better yet, you get a flat tire, you just buy a new car and leave that one there . . . (laughs). I have an old saying: there are only two things wrong with money: too much, or too little . . . Go ahead!

DUVAL: Is it true that during the Great Depression, in the thirties, you seriously thought about holding up banks, like Dillinger?

BUKOWSKI: It entered my mind. And you can never tell how true a thing is until you do it. Before anybody does anything, they first think about it a little bit. This is the beginning of it . . . I think I would have made a good bank robber.

DUVAL: Yeah? Why?

BUKOWSKI: Because I have guts, humor and style (laughs). But I couldn't find anybody who could go with me. You know, two or three good guys. Or maybe just one.

DUVAL: (laughs) Well you should have met me at that time . . .

BUKOWSKI: Oh, you were probably in the cradle . . . Hey baby! you want to hold up the bank? Take your milk! (laughs) . . . Well, that's a joke, okay? You don't have a cigarette, do you?

DUVAL: Sorry, I don't smoke.

BUKOWSKI: Well, I don't have any either, I hoped that . . . (*Linda is trying finding some*)

DUVAL: So during that whole period of your life, you preferred to stay alone, isolated, drinking your wine?

BUKOWSKI: I seem to get more happiness among four walls than when I'm looking at people or listening to them. That's all.

DUVAL: Does that mean that you came to appreciate loneliness more than mixing with people? First, it's hard to be alone. And then you get so used to it that you can't do otherwise, you need it . . .

BUKOWSKI: Well, for me it was never hard to be alone. It always felt best . . . It's natural. Some animals, they dig a hole in the ground, they go underground. I'm kinda like a mole or one of these animals who goes underground. He feels good alone in a hole. It's my natural instinct. When I'm alone, I charge my batteries. I build. That's just that. I feel good. I've never been lonely. I've been depressed. I've been suicidal. But being lonely means another person will solve your problem. Loneliness means you need something or somebody, so I never had a loneliness in that sense. I never felt like another person would solve my problem. I always felt that I would solve my problem. So all I needed was myself. I had myself and I worked with myself, from myself.

DUVAL: And suicide? . . .

BUKOWSKI: Suicide?

DUVAL: Yes, you just mentioned it, but that idea doesn't appear very often in your work.

BUKOWSKI: Suicide is just discouragement with things on hand. You want to roll the dice ticket gamble and try something new. A new deck of cards. You understand, it's a gamble. The idea of suicide comes from there. Then you have got to cut your damned throat, that's messy, you know, it takes nerve. So there is a lot of things that make you want to suicide, and a lot of thoughts that say, hey, wait! Maybe I won't make a clean cut and I'll go around all my life talking with the other side of my mouth. I always thought, when I was thinking of suicide, I could get in a worse place than I am now. How do I know? So it always gave me pause. I finally decided against it. I think I have.

DUVAL: The only people who approached you were losers, you attracted them?

BUKOWSKI: Yeah. I attracted some bad numbers. I attracted some real imbeciles, *(turning to Linda)* like Baldy, you know. Some took me a life time to get rid of.

DUVAL: How do you explain that?

BUKOWSKI: They found somebody who fed them with something. Some kind of strength. Something that made them feel better. And so they hung around me. Sometimes I'd say: Go away! Listen, I'm tired of you, go away! And they would for a while, and they'd come back. So . . . The losers seem to like me. Maybe 'cause I symbolize losers. Or better, I symbolize a loser who hasn't jumped off the cliff yet . . . I get a lot of letters from people in prisons, New Zealand, Orient, various places. They love my books. One guy in New Zealand, he said, no it was the guy in Asia, he said: "You are the only writer the convicts read. They pass the book from cell to cell." To me this is a great honor. Because the hardest people to fool are those in hell. So I feel there is a good gang there reading me. One guy, this is the guy in New Zealand, the guard said to him: "Can I read your book?" He said: "Nooo! Bukowski wouldn't want it!" He said he walked away and his ears were red, he was angry. So you see the guards and the prisoners in New Zealand are fighting over me . . . The losers tend to like me. There are even some winners starting to like me now, I'm getting worried about that. But that's another story.

DUVAL: Do you still feel a loser yourself?

BUKOWSKI: I was never a loser. I was just losing. (*Snap of a cigarette lighter*). Some days I'm a loser, and some days I'm not, I'm like you, depending what happens during that day, or that night. At the track, outside at the track, each day is different. Somedays I feel like a loser, somedays I feel like a winner, somedays I don't feel a damned thing at all! . . . Good wine.

DUVAL: If you are getting fed up, or tired, tell me . . .

BUKOWSKI: Oh hell! You're kidding. Tired? I can talk for eight or ten hours. If there is only enough wine, I can talk for days, like . . .

LINDA: But you must think of this poor man . . . (*laughs*). Maybe he is tired.

BUKOWSKI: When he gets tired, we're done! . . . Like Barbet Schroeder. He shot a documentary on me, and I talked what? for fifty-five hours.

LINDA: No, fifteen hours.

BUKOWSKI: I'm endless. As long as there is something to drink . . . Go ahead!

DUVAL: In your young days, did you drink to prove your manhood?

BUKOWSKI: Yeah, in the worst sense, yeah. We used to think that a man drank, you know. That drinking made a man. Of course, that's entirely untrue. And those ten years I spent just in the bars . . . An awful lot of people who drink aren't men at all, they are hardly anything. And they get on my ear, and they talked the most terrible dribble into my head you've ever heard . . . So drinking doesn't create anything. It's destructive to most people. Not to me, you understand, but to most people.

DUVAL: To you it's not?

BUKOWSKI: No, it's antidestructive.

DUVAL: (*to Linda*) Do you agree, Linda?

166

LINDA: In some ways he is right. Not all the way.

BUKOWSKI: I do all my writing when I'm drunk. Whenever I type, I'm drunk. How can I complain? Should I complain about the royalties? I'm paid for drinking. They're paying me to drink. That's lovely. *(He puts his glass firmly back on the table).*

DUVAL: Mmm, I can't remember what I just wanted to ask you.

BUKOWSKI: You need a drink, you'll remember *(he fills the glasses).*

DUVAL: Thanks.

BUKOWSKI: I was a barfly . . .

DUVAL: A what?

BUKOWSKI: A barfly. In this one bar for about five years, I would run air for sandwiches, you know. I didn't do anything but stay in this bar night and day, and how I survived I have no idea. But one thing that helped, I said, at least I've not worked an eight hour job—it was a twenty-four hour job *(laughs bitterly).* I wasn't pointing at the time clock or anything . . . Just running a little air, and fighting the bartender, and being the bar clown. I was the personality the guy laughed at. The bum. And I was waiting for something to happen. Somebody to say something . . . I was waiting for some magic to occur in this bar . . . It never did. So finally I just walked out. I waited a long time . . . So I wrote a play about it called *Barfly*, a movie script for Barbet Schroeder, and it might be produced, it's getting close, but we'll see.

DUVAL: How did you discover alcohol?

BUKOWSKI: Oh, I had a friend called Baldy. His father was a doctor who lost his license for drinking too much. And one day he took me to his father's wine cellar. I don't know if we were eleven, twelve years old . . . He said, "Hank, try some of this wine!" I said, "oh! Come on." He said, "No! Come on! Stick your head under there, turn that spigot." There was a big barrel. I tried a little, and I said, "eeeeh, it stinks like shit!" He put his head there and got a little wine. And I said, "Let me try some more of that." So I took a big one . . . I grew, I expanded, I was twelve feet tall, I was a giant of a man. And my heart felt wonderful. And life was good. And I was powerful. And I said, "Baldy, this is good stuff." And that was it. I've been hooked ever since.

DUVAL: If you had to choose between wine and women?

BUKOWSKI: *(laughs)* Linda, do you want leave the room?

LINDA: I won't, no.

BUKOWSKI: That's like a friend of mine. His wife said: "Either you have to give up playing the horses, or you give up me." And he said: "Good bye, baby . . ." Ha! ha! ha!

LINDA: True story. *(laughs)*

BUKOWSKI: Yeah, I see him every day sitting in the grandstand. Alone . . . But I would rather have the whole thing: wine and lady. Go ahead!

DUVAL: What about the human heart? Is it good or bad?

BUKOWSKI: The human heart, as of course we all know, is essentially good. But between governments, false Gods, striving for survival, the heart gets mixed up with the head and the feet and the elbows and the intestine. And the peace and the madness. And the heart gets strangled out a bit. It's a good organ and there is complete hope for humanity if it ever gets a little bit straight. It's all there, it's totally there, there is total hope of goodness forever. But we got lost somewhere. How we can ever straighten that out, I don't know.

DUVAL: Do you still have a feeling of wonder towards life?

BUKOWSKI: Wonder? There are times . . . My God, when I'm looking into the eyes of my cat, ha ha—I didn't say my woman . . .

LINDA: Oh!

BUKOWSKI: . . . there are small things . . . I mean, you bet a horse, you got 20 dollars on it, it wins by six lengths . . . There are things that make you feel good. Hell, we wouldn't go on without these little lifts, now and then, that continually occur. You wouldn't go on. But I mean if you always wake up in the morning and say: Oh, life is good, this is gonna be another beautiful day, I don't think there are many people who are awaking that way. Or if they are awaking that way, by the time they're going to sleep, they think an entirely different thing. But what was the original question? *(laughs)*

DUVAL: If you still had a feeling of wonder towards life.

BUKOWSKI: I still like it. I still think it's fine. I'll buy it.

DUVAL: What is your great dream, just now?

BUKOWSKI: Oh, my dream has always been to be a great horse player.

DUVAL: A great horse player!

BUKOWSKI: Yeah, you make money playing the horses. I only pretend to be a writer. To all other people, I'm a writer. Well, truly, I'm a horse player, going to the track everyday, winning money, and just for the fun of it! Having all this money hidden away from the taxman . . .

DUVAL: So you're a horse player more than a writer?

BUKOWSKI: I'm not going to say. *(laughs)* You're gonna have your . . . in a minute . . . I'm a lousy horse player . . . a terrible horse player.

LINDA: *(gently)* That's not true.

BUKOWSKI: *(strongly)* Be quiet, Linda! . . .

LINDA: Okay, he is terrible.

BUKOWSKI: No, it's just a hobby . . . No, no special dreams.

DUVAL: And no special despair?

BUKOWSKI: Mmm, I have the same thing as you have and anybody else has, I have despair, nightmares. But generally, as I said, I accept almost all given situations. I try to do things about them, but I can't do too much. Except drink and type. YOU save the world, and I'll write about you saving the world, okay? Is that a deal?

DUVAL: Writing is also a way to save one's self, isn't it?

BUKOWSKI: Not if you sit down to write, and say, I'm gonna save myself . . . It just has to happen as it happens.

DUVAL: Why aren't your poems translated in French?

BUKOWSKI: Oh? I thought they were *(laughs)*.

Linda stands up and comes back with a few books of Hank's published in French by Le Sagittaire.

BUKOWSKI: Are those extras or the only copies? Oh, shit, too bad, those are originals.

DUVAL: Don't worry. I'll find them in a bookshop.

LINDA: This is *Shakespeare Never Did This* in German, with Michael Montfort photographs. Would you like it?

Buk at the track.

DUVAL: Oh, yeah, thanks. That's where you tell of your trip in Germany and France, don't you? I think you are even more popular in Germany than in France.

BUKOWSKI: Well, I think so, yes. And I've been getting letters from Yugoslavia lately. And then there is Norway, and various places . . . The disease is spreading rapidly.

DUVAL: Whereas in Europe you're famous for your *Tales of Ordinary Madness,* in the States, they don't seem to know much about the novelist, they only know you as a poet . . .

BUKOWSKI: Yes, but I explained that. Poet is a romantic concept.

DUVAL: In France, nobody reads poetry anymore. Do you mean poets are really so appreciated by American people?

BUKOWSKI: They are. But they don't make any money. There are probably two or three poets who can make a living on writing poetry. I'm one of them in the USA. I think there are two others, I'm not sure. I don't even know who they are, it might be five of us, I don't know. Anyhow, that's a small sort. And of course, you can survive by writing very bad poetry too.

DUVAL: Do you meet other writers?

BUKOWSKI: I stay away from them, entirely.

DUVAL: Completely apart?

BUKOWSKI: When I first started writing, they came around, and I would throw them out. And now, they know I don't want to see them. I don't like other writers, because all they do is talk about writing. And about poetry, and about publishers, and about royalties. They talk about everything but something real. I'd rather talk to a plumber. Or a man who catches his fish. Or a boxer. Anybody but a writer. Because they aren't going to say anything. Except how their books are selling in Hollywood, where their next reading is going to be. Writers here are much more of bitches than I am.

DUVAL: Hey, but we spoke quite a little bit about literature, just now!

BUKOWSKI: Oh, you're an interviewer, it's understood that's your job, that's a different thing entirely, forgive me, I don't wanna get you in a . . .

DUVAL: Okay, what about sex? (*Showing a French paperback copy of* Tales of Ordinary Madness, *with a rosebud between the legs of a woman on the cover*). In France, they publish this kind of illustration on the front cover of your books . . .

BUKOWSKI: The kind you find in supermarkets, yeah? (*laughs*)

DUVAL: Well, in bookshops too.

BUKOWSKI: I know. That's nice to see one of my books . . . We never see them. Why don't I see it? Didn't I write it (*laughs*).

LINDA: Here is the original copy, published by Le Sagittaire in Paris.

DUVAL: I hope you get the royalties, at least . . .

BUKOWSKI: The writer is the last one to know, ha! ha! I'm sure I don't get all the money that's got coming to me. I would be a rich man . . . No, I'm sure I've signed some contract or something. But they never sent me a copy of the book.

DUVAL: Okay . . . I asked about sex.

BUKOWSKI: What do you want to know?

DUVAL: Many people in Europe, who haven't really read your books, think you became famous for writing sex stories, especially *Tales of Ordinary Madness*. There is some misunderstanding about all that, I guess.

BUKOWSKI: Well, you see, we go through phases of writing. For a while, I wrote about sex, I explored it. Much of it was done when I first started writing. Because I had to make money fast, because I didn't have any. I was fifty years old, and I quit my job at the post office, and I was in that room in Hollywood. So I drank and I wrote sex stories for the sex magazines, who paid very well at that time. They have changed now, they are not very good. So I made my living writing these short stories for the sex magazines and they were very nice to me, the checks arrived continually, bing, bing, bing, and I kept writing these sex stories. The only thing I did . . . You know, most sex stories in the sex magazines were (*with a strong suggestive tone*): HE HAD A BIG THING, AND HE STUCK IT IN AND HE PUT HIS HAND ON HER ASS, etc. So, I didn't like that. I put sex in it, but I would put a story around it, to please myself. I thought, well, they want sex, but I'll fool them. So this is how the sex stories came about. Even though they have sex, you will find sex is not the story; sex is in there, but there is another story going on. So it was never sex-obsessed. But I had to put sex in to sell the story. I've nothing against sex, except . . . just the other day, this magazine, *Hustler*, they said: send us a story. It is a sex magazine that pays good. So I sent my story. They held it: great story! great story! Finally, they sent it back: not enough sex.

LINDA: They held it for five months!

DUVAL: If sex is not such an obsession, what do you expect of a woman?

BUKOWSKI: All I want out of a woman is peace and quiet. (*Linda starts to laugh*)

DUVAL: What makes you laugh, Linda?

LINDA: (*bursting out laughing*) He picked me!

174

BUKOWSKI: *(laughs)* Maybe I met the wrong one.

LINDA: Oh!

DUVAL: *(to Linda)* So you're not a peaceful and quiet woman, Linda?

BUKOWSKI: Well, she is not always serene.

LINDA: I'm eternally seeking peace and quiet, you might say.

BUKOWSKI: I hope she finds it . . . That's all, peace and quiet. A gentle way to go. Nothing more, nothing less. Just an easy, peaceful quietness. The whole world is out there fighting us. Why should we fight each other?

DUVAL: *(putting the books Linda brought, back on the table)* And which of your books do you prefer?

BUKOWSKI: The last one, always.

DUVAL: Which one is it?

BUKOWSKI: Oh, well . . . *(To Linda)* What the hell is my last book?

LINDA: *War All the Time.*

DUVAL: Short stories?

BUKOWSKI: No, it's poems . . . And there should be another book after summer. More poems, more poems!

DUVAL: Do you feel more a poet or a novelist? . . .

BUKOWSKI: Actually, I feel a poet most of the time. But a poem is so easy to write. It's like rolling off a log . . . It's so easy. So I'm the poet. So I write poems all the time. And they're good. Damned good! I even like them. But I'd like to get back to the short story, just to test myself a little bit. So after this book of poetry comes out, I'm jumping back to the short story.

DUVAL: Okay, what's the meaning of life to you?

BUKOWSKI: Oh, shit, man! Next question . . . Drink as much as you can . . . Next question.

DUVAL: Well, I'm afraid I've no more questions.

BUKOWSKI: All right, we just drink now, ok? Turn it off *(the tape recorder)*. Or leave it on if you wish.

DUVAL: I'll leave it on, you never know.

BUKOWSKI: Yeah, maybe you can make something out of that.

LINDA: This is a different wine, now. It's Beaujolais. A French one.

DUVAL: *(apologizing)* I should have brought a bottle . . .

BUKOWSKI: *(laughs)* We thought you would.

LINDA: What?

BUKOWSKI: He said, "I should have brought the wine."

LINDA: Oh, he did?

BUKOWSKI: No, he didn't . . . He did say that, but he didn't, ha! ha! ha!

DUVAL: I'm so sorry.

BUKOWSKI: Ha! Ha! ha! Jesus Christ! Listen, don't take us too seriously. Take her seriously, but not me. We were down here before you showed up, playing little games. I would go to the door, go out and say *(with a big strong voice, like an ogre)*: JEAN-FRANÇOIS DUVAL IS HERE! and knock, and knock. We were afraid when you came in . . . You understand. We are just not quite right.

DUVAL: What!? What were you afraid of?

BUKOWSKI: We are afraid of everything! There is nothing we do not fear *(laughs)*. Fear makes us great. It makes us think, it makes us tremble, it makes our brain cells turn . . . What is better than fear? . . . Oh, that looks like a good wine. But he doesn't get any? . . .

DUVAL: *(raising his glass)* Where did you buy it?

BUKOWSKI: Around the corner, here. *(Hank is going to refill the glasses)*

LINDA: This one is the new one.

BUKOWSKI: I don't want to pour that in there until you drink that. You wanna mix it? Why do you wait so long? There you go.

DUVAL: *(to Linda)* But YOU don't drink?

LINDA: Not anymore.

DUVAL: *(to Hank)* You aren't convincing enough?

BUKOWSKI: I didn't have to. She outdrank me. We would sit here at nights, it would be 3 o'clock in the morning . . .

LINDA: Chhhht.

BUKOWSKI: . . . She'd say, one more bottle. I said: God, Linda, God, we have had enough. *(Imitating her voice)* No, just one more: we'll watch the sun come up.—Okay. So we would drink that, the sun wouldn't be up yet. She would say: "The sun isn't up yet, let's have one more. This is the last!" Then finally the sun would come, and there we go up the stairway, Rrrrr, she was tough!

DUVAL: So you found your master.

BUKOWSKI: Well, I'm not gonna say that. I'm not saying she outdrank me. I'm saying she was there. She is much smaller than I am. When you drink almost the same amount, it's like drinking twice as much.

LINDA: You have to have a very very brilliant mind to be able to withstand.

BUKOWSKI: Or a very very brilliant body. I think you have a brilliant body. So she drank me two to one.

LINDA: So I just finished drinking. HE is not going to finish yet.

BUKOWSKI: Oh no.

LINDA: He only finishes when he is finished.

BUKOWSKI: Yeah, I'll be finished when I fall in my grave, yeah: "Here, your last drink, old fucker . . ." I wouldn't mind, I'll go "yeah . . ." . . . Oh, God, she wants us in the same casket. Can you imagine that when her bones start screaming "he has got to be the master in the casket!"

Laughs

BUKOWSKI: So do you have any writers in your own country? Hell, yes. Doesn't that happen . . .

DUVAL: Sure we have!

BUKOWSKI: Everywhere. Writers are everywhere. Like roaches. Fucking roaches. (*With a high-pitched voice*) Yeah, I'm a writer, I'm a writer! . . . All you need is a typewriter, right? That makes you a writer. You put a sheet of paper in it: I'm a writer! I'm a poet! (*laughs*)

DUVAL: Who is the greatest living writer in the States, to you? If there is one . . .

BUKOWSKI: He doesn't write anymore. He just vanished off the face of the earth. His name is J. D. Salinger. He wrote two, three books. Nobody has ever heard from him ever since. It's like he is gone. But he is not dead. The latest I heard, he said: I just write for myself. Now this is possible. That's a real saint. But if he says: I just write for myself, doesn't that destroy it? Just saying that? . . . So I don't know. Anyhow, this guy was so good in his early books, and he just stopped all of a sudden. He is a complete mystery. J. D. Salinger. *Catcher In The Rye* is really great. You see, it's about young people going through their thing, but it's so well done . . . Maybe when he got past the young people thing, that was all there was . . . It would be sad if it was so.

LINDA: And he wrote one book of nine short stories as well, they're unbelievable!

BUKOWSKI: He is not dead, is he, Linda?

LINDA: No, he lives in Connecticut.

BUKOWSKI: Now here is an amazing man. Either he knows more than any of us, or he has just drifted off.

LINDA: He is an enigma.

DUVAL: A little bit like Thomas Pynchon, have you heard of him?

BUKOWSKI: I think he is on the best-seller list, you know, the best ten.

LINDA: He was. You see his name on republished paperbacks a lot, and so forth, but nothing new.

BUKOWSKI: I tend to be suspicious of best-seller lists. If you need best-seller lists, it's just like voting for Reagan (laughs).

DUVAL: What about women writers. Take for instance Joyce Carol Oates? Would you say she is a great American female novelist?

BUKOWSKI: She is the human writing machine. Just pages and pages. She has an endless energy for putting words down. But I can't read any of it. Even though she says I'm a great writer, I can't read her craft. It's almost like an endless stream of vomitive words that roll down. It's just like . . . There is a female poet in America who just keeps typing. You find her everywhere. It's like she wakes up in the morning and starts typing of joy, she will have a cup of coffee, and then (breathing in and in one big blow, swelling his voice) SHE'LL TYPE ANOTHER POEM AT ELEVEN THIRTY, and then she'll wait a while, and then—all her divorced husbands, you know, sending her money, and all that—and then SHE WILL BRAND OUT ANOTHER ONE AT THREE THIRTY, AND THEN . . . It's a sickness instead of . . . I guess the best of writing can be a sickness, and the worst too. So, what's the hell is the difference?

179

DUVAL: So there isn't any good female writer?

BUKOWSKI: Women writers, there is one, Carson McCullers. She's dead now. She died of alcoholism. *The Heart Is A Lonely Hunter*. When you've read her talk about pain, you can feel the pain across each line. She was really . . . There was one story about a midget that is so painful and so heart-rending . . . Carson McCullers can really write . . . *The Heart Is A Lonely Hunter*, that's just the way she felt. So she died of alcoholism. I think, if I have it right, on a ship, on a transatlantic journey. She was on her deckchair, drinking . . . And they just found her there, stiff and dead. Great woman writer. Women can write too. *

Clac ! The tape has come to an end.

DUVAL: Let me change it.

BUKOWSKI: Hey man! You can sell that tape for five dollars. Or fifteen dollars . . .

DUVAL: *(laughs)* It wouldn't even pay the taxi that took me here.

BUKOWSKI: Oh, we were thinking about that, Linda and me. My God! From L.A. downtown . . . Must be a hundred twenty dollar taxi, at least.

DUVAL: How much do you think it was?

BUKOWSKI: Seventy-five dollars!

LINDA: No, no, no, Hank! It's only a few minutes away! I would say twenty-five, at the most. How much was that?

DUVAL: It was a special cab, a real limousine in fact, with TV and bar. The driver said he would take me for the same price as an ordinary cab . . . I was jubilant at the idea to arrive at Charles

---

*Bukowski was mistaken: Carson McCullers died of a cerebral hemorrhage in Nayack Hospital, on September 29, 1967.

Bukowski's place in such a magnificent thing . . . It was thirty-five dollars.

BUKOWSKI: That's not bad.

LINDA: That's great!

BUKOWSKI: From here to the airport, we had to pay FIFTY dollars!

LINDA: Well, it's much further to the airport!

BUKOWSKI: Yeah, but that was ten years ago . . . You know, the funniest thing, I told Linda, "he pulled up in a limousine cab," remember that? But I was making fun, and you did (laughs). Whoa!

DUVAL: That was sheer luck.

LINDA: Oh, boy, wonderful!

BUKOWSKI: There is the bathroom.

LINDA: Oh yes, if you want to . . .

DUVAL: Well, thanks but . . .

BUKOWSKI: I'll go first, the old before the interviewer . . . I would rather be the interviewer than the interviewed.

DUVAL: (laughs) No problem. I hope to be the interviewed some day.

BUKOWSKI: (going to the bathroom) I'll interview you then.

DUVAL: Let's say in 20 years maybe (laughs).

LINDA: (taking the opportunity of this interlude) Whom did you interview before Hank?

DUVAL: I met Woody Allen at his place in New York.

LINDA: Oooh, you're serious! We love Woody Allen! Oh, I envy you, that's somebody I would like to meet . . .

BUKOWSKI: *(coming back)* Woody? He has got it. He is got so . . . he has sad little eyes . . .

LINDA: Was Mia Farrow with him?

DUVAL: No, I think they both have their own apartment.

BUKOWSKI: *(pouring wine)* Oh, Woody . . .

DUVAL: He had just finished shooting *Radio Days* the day before. He had a cold and was looking very pale . . . Not at all as lively as in his movies.

BUKOWSKI: Maybe he just gets turned on in his movies, maybe he only lives in his movies. And he rests in-between his movies . . . You know, self love . . . They don't wanna bother with talking . . . because you're not important and for them that doesn't matter. If it's a reporter from *Life* or *Time*, maybe they will perk up . . . Because you are not so important . . . This may be true and it may not be true, I don't know. I don't know everything, do you? *(To Linda)* What do you think?

LINDA: On actors?

BUKOWSKI: Yeah.

LINDA: I think that a lot of actors are very private people and . . .

BUKOWSKI: Oh shit! They are no more private than a plumber.

LINDA: Or they WANT privacy.

BUKOWSKI: Fuck! They are on the screen, they are seen by millions!

LINDA: When they are not on the screen, they want their privacy.

BUKOWSKI: Some are like that, and some aren't, right?

LINDA: I suppose most of them definitely want their privacy when they are not in front of the camera.

BUKOWSKI: Oh, I thought it was the other way, they wanted more and more to be there.

LINDA: *(obstinate)* No. I don't think so.

BUKOWSKI: We have met different types of people all our lives. That's been one of our major problems, she knows that. She sees something. She says "it's black," and I say "no, it's gold." And then the argument begins. And she accuses me of not having good parents; that distorts my visual viewpoint. Which might be true. But how were your parents, Linda? Better than mine?

LINDA: *(in a murmur)* I wouldn't say that. You can't compare.

BUKOWSKI: *(to me)* How were your parents?

DUVAL: Well, I think she is right, you cannot compare . . .

BUKOWSKI: *(dramatically, in a low voice)* God, I'm trapped. You both say: I can't compare. *(Strongly)* ALL I CAN DO IS COMPARE! Look! Here is my left foot, here is my right foot. I'm comparing: they are both different.

LINDA: They are different, exactly. So why compare?

BUKOWSKI: With all this philosophical jargon, you can really trap me. But it doesn't mean anything, you see. It's just wordage that floats and goes off, and vanishes . . . *(Changing subject)* That's just like that guy who couldn't choose between two girls, hey, baby, get married, what a fuck!

DUVAL: Well, you've got to choose and decide.

BUKOWSKI: Nobody chooses and decides. They only think they choose and decide. Everything is chosen and decided for you. *(Ironical)* By some elemental ignorant force called life . . . Some ignorant Godhead called life. You think you're choosing. Come on, baby, choose some wine. That's the only thing you can choose. *(After a while)* Listen, I haven't been too bad, I mean, I haven't said fuck you, or I'm gonna kill you, cut your balls . . . No, no, I like the kid. He is nice. He is gentle. You don't have much hatred in you, I can tell you . . . You're a good sort, baby.

DUVAL: Thanks.

BUKOWSKI: You're welcome.

Meditative for a while.

BUKOWSKI: So . . . I can't stand Faulkner. You tried to read William Faulkner? The good thing about reading him is how difficult he can make writing seem. It's like each of his sentences is under a great strain to get the rhythm down. And this is a nice thing, too, you appreciate that, you say: GOD ALMIGHTY, HE IS STRAINING LIKE HELL TO WRITE THIS SENTENCE AND THAT SENTENCE . . . IT MUST BE GREAT ART! Because he is straining his fucking guts out. How can it be bad art, when he is straining his guts out? So that's kind of a circus act, too, you know. But he was a character. He drank whisky by the gallon. One time— he lived in a small southern town—there was a guy lying in the gutter, just along the gutter. And somebody said: who's that?—That's William Faulkner, a great writer. There he was . . . I don't see how a guy can drink whisky and keep writing. He must have had a great brain for it all, because whisky, you know . . . you keep writing and, all of a sudden, man, you get a tear in your head, you can't see anymore . . .

DUVAL: If it's just for one hour writing and the hour is good, it's worth it, no?

BUKOWSKI: Yeah, you're right, whisky is good for one hour only, no more. But if you take it for six hours . . .

LINDA: Do you drink whisky when you write, Jean-François?

BUKOWSKI: We're interviewing him now.

DUVAL: Well, it happens.

184

LINDA: I mean, is it part of the process of writing?

DUVAL: *(laughs)* Without a doubt!

BUKOWSKI: I say!

DUVAL: When you've got a deadline and . . .

BUKOWSKI: Finish it? right? I like deadlines. I used to have a deadline for a short story a week. The deadline was there, I wrote for a newspaper, *Open City*. I'd lay around, I'd lay around, and I'd say, well, if you don't do it tonight, it's not going to get done. I was suddenly sitting in front of this white sheet of paper, and it would come. Cause the deadline was there. And you would think, writing just for a deadline, you get a piece of shit, right? And sometimes it's dead *(laughs)*. But a lot of times, if the deadlines weren't there, I never would have written, and come up with something really lucky, you know? In fact, along time, the deadline was approaching, and I said, I can't write it, so I said, well I'll just start with the title, to see what happens, I'll make up a title. So I made up a title, something like: "Twelve flying monkeys copulating under a dead moon." The title is near that, I haven't it quite in mind. So with the title I said: Now I've got to write the story under that title. And I made up a story about twelve monkeys . . . So deadline can get you off your dead ass, into rhythm. On the other hand, they can drain you, too, and kill you. Anything and everything can happen at any given time. All of a sudden I can take your arm, just rip it off and suck it! And it's rolling around my head through and out the window! . . . right? *(laughs)*

LINDA: *(laughs)* Poor Jean-Fr—

BUKOWSKI: Oh shit! I'm just trying to give him a little bit of jazz, for Christ's sake! He expects a little devious bullshit. I have to feed him a little bit of . . . you don't mind, do you? At my age, may I luckily rip my honor . . .

DUVAL: What's your age, now?

BUKOWSKI: Sixty-six.

LINDA: Sixty-five, Hank . . .

BUKOWSKI: Yes, sixty-five and still alive.

DUVAL: A few years ago, didn't you meet a French journalist, Jean-François Bizot, who translated *Tales of Ordinary Madness,* and helped make you known in France?

LINDA: Bizot?

BUKOWSKI: Linda knows more about that.

DUVAL: He said there were bottles of beer everywhere, and I don't see any around . . . That's not the style of this place, quite clean in fact . . .

LINDA: Oh, that was in East Hollywood, before Hank came here.

DUVAL: How long have you been here?

BUKOWSKI: Six years.

LINDA: Almost.

BUKOWSKI: We cleaned up our act now. Except, you know, when we first moved in here, the neighbors would say hello to us, they'd say, if you need anything, give us a call. We would say yeah . . . Everybody liked these little children and said hello. We were here about a week, and there was screaming and drinking and crushing the bottles,

and—it was four-thirty in the morning—the sun was just coming up, and Linda is running around up there and I am naked, with my balls and my cock, I was throwing dirty clothes at her and saying, you whore, I'll kill you. So, after that . . .

LINDA: That was seven-thirty in the morning, after going all night long . . .

BUKOWSKI: Oh, I thought it was three-thirty?

LINDA: No, seven.

BUKOWSKI: Now, the neighbors, they say, well, you know, we hear things, but we don't call the police. I said thank you . . . But we are not so bad, lately, are we?

LINDA: No, no.

BUKOWSKI: There are just minor eruptions now. Just like . . . we were quietly waiting for the big blows. *(laughs)*.

LINDA: *(laughs)* Are we one instigator or two?

BUKOWSKI: I think you are the one *(laughs)*. I'm sitting on top of it, waiting along.

DUVAL: Do people around know who you are?

LINDA: Some of them.

BUKOWSKI: Yeah, they are gradually finding out. One neighbor, when we first moved in, he says: "Hey, my brother reads your stuff, you're Charles Bukowski, my brother is crazy about you . . ." Well, the brother was nice, he never showed up. And then, you know, we go to supermarkets and all of a sudden, there is all this cackling, *(he starts singing with a sharp opera voice)* OHOOH, I WENT TO EUROPE, I SAW YOU IN A MAGAZINE . . . And you know, we were just two old folks who came in a supermarket, getting our box of salt. All of the sudden they see this tired old guy with this young woman, and they giggle: Wouahhhh. So you know, we are hiding out in San Pedro, but now and then they discover a little bit. But generally, they'd leave us alone. Nobody knows who I am, I don't know who they are. And it's really nice . . . You know, they can do whatever they wanna do, as far as they are not around me. They can burn cities, and go up in balloons, and go under the sea. As long as they don't do it around me.

LINDA: I'm remembering a thing too.

BUKOWSKI: Oh, yeah. The guy wanted to know her age.

LINDA: *(showing a German newspaper)* He was in Germany. He never knew, and all of a sudden, he saw that! *(laughs)*.

BUKOWSKI: And when he sees it, he goes nuts. I hope he gets over again . . . But you see, this is a great town to hide. Or it has been . . . It's nice and quiet here. Nobody comes here. We have five cats—and if anybody comes around, the five cats—they all run in different directions. You came around, and they have gone.

LINDA: No, there is one!

DUVAL: *(having a look at the article in the German newspaper)* I see they did interview you for that article . . .

LINDA: No, why?

DUVAL: Well, you're saying that . . .

LINDA: Nobody interviewed us, so, they made it up, whatever it is.

DUVAL: "Und Linda ergänzt . . ." That means "and Linda says" . . . You never said anything of that?

LINDA: We don't know . . . What does it mean! They gave me a different age, though.

DUVAL: *(looking up from the article)* At least there is a nice photograph of you. Hey, would you mind if I took one or two photographs of you?

188

BUKOWSKI: You've got a camera?

DUVAL: Yes, I've got one. Linda, would you sit next to Hank?

BUKOWSKI: Okay, (laughs) and then I'll take one of you with Linda.

LINDA: (laughs) And I'll take you with Hank.

Movement and noises from the sofa. Photographs are taken. Hank makes a dedication and a little drawing on a French copy of Tales of Ordinary Madness.

BUKOWSKI: Now, your name, with one L? (detaching each syllable with a strong voice) Oh shit! I already misspelled it!

DUVAL: Oh, it's too long a name . . . Just put my last . . . my first name, I always confuse the two.

BUKOWSKI: So do I. Surname and all that, right, I don't know either what are names . . . An uneducated man, that's what I am. Jesus Christ! It just looks like a J, you want a J or a C?

DUVAL: There? It should be a Ç.

BUKOWSKI: Oh, a Ç. What about Duvall, one L? . . . Oh shit! I already put three!

LINDA: Three Ls!

BUKOWSKI: Okay. Jesus Christ! Man, you'd better be, you mother fucker! Give me all American bullshit. JEAN-FRANÇOIS.

DUVAL: That's it, thanks.

BUKOWSKI: Listen, we're gonna have to call you a cab, right? The bottle is nearly empty.

DUVAL: I think Linda is doing so . . .

BUKOWSKI: I'm not trying to get rid of you, I'm trying to plan your future.

DUVAL: And you're right, I've still some work ahead.

BUKOWSKI: Oh! You are interviewing somebody else! I don't like that! Roaaar. You need somebody else to talk to after me?

DUVAL: (laughs) Well, not tonight . . . Tomorrow.

BUKOWSKI: Oh, tomorrow is better . . . Okay, that's not so bad (laughs). Well, shit! Doing what you're doing, you know that beats the eight hour job, don't you baby. It beats the eight hours job, doing what you are doing. It's better than the eight hour job. Don't you think?

DUVAL: Sure . . .

BUKOWSKI: You're not in a factory. You play your game.

DUVAL: My game? Which game?

BUKOWSKI: Your game is to leech off the poor souls of writing (laughs). You're feasting off of other lives and going back to your country . . .

DUVAL: Hey, that's not nice!

BUKOWSKI: Oh, shit, I'm just playing with you. Don't you understand, I'm not serious.

DUVAL: (laughs) Sure?

BUKOWSKI: Oh, Christ . . . Relax, I'm just playing. I know you won't take me as serious.

Linda comes back.

BUKOWSKI: You know I started playing with him. He took me seriously. I said he is feasting off of other lives . . .

DUVAL: I am only doing like you: looking for a book, looking for a man.

BUKOWSKI: A new great writer? . . . It seems everything is so drawn, nothing is occurring, it just seems to go on and on, it's awfully sad, there is no new fresh blood. There is nothing to shape the tree branches. There is only me here. And I am bad, but I am not bad enough, ha! ha! ha! So we are hoping for better writers, better interviewers, and quicker taxi cabs! *(laughs)*.

DUVAL: What more could we say?

BUKOWSKI: You asked me earlier: is there any hope for the human heart? Right? I said yes, but that was a very tiny yes. A very very tiny yes . . . I'll have another drink.

The interview took place in San Pedro, California, on February 17, 1986.

"I am no longer frightened, but I am tired and angry. I guess that I should be, that my life was wasted . . ." —Charles Bukowski, from a letter to his daughter, Marina 1966.

". . . It's about time I had luck with a good woman. Linda Lee is a good match for me." —Charles Bukowski 1979.

NOTES

The Beat Revival

1   *Libération*, Paris, 3 January 1995.

Bukowski, the Counterculture Dissident

1   Neeli Cherkovski, *Bukowski: A Life*, Vermont, Steerforth Press, 1997, p. 298.

2   Charles Bukowski, *Screams from the Balcony: Selected Letters 1960-1970*, edited by Seamus Cooney, Santa Rosa, Black Sparrow Press, 1993, pp. 287-288.

3   Charles Bukowski, *Women*, Santa Rosa, Black Sparrow Press, 1994, pp. 183-184.

4   Gerald Nicosia, *Memory Babe: A Critical Biography of Jack Kerouac*, Berkeley and Los Angeles, University of California Press, 1994, p. 629.

5   Ron Mann, *Poetry in Motion*, New York, The Voyager Company, 1992, 1994.

6   Article published in *Libération* (Paris) on April 28, 1995 entitled "Bit génération pour les poètes américains," by Francis Mizio.

7   Russell Harrison, *Against the American Dream: Essays on Charles Bukowski*, Black Sparrow Press, 1994. According to Jules Smith, author of *Art, Survival and So Forth: The Poetry of Charles Bukowski*, "Harrison's own reading of Bukowski's work is a distinctly selective one . . . Certain poems are singled out, but it's clear that Harrison's main interest is not in them, or aesthetics, but in their larger social view . . . The evidence in Bukowski's poetry is that Bukowski is not interested in the working class as a group, only as individuals."

8   Allen Ginsberg, interview with Jean-François Duval, New York, 9 November 1994.

9   *Le Monde des livres* dated Friday 19 July 1996 entitled "La beat (re)generation" by Samuel Blumenfeld. In this article Samuel Blumenfeld notably mentions a triple CD released by Rhino Records in 1992, *The Beat Generation*, Santa Monica, Rhino/Word Beat, 1992.

10 Ibid.

11 James Campbell, "Charles Bukowski and the Beats," in *Bananas*, London, circa 1981, pp. 48-50.

12 "Paying for Horses: An Interview with Charles Bukowski," by Robert Wennersten, in: *London Magazine*, December 1974—January 1975.

13 Charles Bukowski, *Screams from the Balcony*, op. cit., p. 275.

14 Charles Bukowski, *Reach for the Sun: Selected Letters 1978-1994*, edited by Seamus Cooney, Santa Rosa, Black Sparrow Press, 1999, p. 227.

15 Ibid., p. 210.

16 "Paying for Horses: An Interview with Charles Bukowski," by Robert Wennersten, op. cit.

17 Charles Bukowski, *Screams from the Balcony*, op. cit., p. 40.

18 Ibid., p. 90.

19 Ibid., p. 197.

20 Ibid., p. 194.

21 Neeli Cherkovski, *Bukowski: A Life*, op. cit., p. 166.

22 Charles Bukowski, *Screams from the Balcony*, op. cit., p. 219.

23 Ibid., p. 275.

24 Ibid., p. 245.

25 Charles Bukowski, *Reach for the Sun*, op. cit., p. 228.

26 Charles Bukowski, *Living on Luck: Selected Letters 1960s-1970s*, volume 2, edited by Seamus Cooney, Santa Rosa, Black Sparrow Press, 1995, p. 75.

27 Anne Waldman, interview with Jean-François Duval, Boulder, Colorado, 5 December 1996.

28 Charles Bukowski, *Screams from the Balcony*, op. cit., p.339.

29 Michael Schumacher, *Dharma Lion: A Critical Biography of Allen Ginsberg*, New York, St. Martin's Press, 1992, p. 509.

30 Ibid., p. 511.

31 Charles Bukowski, *Notes of a Dirty Old Man*, San Francisco, City Lights Books, First City Lights edition published 1973, pp. 65.

32 Charles Bukowski, *Screams from the Balcony*, op. cit., p. 315.

Kerouac: Beat and Reactionary

1 Tom Wolfe, *The Electric Kool-Aid Acid Test*, New York, Bantam Books, 1969, p. 93 (First edition: New York, Farrar, Straus, 1968).

In this book, Ken Kesey becomes the Neal Cassady of the '60s. Wolfe recounts in detail Kesey and the Merry Pranksters' trip across the USA to preach the benefits of LSD experience to all. The most striking point of the trip was their visit to Millbrook Farm in New York to greet the high master, Timothy Leary, who carried out his experiments with LSD at this property. The meeting of the two sacred monsters, Kesey and Leary, and the Pranksters and Leary-ites, promised to be the most memorable encounter of the psychedelic era. Unfortunately it was a failure. Leary, suffering from the flu, casually told his visitors, who were bursting with impatience, that he was on a trip for three days, an experience too serious for him to be disturbed . . . Cold shower for the Merry Pranksters who had made a thunderous entrance to the gothic style austere property lent to Leary by the Hitchcock family: flamboyant bus with American flags flapping in the wind, loud-speakers blasting rock 'n' roll, green smoke exploding from all sides.

2 In Allen Ginsberg's album of Beat photos there is a photograph of Neal Cassady in the bus, next to a smiling Timothy Leary, *Snapshot Poetics*, San Francisco, Chronicle Books, 1993.

3 William Plummer, *The Holy Goof: A Biography of Neal Cassady*, New York, Parangon House, 1990, p. 11.

4   Ibid., p. 122.

5   Gerald Nicosia, *Memory Babe: A Critical Biography of Jack Kerouac*, Berkeley and Los Angeles, University of California Press, 1994, p. 653.

6   Wolfe, op. cit., p. 90.

7   Ibid., p. 90.

8   Nicosia, op. cit., p. 653.

9   Wolfe, op. cit., p. 90.

10   Allen Ginsberg, *The Visions of the Great Rememberer*, Amherst, Massachusetts, Mulch Press. Also see Jack Kerouac, *Visions of Cody*, translated into French by Brice Mathieussent, Paris, 10/18, 1997, preface by Allen Ginsberg, p. 17.

11   Jack Kerouac, "The Origins of the Beat Generation," *Playboy*, June 1959. Included in *Good Blonde & Others*, San Francisco, Grey Fox Press, 1994, p. 56.

12   See Nicosia, op. cit., pp. 630-631.

13   Jack Kerouac, "What Am I Thinking About?" published with the title "After me, the Deluge," *Chicago Tribune Magazine*, 28 September 1969. Included in *Good Blonde & Others*, op. cit., p. 184.

14   Jack Kerouac, "Aftermath: The Philosophy of the Beat Generation," *Esquire*, March 1958. Included in *Good Blonde & Others*, op. cit., p. 48.

15   Thomas Pynchon, *Slow Learner*, Boston, New York, London, Little, Brown and Company, Back Bay Books, 1998, pp. 8-9.

16   Joyce Johnson, *Minor Characters*, Boston, Houghton and Mifflin, 1983, p. 185; New York, Anchor Books, Doubleday, 1994, p. 185.

17   Jack Kerouac, "Aftermath: The Philosophy of the Beat Generation," *Esquire*, March 1958. Included in *Good Blonde & Others*, op. cit., pp. 48-49.

18   Jack Kerouac, "The Origins of the Beat Generation," *Playboy*, June 1959. Included in *Good Blonde & Others*, op. cit., pp. 63-65.

19   Nicosia, op. cit., p. 620.

Buk Goes Down in Legend with the Beats

1   See Gérard Guégan's postscript to his translation of Charles Bukowski's *Notes of a Dirty Old Man, Journal d'un vieux dégueulasse*, Grasset, 1996. p. 312.

2   Charles Bukowski, *Notes of a Dirty Old Man*, San Francisco, City Lights Books, 1973, pp. 31-32.

3   Charles Bukowski, *Living on Luck*, op. cit., p. 198.

4   Neeli Cherkovski, *Bukowksi: A Life*, op. cit., p. 194.

5   Ibid., p. 159.

6   Ibid. pp. 159-160.

7   Ibid., p. 205.

8   Harold Norse, E-mail to Jean-François Duval, January 19, 2001.

9   Charles Bukowski, *Screams from the Balcony*, op. cit., p. 315.

10 Harold Norse, *Memoirs of a Bastard Angel: A Fifty-Year Literary and Erotic Odyssey*, preface by James Baldwin, New York, William Morrow, 1989, p. 415.

11 Ibid., p. 420.

12 Harold Norse, E-mail to Jean-François Duval, January 19, 2001.

13 Harold Norse, *Memoirs of a Bastard Angel*, op. cit., p. 420.

14 Ibid., p. 421.

15 Ibid., p. 421.

16 Ibid., p. 429.

17 Cherkovski, *Bukowksi: A Life*, op. cit., p. 256.

18 Ibid., p. 257

19 Ibid., p. 257-258.

20 Linda King, Letter to Jean-François Duval, February 2001.

21 Neeli Cherkovski, *Whitman's Wild Children*, San Francisco, The Lapis Press, 1988, pp. 131-132.

22 Neeli Cherkovski, *Whitman's Wild Children*, op. cit., p. 132. And *Bukowksi: A Life*, op. cit., p. 166.

23 Harold Norse, "Laughter in Hell." In: *Drinking with Bukowski*, ed. by Daniel Weizmann, New York, Thunder's Mouth Press, 2000, p. 92.

24 "Paying for Horses: An Interview with Charles Bukowski," by Robert Wennersten, *London Magazine*, December 1974—January 1975.

25 Charles Bukowski, *Notes of a Dirty Old Man*, op. cit., p. 46.

26 Fernanda Pivano, *Quello che mi importa e grattarmi sotto le ascelle: Fernanda Pivano intervista Bukowski*, Milan, SugarCo Edizioni, 1991, Collana Tasco 56, p. 130.

27 Jack Kerouac, "Lamb, no Lion," in *Pageant*, February 1958. Included in *Good Blonde & Others*, op. cit., p. 53.

28 Gerald Locklin, *Charles Bukowski: A Sure Bet*, Sudbury, Water Row Press, Massachusetts, 1996, p. 66.

29 Ibid., p. 69.

Buk and Neal Cassady

1 Ann Charters, *The Portable Beat Reader*, edited by Ann Charters, New York, Viking Penguin, 1992, p. 438.

2 Harold Norse, E-mail to Jean-François Duval, January 2001.

3 Charles Bukowski, *Notes of a Dirty Old Man*, op. cit., p. 24.

4 Johnson, op. cit., p. 182.

5 Plummer, op. cit., p. 64.

6 Ibid., p. 154.

7 Timothy Leary, *Flashbacks: A Personal and Cultural History of an Era. An Autobiography*. Preface by William Burroughs, New York, Tarcher/Putnam, 1983 and 1990, p. 53.

8 Wolfe, op. cit., p. 89.

9 Plummer, op. cit., p. 125.

Neal at Vanishing Point

1 Carolyn Cassady, *Off the Road: My Years with Cassady, Kerouac and Ginsberg*, New York, Penguin Books, 1991, p. 2 (First edition, New York, William Morrow, 1990).

2   Ibid., p. 18.

3   Ibid., p. 19.

4   Brenda Knight, *Women of the Beat Generation: The Writers, Artists and Muses at the Heart of Revolution*, edited by Brenda Knight, foreword by Anne Waldman, afterword by Ann Charters, Berkeley, Conari Press, 1996.

5   Jack Kerouac, "Essentials of Spontaneous Prose," *Black Mountain Review*, Autumn 1957. Included in *Good Blonde & Others*, op. cit., pp. 70-71.

6   Carolyn Cassady, op. cit., p. 49.

7   Plummer, op. cit., p. 48.

8   Carolyn Cassady, op. cit., p. 29.

9   Ibid., p. 163.

10   Ibid., p. 166.

11   Ibid., p. 167.

12   "Paying for Horses: An Interview with Charles Bukowski," by Robert Wennersten, *London Magazine*, December 1974—January 1975.

13   Charles Bukowski, *Women*, Santa Rosa, Black Sparrow Press, 1994, p. 221.

14   Charles Bukowski, *Notes of a Dirty Old Man*, op. cit., p. 132.

15   Philippe Djian, Interview with Jean-François Duval, Paris, March 24, 2000.

On Style

1   Jack Kerouac, "Biographical Notes for The New American Poetry," Grove Press, 1960. Included in *Good Blonde & Others*, op. cit., pp. 92-93.

2   Carolyn Cassady, op. cit., p. 49.

3   Ann Charters, *The Portable Beat Reader*, op.cit., p. 197.

4   Ibid., pp. 208-210.

5   Cherkovski, op. cit., p. 166.

6 Gérard Guégan, postscript to French translation of *Notes of a Dirty Old Man, Journal d'un vieux dégueulasse*, Paris, Grasset, 1996, p. 312.

7 Charles Bukowski, *Post Office*, translated into French by Philippe Garnier, Paris, Grasset, 1986. See the Preface.

8 Neeli Cherkovski, *Whitman's Wild Children*, op. cit., pp. 10 and 21.

9 Robert Creeley's preface to Jack Kerouac's *Good Blonde & Others*, op. cit., p. XI.

10 Jack Kerouac, *Selected Letters 1940-1956*, edited by Ann Charters, New York, Viking Penguin, 1995, p. 516.

11 Steve Turner, *Angelheaded Hipster: A Life of Jack Kerouac*, London, Bloomsbury, 1996, p. 19.

12 Jack Kerouac, "Written Address to the Italian Judge," *Evergreen Review*, October—November 1963. Included in *Good Blonde & Others*, op. cit., pp. 81-82.

13 Jack Kerouac, *Selected Letters 1940-1956*, op. cit., p. 246.

14 Johnson, op. cit., p. 229.

15 Anne Waldman, interview with Jean-François Duval, Boulder, Colorado, December 5, 1996.

16 Philippe Djian, Interview with Jean-François Duval, Paris, March 24, 2000.

17 Anne Waldman, interview with Jean-François Duval, Boulder, Colorado, December 5, 1996.

18 James Campbell, op.cit., p. 50.

19 ibid., pp. 49-50.

20 Charles Bukowski and Sheri Martinelli, *Beerspit Night and Cursing: The Correspondence of Charles Bukowski and Sheri Martinelli 1960-1967*. Edited by Steven Moore. Black Sparrow Press: Santa Rosa, 2001, p. 278.

Angels and the Gargoyle

1 Jack Kerouac, "The Last Word," *Escapade*, June 1959—April 1960. Included in *Good Blonde & Others*, op. cit., p. 152.

2   Charles Bukowski, *Screams from the Balcony*, op. cit., pp. 96-97.
3   Jack Kerouac, *Vanity of Duluoz*, Flamingo, 1994, pp. 86-87.
4   Charles Bukowski, *Screams from the Balcony*, op. cit., p. 326.
5   Nicosia, op. cit., p. 565.
6   Turner, op. cit., p. 205.
7   Pivano, op. cit., p. 148.
8   Allen Ginsberg, preface to *The Beat Book*, edited by Anne Waldman, Boston, Shambhala, 1996, p. XIII.

The Counterpuncher

1   Neeli Cherkovski, *Whitman's Wild Children*, op.cit., p. 26.
2   Roddy Doyle, introduction to *Ham on Rye* by Charles Bukowski, Edinburgh, Rebel Inc., an imprint of Canongate Books, 2000, p. VIII.
3   Roland Jaccard, in: *Le Monde*, Paris, circa 1988.
4   Harold Norse, *Memoirs of a Bastard Angel*, op. cit., p. 420.
5   Neeli Cherkovski, *Whitman's Wild Children*, op. cit., p. 26.
6   James Campbell, op. cit., p. 50.
7   Charles Bukowski, *Hollywood*, Santa Rosa, Black Sparrow Press, 1989, p. 172.
8   Ibid., p. 187.
9   Ibid., p. 25.
10   Joyce Johnson, interview with Jean-François Duval, New York, November 23, 1996.
11   Charles Bukowski, "Tough Guys Write Poetry," an interview with Sean Penn, in: *Drinking With Bukowski*, Thunder's Mouth Press, New York, 2000, p. 196.
12   Charles Bukowski, *Hollywood*, op. cit., p. 150
13   Robert Crumb. Letter to Jean-François Duval, December 22, 2000.
14   Linda Lee Bukowski. Phone interview with Jean-François Duval, January 9, 2000.
15   Charles Bukowski, *Hollywood*, op. cit., p. 29.

16 Raymond Carver, *Fires: essays, poems, stories*, New York, Vintage Contemporaries, 1989, pp. 75-79.

17 Jean-Luc Godard, telephone conversation with Jean-François Duval, January 18, 2001.

18 Jack Kerouac, "Aftermath: The Philosophy of the Beat Generation," *Esquire*, March 1958.

19 Howard Sounes, *Charles Bukowski: Locked in the Arms of a Crazy Life*, Edinburgh, Rebel Inc., 1998, p. 142.

20 Steve Richmond, *Spinning Off Bukowski*, Northville (MI), Sun Dog Press, 1996, p. 21.

21 Linda Lee Bukowski, phone interview with Jean-François Duval, January 9, 2000.

22 Ibid.

23 Ibid.

24 Ibid.

Buk at the End: Beyond the Myth

1 Linda Lee Bukowski. Interview with Jean-François Duval. San Pedro, California, 4 December 1997.

2 Ibid.

3 See *Beat Scene* (27 Court Leet, Binley Woods, Nr Coventry CV3 2JQ, Warwickshire, England) No 22, "Hank and Georgia," pp. 24-26.

4 Linda Lee Bukowski. Interview with Jean-François Duval. San Pedro, California, 4 December 1997.

5 Ibid.

6 Ibid.

7 Ibid.

8 Ibid.

9 Ibid.

10 James Campbell, op.cit., p. 48.

11 Charles Bukowski, *Reach for the Sun*, op. cit., p. 225.

BUK BIBLIO

Works

Bukowski, Charles. *A Bukowski Sampler*. Madison, Wisc.: Quixote Press, 1969.

———. *A Love Poem*. Black Sparrow Press, 1979. Printed as a New Year's Greeting.

———. *All the Assholes in the World and Mine*. Benseville, Ill.: Ole Press, 1966.

———. *A New War*. Black Sparrow Press, 1997. Printed as a New Year's Greeting.

———. *Art*. Black Sparrow Press, 1977. Printed as a New Year's Greeting.

———. *At Terror Street and Agony Way*. Los Angeles: Black Sparrow Press, 1968.

———. *Beerspit Night and Cursing: The Correspondence of Charles Bukowski and Sheri Martinelli 1960-1967*. Santa Rosa: Black Sparrow Press, 2001.

———. *Betting on the Muse: Poems and Stories*. Santa Rosa: Black Sparrow Press, 1996.

———. *Bone Palace Ballet: New Poems*. Santa Rosa: Black Sparrow Press, 1997.

———. *Bring Me Your Love*. Illustrations by R. Crumb. Santa Rosa: Black Sparrow Press, 1983, 1996.

———. *The Bukowski/Purdy Letters : 1964-1974*. Paget Press, 1983.

———. *Burning in Water, Drowning in Flame: Selected Poems 1955-1973*. Santa Barbara: Black Sparrow Press, 1974.

———. *The Captain Is Out To Lunch And The Sailors Have Taken Over The Ship*. The last journals of Charles Bukowski, Illustrated By R. Crumb in a signed handbound edition of 175 Copies. Santa Rosa: Black Sparrow Press, 1997. Limited edition at 650 dollars per copy. Current edition, 1998.

————. *Charles Bukowski, Philip Lamantia, Harold Norse.* Penguin Modern Poets 13. London: Penguin Books, 1969.

————. *Cold Dogs in the Courtyard.* Chicago: Literary Times-Cyfoeth, 1965.

————. *Confession of a Coward.* Black Sparrow Press, 1995. Printed as a New Year's Greeting.

————. *Confession of A Man Insane Enough To Live with Beasts.* Benseville, Ill.: Ole Press, 1965.

————. *Crucifix in a Deathhand.* New Orleans: Loujon Press, 1965.

————. *The Cruelty of Loveless Love.* New York: Kunst Editions New York, 2001. 18 Poems by Charles Bukowski and 18 original photographs by Joan Levine Gannij. Foreword by Carl Weissner. A numbered edition in portfolio priced at 1000 dollars per copy.

————. *The Curtains are Waving and People Walk Through/The Afternoon/Here and in Berlin and in New York City and in Mexico.* Black Sparrow Press, 1967.

————. *Dangling in the Tournefortia.* Santa Barbara: Black Sparrow Press, 1981.

————. *The Day It Snowed in LA.* Paget Press, 1986. A series of cartoons by Bukowski and a brief text.

————. *The Days Run away Like Wild Horses over the Hills.* Los Angeles: Black Sparrow Press, 1969.

————. *Dear Mr. Bukowski.* Garage Graphics, 1979. A series of cartoon drawings by Bukowski. 50 copies.

————. *Erections, Ejaculations, Exhibitions and General Tales of Ordinary Madness.* San Francisco: City Lights Books, 1972. Republished by City Lights Books, 1983, in two volumes: *The Most Beautiful Woman in Town* and *Tales of Ordinary Madness.*

————. *Factotum.* Santa Barbara: Black Sparrow Press, 1975.

————. *Fire Station.* Capricorn Press, 1970. A limited edition of one poem.

————. *Flower, Fist and Bestial Wail.* Eureka, Calif.: Hearse Press, 1960.

————. *The Genius of the Crowd.* Cleveland: 7 Flowers Press, 1966.

————. *Ham On Rye.* Santa Barbara: Black Sparrow Press, 1982.

———. *Heat Wave*. Illustrated by Ken Price. Santa Rosa: Black Sparrow Graphic Arts, 1995. A limited edition illustrated by Ken Price. 1250 dollars per copy.

———. *Hollywood*. Santa Rosa: Black Sparrow Press, 1989.

———. *Horsemeat*. Black Sparrow Press, 1982. A limited edition with photographs by Michael Montfort of Bukowski at the race track.

———. *Hot Water Music*. Santa Barbara: Black Sparrow Press, 1983.

———. *If We Take*. Black Sparrow Press, 1970. Printed as a New Year's Greeting.

———. *In the Shadow of the Rose*. Black Sparrow Press, 1991. A limited edition dedicated to Bukowski's friend, Sean Penn.

———. *It Catches My Heart in Its Hands*. New Orleans: Loujon Press, 1963.

———. *Jaggernaut*. A short story by Charles Bukowski. Coventry, Beat Scene Press, 1995. Booklet. Limited to 200 copies.

———. *The Last Generation*. Black Sparrow Press, 1982. Printed as a New Year's Greeting.

———. *The Last Night of the Earth Poems*. Santa Rosa: Black Sparrow Press, 1992.

———. *Living on Luck: Selected Letters 1960s-1970s*, Volume 2. Edited by Seamus Cooney. Santa Rosa: Black Sparrow Press, 1995.

———. *Longshot Pomes for Broke Players*. New York: 7 Poets Press, 1962.

———. *Love Is a Dog from Hell: Poems 1974-1977*. Santa Barbara: Black Sparrow Press, 1977.

———. *Me and Your Sometimes Love Poems*. Kisskill Press, 1972; 1994. Collection of poems published at the author's expense by Bukowski and Linda King.

———. *Mocking Bird Wish Me Luck*. Los Angeles: Black Sparrow Press, 1972.

———. *The Movie: Barfly*. Santa Rosa: Black Sparrow Press, 1987.

———. *Notes of a Dirty Old Man*. North Hollywood: Essex House, 1969. Republished by City Lights Books, San Francisco, 1973.

———. *The Night Torn Mad with Footsteps: New Poems*. Santa Rosa: Black Sparrow Press, 2001.

————. *Open All Night: New Poems*. Santa Rosa: Black Sparrow Press, 2000.

————. *Play the Piano Drunk Like a Percussion Instrument Until the Fingers Begin to Bleed a Bit*. Santa Barbara: Black Sparrow Press, 1979.

————. *Poems Written before Jumping out of an 8-Storey Window*. Glendale, Calif.: Poetry X/Change/Litmus, 1968.

————. *Post Office*. Los Angeles: Black Sparrow Press, 1970.

————. *Pulp*. Santa Rosa: Black Sparrow Press, 1994.

————. *Reach for the Sun: Selected Letters 1978-1994*, Volume 3. Edited by Seamus Cooney. Santa Rosa: Black Sparrow Press, 1999.

————. *Relentless as the Tarantula*. Detroit: Planet Detroit Chapbooks, 1986. Stapled wrappers. Unauthorized collection of Bukowski poems banned from distribution soon after publication.

————. *The Roominghouse Madrigals: Early Selected Poems 1946-1966*. Santa Rosa: Black Sparrow Press, 1988.

————. *Run With the Hunted*. Chicago: Midwest Press, 1962.

————. *Run With the Hunted: A Charles Bukowski Reader*. Edited by John Martin. New York: HarperCollins, 1993.

————. *Scarlet*. Black Sparrow Press, 1976. Reprinted in *Love Is a Dog from Hell*.

————. *Screams from the Balcony: Selected Letters 1960-1970*. Edited by Seamus Cooney. Santa Rosa: Black Sparrow Press, 1993.

————. *Septuagenarian Stew*. Santa Rosa: Black Sparrow Press, 1990.

————. *Shakespeare Never Did This*. San Francisco: City Lights Books, 1979. Santa Rosa: Black Sparrow Press, 1995, augmented edition.

————. *The Singer*. Black Sparrow Press, 1999. Collection of six previously unpublished poems issued as a New Year's Greeting by the Press.

————. *South of No North*. Los Angeles: Black Sparrow Press, 1973.

————. *Sparks*. Black Sparrow Press, 1983. Printed as a New Year's Greeting.

————. *There's No Business*. Illustrations by R. Crumb. Santa Rosa: Black Sparrow Press, 1984, 1994.

———. *Those Marvelous Lunches*. Black Sparrow Press, 1993. Printed as a New Year's Greeting.

———. *Three by Bukowski*. Black Sparrow Press, 1992. A limited edition.

———. *To Lean Back Into It*. Santa Rosa: Black Sparrow Press, 1998. A collection of five Bukowski poems published for the first time. Issued as New Year's greeting by the press.

———. *Tough Company*. Black Sparrow Press, 1976. Printed as a New Year's Greeting.

———. *Two Poems*. Black Sparrow Press, 1967.

———. *War All the Time: Poems 1981-1984*. Santa Barbara: Black Sparrow Press, 1984.

———. *The Wedding*. Brown Buddha Books, 1986. A rare limited edition printed to celebrate Bukowski's marriage to Linda Lee Beighle. Text by Bukowski, photographs by Michael Montfort.

———. *What Matters Most Is How Well You Walk Through the Fire*. Santa Rosa: Black Sparrow Press, 1999.

———. *Women*. Santa Barbara: Black Sparrow Press, 1978.

———. *You Get So Alone at Times That It Just Makes Sense*. Santa Rosa: Black Sparrow Press, 1986.

About Bukowski

Barker, David. *The King of San Pedro*. Richard G. Wong & Co, 1985. Short book summarizing Bukowski's biography.

Brewer, Gay. *Charles Bukowski*. New York: Twayne, 1997. Literary study.

Carver, Raymond. "You Don't Know What Love Is," a poem in which Carver parodies Bukowski at a reading which he attended. In: *Fires: Essays, Poems, Stories*. Capra Press, 1983, Vintage Books, 1984, 1989.

Cherkovski, Neeli. *Bukowski: A Life*. South Royalton, Vermont: Steerforth Press, 1997. Revised and corrected edition of *Hank: The Life of Charles Bukowski*, 1991.

————. *Hank: The Life of Charles Bukowski.* New York: Random House, 1991.

————. *Whitman's Wild Children.* San Francisco: The Lapis Press, 1988. Essay in 10 chapters: Bukowski, Ginsberg, Corso, Lamantia, Norse, Kaufman, Ferlinghetti, etc.

Christy, Jim, and Powell, Claude. *The Buk Book: Musings On Charles Bukowski.* Toronto: ECW Press, 1997. With 24 amazing and rare photos of Charles Bukowski taken by Claude Powell. Beautiful Gina consoles him, doing a striptease on his lap.

Dorbin, Sanford. *A Bibliography of Charles Bukowski.* Los Angeles: Black Sparrow Press, 1969. A listing of Bukowski primary and secondary works up to 1969.

Dougherty, Jay. "Charles Bukowski and the Outlaw Spirit." In: *Gargoyle* 35 (1988), pp 92-103. An interview with Bukowski.

————. "Translating Bukowski and the Beats." In: *Gargoyle* 35 (1988), pp. 66-86. An interview with Carl Weissner, Bukowski's German translator and agent.

Duval, Jean-François. *Buk et les Beats suivi de Un Soir chez Buk, entretien inédit avec Charles Bukowski.* Paris: Michalon, 1998. *Buk e i Beat. Con una intervista inedita a Charles Bukowski.* Traduzione di Guido Lagomarsino. Milano: Archinto, 1999.

Elms Lesters Celebrates Charles Bukowski, 12-24 August 1996. The first ever multimedia exhibition celebrating the life and work of American realist writer Charles Bukowski. London, Flitcroft Street (Soho), 1996. Catalogue of the Exhibition at Elms Lesters Painting Rooms.

Fante, John. *Ask the Dusk.* Santa Barbara: Black Sparrow Press, 1980. Foreword by Charles Bukowski.

Fogel, Al. *Charles Bukowski: A Comprehensive Checklist (1946-1982).* The Sole Proprietor Press, 1982.

————. *Charles Bukowski: A Comprehensive Price-Guide and Checklist 1944-1999.* Surfside, Florida: The Sole Proprietor Press, 2000. 1000 numbered copies.

Fox, Hugh. *Charles Bukowski: A Critical and Bibliographical Study.* Somerville, Mass.: Abyss Publications, 1969. Limited edition, 300 copies.

Francheschini, Enrico. *I'm Bukowski, and then.* Binley Woods Nr Coventry: Beat Scene Press, Pocket Books Series, 1997. A short seventeen-page testimony.

Freyermuth, Gundolf. *Das War's: Letzte Worte mit Charles Bukowski.* Hamburg: Rasch und Röhring Verlag, 1996. With photographs by Michael Montfort.

Fulton, Lee. "See Bukowski Run." In: *Small Press Review* 4.4 no. 16 (May 1973).

Glazier, Loss Pequeno (ed). *All's Normal Here.* Fremont, Calif.: Ruddy Duck Press, 1985. A tribute to Charles Bukowski by some of his friends.

Glover, David. "A Day at the Races: Gambling and Luck in Bukowski's Fiction." In: *Review of Contemporary Fiction* 5.3 (Fall 1985), pp. 32-33.

Harrison, Russell. *Against the American Dream: Essays On Charles Bukowski.* Santa Rosa: Black Sparrow Press, 1994. Edinburgh: Rebel Inc., 2001.

———. "The Letters of Charles Bukowski." In: *Sure, the Charles Bukowski Newsletter* 8-9 (1993), pp. 17-29.

Hodenfeld, Chris. "Gin-Soaked Boy: Charles Bukowski Interviewed." In: *Film Comment,* July-August 1987. Interview with Bukowski on the occasion of the release of *Barfly.*

Hollywood, Rikki (Editor). *Bukowski Unleashed, Essays On a Dirty Old Man.* Bukowski Journal Volume 1. London: Little Lagoon Press, circa 2000.

Johnson, Kay. *Kaja.* New Orleans: Perdido Press, 1998. 150 numbered copies. Contains poem "Dead Cat—Poem for Bukowski."

Joyce, William. *Miller, Bukowski & Their Enemies.* Greensboro, North Carolina, 1996.

Krumhansl, Aaron. *A Descriptive Bibliography of the Primary Publications of Charles Bukowski.* Compiled by Aaron Krumhansl. Santa Rosa, Black Sparrow Press, 1999.

Locklin, Gerald. *Charles Bukowski: A Sure Bet.* Sudbury (MA): Water Row Press, 1996. Testimony. Cover illustrated by Crumb.

Long, Philomene. *Bukowski in the Bathtub*. Recollections of Charles Bukowski, with John Thomas. Sudbury: Water Row Press, 1998. Transcripts of conversations between Philomene Long, John Thomas and Charles Bukowski.

Micheline, Jack. *Sixty-Seven Poems for Downtrodden Saints*. FMSBW, 1997. Collection of poems by Micheline, in which Bukowski is mentioned.

Montfort, Michael. *Bukowski*. Michael Montfort, 1993. Photographs. Limited edition.

————. *Bukowski: Photographs 1977-1987*. Graham Mackintosh, 1987. Catalogue of Monfort's exhibition at Hamburg, Germany.

Norse, Harold. "To Know You Has Been Grace." In: *Small Press Review* (May 1973), pp. 7-8. Norse on his relationship with Buk and his work.

O'Neil, Amber (pseudonym). *Blowing My Hero*. Amber O'Neil Productions, 1995. By one of his ex-conquests, described by Buk in *Women*.

Packard, William. "Notes on Bukowski." In: *Small Press Review* (May 1973), pp. 9-20.

————. *The Poet's Craft: Interviews from the New York Quarterly*. New York: Paragon House, 1987. Includes William Packard's interview with Buk, originally published in the *New York Quarterly*.

Penn, Sean. "Tough Guys Write Poetry." In: *Interview* (September 1987), pp. 94-100. Bukowski interviewed by the actor Sean Penn.

Pivano, Fernanda. *Quello che mi importa e grattarmi sotto le ascelle: Fernanda Pivano intervista Bukowski*. Milan, SugarCo Edizioni, 1982, 1991. *Laughing With the Gods: Fernanda Pivano Interviews Charles Bukowski*. Northville, Michigan: Sun Dog Press, 2000.

Polimeni, Carlos. *Bukowski for Beginners*. Illustrated by Miguel Rep. New York: Writers and Readers Publishing Inc., 2000. A Writers and Readers Documentary Comic Books.

Purdy, Al. *Lament for Bukowski*. Sun Dog Press/Harbour Publishing, 1997. Poems dedicated to Bukowski by his friend Al Purdy. With rare photographs.

Richmond, Steve. *Charlene Rubinski*. By Gretchen Willits as told to Steve Richmond. Cape Elisabeth: Maelstrom Press, 1983. Published with Dry County in Texas by Chuck Taylor. Steve Richmond's first memoir of Charles Bukowski.

————. *Spinning Off Bukowski*. Northville, Michigan: Sun Dog Press, 1996. Testimony.

Rolfe, Lionel. "Tales of an Extraordinary Madman." In: *In Search Of . . . Literary L.A.* Los Angeles, California Classics Books, 1991, pp. 33-45.

Schultheiss/Bukowski. *Folies ordinaires*. Glénat, 1985. Fine comic strip, adaptation of some of Bukowski's short stories.

Sherman, Jory. *Bukowski: Friendship, Fame and Bestial Myth*. Augusta, Ga.: Blue Horse Publications, 1981.

Smith, Joan Jobe. *Bukowski Boulevard*, Pearl Editions.

————. (ed.) *Das Ist Alles: Charles Bukowski Recollected*. Long Beach, Calif.: Pearl Editions, 1995. Collection of poems by friends and admirers.

Smith, Jules. *Art, Survival and so Forth: The Poetry of Charles Bukowski*. North Cave, East Yorkshire (U.K.): Wrecking Ball Press, 2000. Based on extensive research, it places Bukowski's poetry in its American cultural context.

Smith, Julian. "Charles Bukowski and the Avant-Garde." In: *Review of Contemporary Fiction* 5.3 (Fall 1985), pp. 56-59. Buk's work viewed as an intentionally burlesque parody of Hemingway's work.

Sounes, Howard. *Locked in the Arms of a Crazy Life: A Biography of Charles Bukowski*. Edinburgh: Rebel Inc., an imprint of Canongate Books, 1998. Biography with very interesting photographs: particularly notable are pictures of Bukowski as a child, and photos of his many women.

————. *Bukowski in Pictures*. Edinburgh: Rebel Inc., an imprint of Canongate Books, 2000. A handsome and well produced book.

Weizmann, Daniel (Editor). *Drinking With Bukowski: Recollections of the Poet Laureate of Skid Row*. New York: Thunder's Mouth Press, 2001. A good book to get a rounded view of Bukowski from, written by varied people who knew him as fans or friends.

Winans, A.D. *Charles Bukowski: The Second Coming Years*. Binley Woods Nr Coventry (G.B.): Beat Scene Press, 1996.

———. *Remembering Bukowski*. San Pedro: Lummox Press, 1999.

———. *The Holy Grail: The Charles Bukowski/Second Coming Revolution*. Paradise, Calif.: Dustbooks, 2002.

Reviews

Atom Mind. 4.14. (Summer 1994). Ed. by Gregory Smith. Following Bukowski's death, 16 pages of tributes by Steve Richmond, A. D. Winans, Harold Norse, et al.

The Beat Journals. Vol 1. Binley Woods Nr Coventry (G.B.): Beat Scene Press, 1996. First volume of a continuing series, with contributions on Bukowski. Write to *Beat Scene*.

Beat Scene. 27 Court Leet, Binley Woods, Nr Coventry CV3 2JQ, Warwickshire, England. Tel: (01203) 54 36 04. Packed with previously unpublished information. Bukowski appears alongside the Beats in almost every issue. 39 issues have been published to date (Spring 2001). *Beat Scene 20* (1994) is entirely devoted to Bukowski.

The Bukowski Journal. Edited by Rikki Hollywood. Vol. 1: *Bukowski Unleashed, Essays On a Dirty Old Man*. London: Little Lagoon Press, circa 2000.

Bukowski Zine. Four issues. Write to: Rikki Hollywood. PO Box 11271, Wood Green, London, N22 4BF. The *Bukowski Journal* picks up where *Bukowski Zine* Nr 4 left off.

The Charles Bukowski Review. An annual publication. First issue: August 2001. Contact Joan Jobe Smith, 3030 East 2nd Street, Long Beach, California 90803, USA.

Chiron Review. Edited by Michael Hathaway. 702 North Prairie, St. John, Kansas 67576-1516, USA.

The New Censorship. Edited by Yvan Suvanjieff. Three issues devoted to Bukowski: 2.3 (June 1991), 3.1 (April 1992), 4.2 (May 1993). Contact Ivan Suvanjieff, 2953 Wyandot, Denver CO 80211-3844.

New York Quarterly. Edited by William Packard. Over the years, has regularly published Buk's poems.

ONTHEBUS. Edited by Jack Grapes. Literary review published in Los Angeles. In particular, see nos 6 and 7 (1990-1991), 10 and 11 (1992), 12 (1993).

Pearl. Edited by Joan Jobe Smith, Barbara Hauk and Marilyn Johnson. 3030 E. Second Street, Long Beach, California 90803, USA.

The Reater No 3. North Cave, Brough, East Yorkshire: Wrecking Ball Press, 1999. There's the very first interview with Charles Bukowski from 1963.

Review of Contemporary Fiction 5.3 (Fall 1985). Devoted to Charles Bukowski and Michel Butor, this issue of the academic review includes some of the most interesting contributions on Bukowski's work. Unfortunately, this issue is no longer available.

Second Coming 2.3 (1974). Edited by A. D. Winans. Issue devoted to Bukowski, with Gerald Locklin, Hugh Fox, Linda King, Harold Norse, et al.

Small Press Review 4.4 no 16 (May 1993). Edited by Tony Quagliano. Issue devoted to Bukowski, with contributions from Quagliano, Harold Norse, William Packard, et al.

The Stylus. No 2 (1994) and No 3 (1997). An amateur journal published by Roger Reus, 9412 Huron Ave., Richmond, Virginia 23 294.

Sure, the Charles Bukowski Newsletter. Edited by Edward L. Smith. Ten issues of a review generally devoted to Bukowski, published between 1991 and 1994 by Ed Smith. Double issue 5-6 entitled "Further Buk News" is particularly noteworthy. Contact Ed Smith, PO Box 4785, Rolling Bay, Washington 98061, USA.

Transit Magazine. Issues 1 (1993), 6 and 8 (1998), in particular, are devoted to Bukowski. Contact Kevin Ring, Beat Scene. 27 Court Leet, Binley Woods, Nr Coventry CV3 2JQ, Warwickshire, England.

Wormwood Review. Edited by Marvin Malone. From 1962 up until the death of its editor, this review regularly published Bukowski's poems.

Audio CD

Bukowski, Charles. *At Terror Street and Agony Way*. London: King Mob KM0B2, 1998. Recorded in February 1969. Barry Miles has sat upon this recording till 1998, and finally did put it out.

———. *Bukowski Reads His Poetry*. Santa Rosa, Calif.: Black Sparrow Graphic Arts, 1995.

———. *Charles Bukowski King of Poets*. Chinaski Records. Home recording, New Orleans, 1970.

———. *Charles Bukowski Uncensored: From the Run with the Hunted Session*. Harper Audio, Audio CD 2000.

———. *Hostage*. California, 1980. Los Angeles: Rhino Records Inc., 1985, 1994. Recorded live during a reading at the Sweetwater, Redondo Beach, April 1980.

———. *Poems and Insults*. Grey Matter. Live reading at City Lights Poets Theater, San Francisco, September 14, 1973.

Rodway, Keith. *The Life and Hazardous Times of Charles Bukowski*. New Malden, Surrey: Chrome Dreams, circa 2000. A compact disk biography of Charles Bukowski.

Thiltges, Alexandre. *Betraying Charles Bukowski*. An intriguing experiment with soundscapes and the voice of Charles Bukowski, 1998. Write to Alex Thiltges, 4 rue des Moulineaux, 27 668 Bezu Saint Eloi, France.

Audio Cassettes and Records

Bukowski, Charles. *A Bukowski Sampler*. Three interviews from the late 1980s. Bukowski reads extracts from his work. No information about the publisher.

———. *American Hostage*. Recorded live during a reading at the Sweetwater, Redondo Beach, CA, April 1980. 1 cassette. No information about the publisher.

————. *Cassette Gazette Special: Charles Bukowski*. Recorded in 1970 by Robert Head and Darlene Fife, New Orleans. Produced by Jim Haynes. Paris: Handshake Editions.

————. *Do You Use a Notebook*. Amer Audio Prose Library, 1980.

————. *The Early Years*. Bukowski reads 20 or so of his poems. Recorded in the 1970s. 1 cassette. No information about the publisher.

————. *The Home Recordings (1969-1970)*. Bukowski reads early gritty poems at home drinking and ad-libbing! Write to: R. Hollywood. PO Box 11271 Wood Greeb, London, N22 4BF.

————. *Hostage*. Los Angeles: Rhino/Word Beat, 1994.

————. *Love & Fame & Death/I've Always Had Trouble With Money*. Beat Scene Magazine, 1998. Flexi record of Bukowski reading his poems, in photo sleeve & plastic jacket/mint.

————. *The Meaning of Life*. Bukowski readings from Hamburg. L.A. cassette.

————. *90 Minutes in Hell*. Santa Monica: EarthBooks, 1977.

————. *Run With the Hunted* (Charles Bukowski Reader). Published by Harper Audio, 1993.

————. *Run With The Hunted*. Bukowski reads extracts from *Ham On Rye* and "The Genius Of Crowd." 1 cassette. 60 min. No information about the publisher.

————. *Screaming Life Of . . . Bukowski*. 2 cassettes. 120 min. No information about the publisher. Write to: Rikki Hollywood. PO Box 11271 Wood Greeb, London, N22 4BF.

————. *There Goes The Neighbourhood*. 2 tapes. Tape 1, Side A: Hamburg (1978), Side B: Los Angeles (1980). Tape 2, Side A: Redondo Beach (1980), Side B: Redondo Beach (1980). No information about the publisher. Write to: R. Hollywood. PO Box 11271 Wood Greeb, London, N22 4BF.

CD-ROM

Ron Mann. *Poetry In Motion*. Ed. Ron Mann. New York: The Voyager Company, 1992, 1994, 1995. 2 CD-ROM. CD-ROM version of the film of the same title. Bukowski appears on this CD-ROM alongside numerous Beat poets.

Films and Video

The Best Hotel on Skid Row. TV show, 1990.

Bouchitey, Patrick. *Lune Froide*, 1991 (France), 90 minutes. Full-length film adapted from "The Copulating Mermaid of Venice."

Bukowski at Bellevue 1970. Santa Rosa: Black Sparrow Press, 1998. Licensed to Visionary Communications Ltd, Lytham St.Annes, FY8 1RL England. Video cassette.

Deruddere, Dominique. *Crazy Love*. Mainline Pictures, 1987. Adaptation of three of Buk's short stories (*Love Is A Dog From Hell*).

Ferreri, Marco. *Tales of Ordinary Madness*, 23 Giugno/Ginis Film, 1983, color, 108 minutes. With Ben Gazzara.

Godard, Jean-Luc. *Sauve qui peut (la vie)* (*Every Man for Himself*), 1979, color, 87 minutes.

Hackford, Taylor. *Bukowski*. KCET (TV station in Los Angeles), 1973. Black and white documentary.

Hodgson, Jonathan. *The Man With the Beautiful Eyes*. Channel Four, 1999. A short film adapted for television from a poem by Bukowski.

Innis, Chris. *Love Pig*. Produit par Arroz con Pollo Productions, 1990. 14 minutes. In the manner of *Bring Me Your Love*.

Mann, Ron. *Poetry In Motion*. Produced by Ron Mann Sphinx Productions. New York: Girono Poetry Systems, n. d.

The Ordinary Madness of Charles Bukowski. British Broadcasting Corporation, 1995. BBC documentary, part of its Bookmark series on modern writers.

Roth, Daniel. *The Killers*, 1984, 60 minutes. Written by and with Charles Bukowski.

Schmitt, Thomas. *Charles Bukowski—East Hollywood*. Black and white documentary.

———. *I'm Still Here*. Tag/Traum, 1990. Color documentary for German television.

Schrœder, Barbet. *Barfly*. Cannon, 1987. Screenplay by Bukowski.

———. *The Charles Bukowski Tapes*. Les Films du losange, 1987. Two video cassettes, both 120 minutes, cut in to 52 short sequences.

Sikora, Jim. *Walls in the City*. Available on film and video cassette. Licensed to Visionary Communications Ltd, Lytham St.Annes, FY8 1RL England. (Write to Screen Edge, PO Box 30, Lytham St Annes, Lancs FY8 1RL, Great Britain).

Bukowski on the Internet

Oyster Boy Review Bukowski Page
http://www.levee67.com/bukowski/

http://www.mjptv.com/writers/bukowski

Black Sparrow Press (Bukowski's Publishing House)
http://www.blacksparrowpress.com/

Wino Xins
http://www.picpal.com/cbsyn.html

buk's page
http://realbeer.com/buk/

sure: the bukowski newsletter
http://realbeer.com/buk/sure.html

sure: the Charles Bukowski Newsletter
http://www.picpal.com/cbart.html

http://www.charm.net/~brooklyn/Buk/sure.html

rikki hollywood's buk zine
http://members.aol/sbaker1357/

http://www.obscure.org/obscene-latin/

http://www.bukowski-gesellschaft.de/

Folie ordinaire: un site pour Charles Bukowski
http://www.mygale.org/~brake/

http://www.aubry.free.fr/Bukowski.htm

BEAT BIBLIO

Works

Amburn, Ellis. *Subterranean Kerouac: The Hidden Life of Jack Kerouac.* New York: St. Martin's Press, 1998.

Baraka, Amiri (LeRoi Jones). *The Autobiography of LeRoi Jones/Amiri Baraka.* New York: Freundlich Books, 1984.

———. *Dutchman and the Slave.* New York: William Morrow, 1971.

———. *The LeRoi Jones/Amiri Baraka Reader.* Edited by William J. Harris. New York: Thunder's Mouth, 1991.

———. *Transbluesency: Selected Poems 1961—1995.* New York: Marsilio, 1995.

Burroughs, William S. *Ah Pook Is Here and Other Texts.* Calder, 1979.

Burroughs, William S. *The Burroughs File.* San Francisco: City Lights Books, 1984.

———. *Cities of the Red Night.* Holt, 1981.

———. *Exterminator!* New York: Viking Press, 1973.

———. *Interzone.* New York: Viking Press, 1989.

———. *Junky.* New York: Ace Books, 1953.

———. *Last Words: The Final Journal of William S. Burroughs.* New York: Grove Press, 2000.

———. *The Last Words of Dutch Schultz: A Fiction in the Form of a Film Script.* Cape Goliard Press, 1970.

———. *The Letters of William S. Burroughs 1945-1959.* Edited and with an introduction by Oliver Harris. New York: Viking Penguin, 1993.

———. *Letters to Allen Ginsberg.* New York: Full Court Press, 1982.

———. *My Education: A Book of Dreams.* New York: Viking Penguin, 1995.

———. *Naked Lunch.* Paris: Olympia Press, 1959.

————. *Nova Express*. New York: Grove, 1964.

————. *Port of Saints*. Convent Garden Press, 1975.

————. *Queer*. New York: Viking Press, 1985.

————. *Roosevelt After Inauguration*. San Francisco: City Lights Books, 1979.

————. *The Soft Machine*. Paris: Olympia Press, 1961.

————. *The Ticket that Exploded*. Paris: Olympia, 1962.

————. *The Western Lands*. New York: Viking Penguin, 1988.

————. *The White Subway*. Aloes Books, 1965.

————. *The Wild Boys: A Book of the Dead*. New York: Grove Press, 1971.

————, and Ginsberg, Allen. *The Yage Letters*. San Francisco: City Lights Books, 1963.

Burroughs Jr, William. *Kentucky Ham*, 1973. Published in 1984 by The Overlook Press.

————. *Speed*, 1970.

Campbell, James. *This Is the Beat Generation: New York—San Francisco—Paris*. London: Secker & Warburg, 1999.

Cassady, Carolyn. *Heart Beat: My Life with Jack and Neal*. Berkeley: Creative Arts Book Company, 1976 ; Pocket Books, 1978.

————. *Off the Road: My Years with Cassady, Kerouac and Ginsberg*. New York: William Morrow, 1990; Penguin Books, 1991.

Cassady, Neal. *The First Third & Other Writings*. Revised and Expanded Edition, together with a new Prologue. San Francisco: City Lights Books, 1971, 1981.

————. *Grace Beats Karma: Letters from Prison, 1958-60*. Published by Blast Books, 1993.

————, and Ginsberg, Allen. *As Ever: The Collected Correspondence of Allen Ginsberg and Neal Cassady*. Edited by Barry Gifford. Berkeley: Creative Arts, 1977.

Cavaney, Graham. *Screaming with Joy: The Life of Allen Ginsberg*. London: Bloomsbury Press, 1999.

Charters, Ann. *A Bibliography of the Works of Jack Kerouac*. New York: The Phoenix Book Shop, 1975.

————. *Kerouac*. San Francisco: Straight Arrow Publishers, 1973.

Christopher, Tom. *Neal Cassady*. Vol. One 1926-1940. Vol. Two 1941-1946. Vashon, WA, 1995, 1998. Brochures.

Clark, Tom. *Jack Kerouac: A Biography*. New York: Marlowe, 1984. London: Plexus, 1997.

Coolidge, Clark. *Now It's Jazz: Writings on Kerouac & the Sounds*. Living Batch Press, 1999.

Corso, Gregory. *The American Express*. Paris: Olympia Press, 1961.

————. *Bomb*. San Francisco: City Lights Books, 1958.

————. *Gasoline, The Vestal Lady on Brattle and Other Poems*. Pocket Poets Series No 8. San Francisco: City Lights, 1958.

————. *The Happy Birthday of Death*. New York: New Directions, 1960.

————. *Herald of the Autochtonous Spirit*. New York: New Directions, 1981.

————. *Long Live Man*. New York: New Directions, 1962.

————. *Mindfield, New and Selected Poems*. New York: Thunder's Mouth, 1989.

Cowen, Elise. Some of her poems have been collected in Brenda Knight's anthology, *Women of the Beat Generation*, Berkeley, Conari Press, 1996.

Crumb, Robert. *Your Vigor for Life Appalls Me: Robert Crumb Letters 1958–1977*. Seattle: Fantagraphics Books, 1998.

Deakin, Richard. *Jack and Neal, Angels Still Falling: The Story of Kerouac & Cassady*. A play. Binley Woods Nr Coventry: Beat Scene Press, 1997.

DiPrima, Diane. *Dinners and Nightmares*. New York: Corinth Books, 1961.

————. *Loba*, Part. I. Santa Barbara: Capra, 1973.

————. *Loba*, Parts I-VII. Berkeley: Calif.: Wingbone, 1978.

————. *Memoirs of a Beatnik*. Paris: Olympia/Traveler's Companion, 1969.

————. *Pieces of a Song: Selected Poems*. San Francisco: City Lights, 1990.

————. *Recollections of My Life as a Woman: The New York Years*. New York: Viking Press, 2001.

————. *Revolutionnary Letters*. San Francisco: City Lights, 1971.

————. *Selected Poems: 1956-1975*. Plainfield, Vermont: North Atlantic, 1975.

————. *This Kind of Bird Flies Backward*. New York: Totem Press, 1958.

Dister, Alain. *La Beat Generation*. Paris: Gallimard, 1997. Coll. Découvertes.

Dorfner, John. *Kerouac: Visions of Lowell*. Cooper Street Publications, 1993. Foreword by Allen Ginsberg.

Duval, Jean-François. *Buk et les Beats, suivi de Un Soir chez Buk, entretien inédit avec Charles Bukowski*. Paris: Michalon, 1998. Translated in Italian as *Buk e i Beat*. Milano: Archinto, 1999.

Edington, Stephen. *Kerouac's Nashua Connection*. Nashua, New Hampshire: Transition Publishing, 1999.

Ellis, R. J. *Liar! Liar!: Jack Kerouac: Novelist*. London: Greenwich Exchange, 2000.

Ferlinghetti, Lawrence. *A Coney Island of the Mind*. Norfolk, Connecticut: New Directions, 1958.

————. *Pictures of The Gone World*. San Francisco: City Lights Books, 1955.

————. *These Are My Rivers: New and Selected Poems 1955-1993*. New York: New Directions, 1993.

Frank, Robert. *The Americans*. Introduction by Jack Kerouac. New York: Grove Press, 1959.

Gifford, Barry. *Kerouac's Town*. Santa Barbara, Calif.: Capra, 1973.

Gifford, Barry, and Lee, Lawrence. *Jack's Book: An Oral Biography of Jack Kerouac*. New York: St. Martin Press, 1978. Revised 1994 and updated with a new preface by Barry Gifford.

Ginsberg, Allen. *As Ever: The Collected Correspondence of Allen Ginsberg and Neal Cassady*. With Neal Cassady. Edited by Barry Gifford. Berkeley, Calif.: Creative Arts, 1977.

————. *Cosmopolitan Greetings: Poems 1986-1992*. New York: HarperCollins, 1994.

————. *Deliberate Prose: Selected Essays 1952-1995*. HarperCollins, 2000.

————. *Howl and Other Poems*. Introduction by William Carlos Williams. San Francisco: City Lights Books, 1956.

————. *Howl: Original Draft Facsimile, Transcripts & Variant Versions.* Fully Annotated by Author, with Contemporaneous Correspondence. Account of First Public Reading, Legal Skirmishes, Precursor Textes & Bibliography. Edited by Barry Miles. New York: Harper & Row, 1986.

————. *Indian Journals.* San Francisco: Dave Haselwood Books and City Lights Books, 1970.

————. *Journals: Early Fifties Early Sixties.* Edited by Gordon Ball. New York: Grove Press, 1977.

————. *Kaddish and Other Poems 1958-1960.* San Francisco: City Lights Books, 1961.

————. *Mind Breath: Poems 1972-1977.* San Francisco: City Light Books, 1977.

————. *Photographs.* Altadena, Calif.: Twelvetrees Press, 1990.

————. *Planet News, 1961-1967.* San Francisco: City Lights Books, 1968.

————. *Plutonian Ode: Poems 1977-1980.* San Francisco: City Lights Books, 1982.

————. *Reality Sandwiches, 1953-60.* San Francisco: City Lights Books, 1963

————. *Reality Sandwiches.* Fotografien. Herausgegeben von Michael Köhler. Berlin, Nishen, 1989. U.S. edition: *Snapshots Poetics.* San-Francisco, Chronicle Books, 1993.

————. *Selected Poems 1947-1995.* London: Penguin Press, 2001.

————. *Snapshot Poetics.* San-Francisco, Chronicle Books, 1993. U.S. edition of *Reality Sandwiches,* Berlin, Nishen, 1989.

————. *Spontaneous Mind: Selected Interviews of Allen Ginsberg 1958-1996.* New York: HarperCollins Publishers, 2001

————. *The Visions of the Great Rememberer.* With letters by Neal Cassady and drawings by Basil King. Amherst, MA: Mulch Press, 1974.

————. *White Shroud: Poems 1980-85.* New York: Harper & Row, 1986.

————. *The Yage Letters.* With William S. Burroughs. San Francisco: City Lights Books, 1963.

Gysin, Brion. *The Beat Hotel.* Paris: Aitken & Stone.

——. *Minutes to Go*. With William S. Burroughs, Gregory Corso, and Sinclair Beiles. Paris: Two Cities, 1960.

——. *The Third Mind*. With William S. Burroughs. New York: Seaver Books, 1987.

Holmes, John Clellon. *Go*. New York: Charles Scribner's, 1952; Thunder's Mouth Press, 1988, with an afterword by Seymour Krim.

Holton, Robert. *On the Road: Kerouac's Ragged American Journey*. New York: Twayne Publishers, circa 2000. (Twayne's Masterwork Studies 172).

Huncke, Herbert. *The Evening Sun Turned Crimson*. New York: Cherry Valley, 1980.

——. *Guilty of Everything*. Madras and New York: Hanuman Books, 1987. New York: Paragon House, 1990.

——. *The Herbert Huncke Reader*. Edited by Benjamin G. Schafer. Foreword by William S. Burroughs. New York: William Morrow, 1997.

Hunt, Tim. *Kerouac's Crooked Road: The Development of a Fiction*. Archon Books, 1981.

Jack Kerouac's Typescript Scroll of "On the Road." Tuesday 22 May 2001. The sale's catalogue edited by Christie's. New York: Christie's International, 2001. Full description of the scroll.

Jarvis, Charles E. *Visions of Kerouac: The Life of Jack Kerouac*. Lowell: Ithaca Press, 1973.

Johnson, Joyce. *Bad Connections*. Putnam, 1978.

——. *Come and Join the Dance* (as Joyce Glassman), Atheneum, 1962.

——. *In the Night Café*. Dutton, 1989.

——. *Minor Characters: A Young Woman's Coming-of-Age in the Beat Orbit of Jack Kerouac*. New York, Anchor Books, Doubleday, 1994. First published: Boston, Houghton Mifflin, 1983.

——. *What Lisa Knew: The Truth and Lies of the Steinberg Case*. Putnam, 1990.

Johnson, Joyce, and Kerouac, Jack. *Door Wide Open: A Beat Love Affair in Letters, 1957-1958*. Introduction and commentary by Joyce Johnson. New York: Viking Press, 2000.

Jones, Hettie. *How I Became Hettie Jones*. New York: Penguin, 1990.

Jones, James T. *Jack Kerouac's Duluoz Legend: The Mythic Form of an Autobiographical Fiction*. Carbondale, Illinois: Southern Illinois University Press, 1999.

Jones, Jim. *Jack Kerouac's Nine Lives: Essays*. Cityful Press, 2001.

————. *Use My Name: Jack Kerouac's Forgotten Families*. Toronto: ECW Press, 1999.

Kandel, Lenore. *The Love Book*. San Francisco: Stolen Paper Review Editions, 1966.

Kaufman, Bob. *Abomunist Manifesto*. San Francisco: City Lights, 1959.

————. *The Ancient Rain: Poems 1956-1978*. Edited by Raymond Foye. New York: New Directions, 1981.

————. *Golden Sardine*. Pocket Poets Series no. 21. San Francisco: City Lights, 1967.

————. *Selected Poems*. Minneapolis: Coffee House, 1995.

————. *Solitudes Crowded with Loneliness*. New York: New Directions, 1965.

Kaufman, Eileen. *Who Wouldn't Walk With Tigers?* Previously unpublished autobiography; an extract from it appeared in Brenda Knight's anthology, *Women of the Beat Generation*. Berkeley, Calif.: Conari Press, 1996.

Keenan, Larry. *Postcards from the Underground: Portraits of the Beat Era*. Photographs by Larry Keenan. San Francisco: City Lights, 1999.

Kerouac, Edie Parker. *You'll Be Okay*. Unpublished autobiography; a short extract from it appeared in Brenda Knight's anthology, *Women of the Beat Generation*, Berkeley, Conari Press, 1996.

Kerouac, Jack. *Atop an Underwood: Early Stories and Other Writings*. Edited with an Introduction and Commentary by Paul Marion. Viking Penguin, 1999.

————. *Big Sur*. New York: Farrar, Straus and Cudahy, 1962.

————. *Book of Dreams*. San Francisco: City Lights Books, 1961.

————. *Desolation Angels*. New York: Coward-McCann, 1965.

————. *The Dharma Bums*. New York: Viking Press, 1958.

————. *Doctor Sax*. New York: Grove Press, 1959.

————. *Good Blonde & Others*. San Francisco: Grey Fox Press, 1993.

———. *Heaven and Other Poems*. Bolinas: Grey Fox Press, 1977.

———. *Lonesome Traveler*. New York: McGraw-Hill, 1960.

———. *Maggie Cassidy*. New York: Avon Books, 1959.

———. *Mexico City Blues*. New York: Grove Press, 1959.

———. *Old Angel Midnight*. San Francisco: Grey Fox Press, 1993.

———. *On the Road*. New York: Viking Press, 1957.

———. *Pic*. New York: Grove Press, 1971.

———. *Pomes All Sizes*. San Francisco: City Lights Books, 1992.

———. *The Portable Jack Kerouac Reader*. New York: Viking, 1995.

———. *Pull My Daisy*. New York: Grove Press, 1961.

———. *Satori in Paris*. New York: Grove Press, 1966.

———. *Scattered Poems*. San Francisco: City Lights Books, 1971.

———. *The Scripture of the Golden Eternity*. New York: Corinth Books, 1960.

———. *Selected Letters 1940-1956*. Edited by Ann Charters. New York: Viking Penguin, 1995.

———. *Selected Letters 1957-1969*. Edited by Ann Charters. New York: Viking Penguin, 1999.

———. *The Subterraneans*. New York: Grove Press, 1958.

———. *The Town and the City*. New York: Harcourt, Brace and Company, 1950.

———. *Tristessa*. New York: Avon Books, 1960.

———. *Vanity of Duluoz*. New York: Coward-McCann, 1968.

———. *Visions of Cody*. New York: McGraw-Hill, 1972.

———. *Visions of Gerard*. New York: Farrar, Straus and Cudahy, 1963.

Kerouac, Jan. *Baby Driver: A Story About Myself*. New York: St. Martin's, 1981; New York: Thunder's Mouth Press, 1998, expanded edition including letters, poems, and journal selections.

———. *Parrot Fever*. Santa Cruz, Pica Pole Press, 1994. With an introduction by Gerald Nicosia. Extract from her third novel.

———. *Trainsong*. New York: Henry Holt, 1988; New York: Thunder's Mouth Press, 1998, expanded edition including interviews, reminiscences, and poems.

Kerouac, Joan Haverty. *Nobody's Wife: The Smart Aleck and the King of the Beats*. Berkeley: Creative Arts Book Co., 2000. Introduction by

Jan Kerouac. Foreword by Ann Charters. An extract appears in Brenda Knight's anthology, *Women of the Beat Generation*. Berkeley: Conari Press, 1996.

Kesey, Ken. *Demon Box*. New York: Viking Penguin, 1986. Penguin Books, 1987.

————. *The Further Inquiry*. New York: Viking Penguin, 1990.

————. *Kesey's Garage Sale*. New York: Viking, 1973.

————. *One Flew Over the Cuckoo's Nest*. Text and Criticism. Edited by John Clark Pratt. New York, Penguin Books, 1996. First published by The Viking Press, 1962.

————. *Sometimes a Great Notion*. New York: Viking Press, 1964. Viking Penguin, 1977.

Knight, Arthur and Kit. *The Beat Vision: A Primary Sourcebook*. New York: Paragon House, 1987.

————. *Kerouac And The Beats: A Primary Sourcebook*. Edited by Arthur and Kit Knight. Foreword by John Tytell. New York: Paragon House, 1988.

Kyger, Joanne. *The Japan and India Journals 1960-1964*. Bolinas: Calif.: Tombouctou Books, 1981. *Strange Big Moon: The Japan and India Journals 1960-64*. Berkeley: North Atlantic Books, 2000.

————. *Just Space: Poems 1979-1989*. Santa Rosa, Calif.: Black Sparrow Press, 1991.

————. *Some Life*. The Post Apollo Press, 2000.

————. *The Tapestry and the Web*. San Francisco: Four Seasons Foundations, 1965.

Lamantia, Philip. *Destroyed Works*. San Francisco: Auerhahn Press, 1962.

————. *Ektasis*. San Francisco: Auerhahn Press, 1959.

————. *Narcotica*. San Francisco: Auerhahn Press, 1959.

————. *Selected Poems*. San Francisco: City Lights Books, 1967.

Lardas, John. *The Bop Apocalypse. The Religious Visions of Kerouac, Ginsberg and Burroughs*. University of Illinois Press, 2001.

Leary, Timothy. *An Annotated Bibliography of Timothy Leary*. Archon Books, 1988.

————. *Changing My Mind Among Others*. Prentice Hall, 1982.

————. *Chaos and Cyberculture*. Berkeley: Ronin, 1994.

————. *Confessions of a Hope Friend*, 1973.

————. *The Curse of the Oval Room*, 1974.

————. *The Delicious Grace of Moving One's Hand. The Collected Sex Writings*. New York: Thunder's Mouth Press, 1999.

————. *Design for Dying*. With R.U. Sirius. HarperCollins, 1997.

————. *The Dimensions of Intelligence* (M.S. thesis, W.S.U., 1946).

————. *Exo-Psychology: A Manual on the Use of Human Nervous System According to the Instructions of the Manufacturers*. Peace Press, 1977.

————. *Flashbacks: A Personal and Cultural History of an Era*. An Autobiography. Foreword by William Burroughs. New York: Tarcher/Putnam, 1983, 1997.

————. *The Game of Life*. Phoenix, Arizona: New Falcon Publications, 1993.

————. *High Priest*. Berkeley: Ronin, 1968, 1995.

————. *Info-Psychology*. Phoenix, Arizona: New Falcon Publications, 1987. Revised and corrected edition of *Exo-Psychology*.

————. *The Intelligence Agents*. Culver City, Calif.: Peace Press, 1979. New Falcon Publications, 1996.

————. *Interpersonnal Diagnonis of Personality: Functionnal Theory and Methodology for Personality Evaluation*. Published by John Wiley & Sons, 1957.

————. *Jail Notes*, 1971.

————. *Multilevel Measurement of Interpersonal Behavior*, 1956.

————. *Neurologic*, with Joanna Leary. Published by Pieper's Medienexperimente, 1973.

————. *Neuropolitique*. Phoenix, Arizona: New Falcon Publications, 1991.

————. *Politics of Ecstasy*. Berkeley: Ronin, 1990. First published by G. P. Putnam, 1968.

————. *The Psychedelic Experience: A Manual Based On the Tibetan Book of the Dead*. With Ralph Metzner and Richard Alpert. New York: University Books, 1964. Citadel Press, 1995.

————. *Psychedelic Prayers & Other Meditations*. Ronin Publishing, 1997. With a new introduction by Ralph Metzner.

————. *Psychedelic Prayers After the Tao Te Ching*. Published by Academy Editions. First published 1967.

————. *The Psychedelic Reader* (ed. with Weil, 1965). Citadel Press, 1993.

————. *The Social Dimensions of Personality* (Ph. D. dissertation, U.C., 1950).

————. *Starseed: A Psy-Phy Comet Tale*, 1973.

————. *Surfing the Conscious Nets: A Graphic Novel.* Robert Williams (Illustrator). Last Gasp of San Francisco, 1995.

————. *Terra II*, with Joanna Leary and L. W. Benner, 1974.

————. *Timothy Leary's Greatest Hits.* KnoWare, 1990.

————. *Turn On, Tune In, Drop Out.* Berkeley: Ronin, 1999.

————. *What Does WoMan Want ?*, 1976. Phoenix, Arizona: New Falcon Publications, 1996. Revised edition.

Leary, Timothy, and Potter, Beverly A. *Politics of Self-Determination.* Berkeley: Ronin, 2000. (Self-Mastery Series).

Lee, A. Robert. *The Beat Generation Writers.* Edited by A. Robert Lee. London: Pluto Press, 1996.

McClure, Michael. *Antechamber and Other Poems.* New York: New Directions, 1978.

————. *Dark Brown.* London: Auerhahn Press, 1961.

————. *Ghost Tantras.* San Francisco: Four Seasons Foundation, 1969.

————. *Meat Science Essays.* San Francisco: City Lights, 1963.

————. *Rebel Lions.* New York: New Directions, 1991.

————. *Scratching the Beat Surface: Essays on New Vision from Blake to Kerouac.* New York: Penguin, 1994.

————. *Selected Poems.* New York: New Directions, 1986.

McDarrah, Fred. *Kerouac and Friends: A Beat Generation Album.* William Morrow & Co, 1985.

McDarrah, Fred W., Gloria S. *Beat Generation: Glory Days In Greenwich Village.* New York: Schirmer Books, 1996.

McNally, Dennis. *Desolate Angel. A Biography. Jack Kerouac, the Beat Generation and America.* Random House, 1979.

Meltzer, David. *San Francisco Beat: Talking With the Poets.* Edited by David Meltzer. San Francisco: City Lights Books, 2001. Photos by Harry Redl and Larry Keenan.

Miles, Barry. *The Beat Hotel: Ginsberg, Burroughs, and Corso in Paris 1957-1963*. New York: Grove Press, 2000.

———. *Ginsberg: A Biography*. New York: Simon & Schuster, 1989.

———. *Jack Kerouac King of the Beats: A Portrait*. London: Virgin, 1998.

Milewski, Robert. *Jack Kerouac: An Annotated Bibliography of Secondary Sources 1944-1979*. Scarecrow Press, 1981.

Montgomery, John. *Kerouac at the "Wild Boar" and Other Skirmishes*. Compiled by John Montgomery. Fels & Fern Press, 1986.

———. *Kerouac We Knew: Unposed Portraits, Action Shots*. Compiled by John Montgomery. Fels & Fern Press, 1982.

Morgan, Bill. *The Beat Generation in New York: A Walking Tour of Jack Kerouac City*. San Francisco: City Lights Books, 1997.

Nicosia, Gerald. *Memory Babe: A Critical Biography of Jack Kerouac*. Berkeley and Los Angeles: University of California Press, 1994. First published in the USA by Grove Press, 1983.

Norse, Harold. *Beat Hotel*. San Diego: Atticus, 1983.

———. *Memoirs of a Bastard Angel: A Fifty-Year Literary and Erotic Odyssey*. Preface by James Baldwin. New York: William Morrow, 1989.

Odier, Daniel. *The Job: Interviews with William S. Burroughs*. New York: Grove Press, 1974.

Olson, Charles. *Reading at Berkeley*. Berkeley, Calif.: Small Press Distribution, 1966.

Orlovsky, Peter. *Clean Asshole Poems and Smiling Vegetable Songs, Poems 1957-1977*. Pocket Poets Series no. 37. San Francisco: City Lights, 1978. Reprint. Orono, Maine: Northern Lights, 1993.

———. *Leper's Cry*. New York: Phoenix Bookshop, 1982.

Perry, Paul, and Babbs, Ken. *On the Bus: The Complete Guide to the Legendary Trip of Ken Kesey and the Merry Pranksters and the Birth of the Counterculture*. New York: Thunder's Mouth Press, 1990.

Phillips, Lisa. *Beat Culture and the New America 1950-1965*. New York: Whitney Museum of Art, 1995; Paris: Flammarion, 1995. Published on the occasion of the exhibition at the Whitney Museum of American Art, November 9, 1995 - February 4, 1996.

Phillips, Rod. *Forest Beatniks and Urban Thoreaus: Gary Snyder, Jack Kerouac, Lew Welch, and Michael McClure*. Bern (Switzerland): Peter Lang Publishing, 2001.

Pivano, Fernanda. *Amici scrittori: Quarant'anni di incontri e scoperte con gli autori americani*. Milano: Arnoldo Mondadori Editore, 1995.

——. *Album americano: Dalla generazione perduta agli scrittori della realtà virtuale*. Frassinelli, 1997.

Plummer, William. *The Holy Goof: A Biography of Neal Cassady*. Englewood Cliffs, NJ, 1981. New York: Paragon House, 1990, first paperback edition.

The Rolling Stone Book of the Beats: The Beat Generation and American Culture. Ed. by Holly George–Warren. New York, Hyperion, 1999.

Roszak, Theodore. *The Making of a Counter Culture. Reflection on the Technocratric Society and its Youthful Opposition*. Berkeley: University of California Press, 1995. First published: New York: Doubleday, 1969.

Sandison, David. *Jack Kerouac: An Illustrated Biography*. London, Hamlyn Press, 1999. Foreword by Carolyn Cassady.

Schumacher, Michael. *Dharma Lion: A Critical Biography of Allen Ginsberg*. New York: St. Martin's Press, 1992.

Shoaf, Eric C. *Collecting William S. Burroughs In Print: A Checklist*. Rumford, Rhode Island: Ratishna Books, circa 2001.

Skau, Michael. *A Clown in a Grave: Complexities and Tensions in the Works of Gregory Corso*. Carbondale, Illinois: Southern Illinois University Press, 1999.

Snyder, Gary. *Axe Handles*. New York: Farrar, Straus & Giroux, 1982.

——. *The Back Country*. New York: New Directions, 1968.

——. *Earth House Hold: Technical Notes and Queries to Fellow Dharma Revolutionaries*. New York: New Directions, 1969.

——. *Left Out in the Rain*. Berkeley, Calif.: North Point, 1986.

——. *Mountains and Rivers Without End*. San Francisco: Four Seasons Foundation, 1970.

——. *Myths & Texts*. New York: Totem Press/Corinth Books, 1960.

————. *No Nature: New and Selected Poems.* New York: Pantheon, 1992.

————. *Riprap.* Kyoto: Origin, 1959.

Solomon, Carl. *Emergency Messages: An Autobiographical Miscellany.* Edited and with a Foreword by John Tytell. New York: Paragon House, 1989.

————. *Mishaps, Perhaps and More Mishaps.* San Francisco: City Lights Books, 1966.

————. *More Mishaps.* San Francisco: City Lights Books, 1966.

Swartz, Omar. *The View from On the Road: The Rhetorical Vision of Jack Kerouac.* Southern Illinois University Press, 1999.

Timothy Leary: Outside Looking In. Edited by Robert Forte. Park Street Press, 1999. A memorial volume.

Turner, Steve. *Angelheaded Hipster: A Life of Jack Kerouac.* London: Bloomsbury, 1996.

Tytell, John. *Naked Angels: Kerouac, Ginsberg, Burroughs.* Grove Press, 1999. Paperback reprint edition.

————. *Paradise Outlaws: Remembering the Beats.* Photographs by Mellon. New York: William Morrow, 1999.

Un homme grand: Jack Kerouac at the Crossroads of Many Cultures/Jack Kérouac à la confluence des cultures. Edited by Pierre Anctil, Louis Dupont, Rémi Ferland, et al. Ottawa: Carleton University Press, 1990.

The Unbearables. *Crimes of the Beats.* Brooklyn, New York, Autonomedia, 1998.

Vega, Janine Pommy. *Poems to Fernando.* San Francisco: City Lights Books. Poet Pocket Series No 22, 1968.

Waldman, Anne. *Fast Speaking Woman: Chants and Essays.* New Expanded Edition. San Francisco: City Lights Books, 1996. First published 1975.

————. *Helping the Dreamer: New and Selected Poems: 1966-1988.* Minneapolis: Coffee House Press, 1989.

————. *Iovis.* Minneapolis: Coffee House Press, 1993.

————. *Kill or Cure.* New York: Penguin Books, 1994.

————. *Makeup on Empty Space.* Toothpaste Press, 1984.

————. *Marriage: A Sentence.* New York: Penguin Putnam, 2000.

————. *Skin Meat Bones*. Minneapolis: Coffee House Press, 1985.

Watson, Steven. *The Birth of the Beat Generation: Visionaries, Rebels, and Hipsters, 1944-1960*. New York, Pantheon Books, 1995.

Weinreich, Regina. *The Spontaneous Poetics of Jack Kerouac*. Southern Illinois University Press, 1987; Marlowe & Co, 1994.

Whalen, Philip. *The Diamond Noodle*. Berkeley, Calif.: Poltroon, 1980.

————. *Heavy Breathing: Poems 1967-1983*. San Francisco: Four Seasons Foundation, 1980.

————. *On Bear's Head*. New York: Harcourt, Brace and World, 1964.

Winans, A. D. *North Beach Revisited*. New York: Green Bean Press, 2000.

Wolfe, Tom. *The Electric Kool-Aid Acid Test*. New York, Bantam Books, 1969. First published: New York, Farrar, Straus, 1968.

Anthologies

Allen, Donald. *The New American Poetry 1945-1960*. Ed. by Allen Donald. New York: Grove Press, 1960.

Blazek, Douglas. *Ole Anthology*. Edited by Douglas Blazek. Glendale: Poetry/X Change, 1967.

Charters, Ann. *Beat Down to Your Soul: What Was the Beat Generation? Poems, Essays, Memoirs, Notes, Protests, Attacks, and Apologies—from the Beat Explosion That Rocked the World*. Edited with an introduction by Ann Charters. New York: Penguin, 2001.

————. *The Portable Beat Reader*. Edited by Ann Charters. New York: Viking Penguin, 1992.

Knight, Brenda. *Women of the Beat Generation: The Writers, Artists and Muses at the Heart of Revolution*. Edited by Brenda Knight. Foreword by Anne Waldman, afterword by Ann Charters. Berkeley: Conari Press, 1996.

Peabody, Richard. *A Different Beat Writings by Women of the Beat Generation*. Edited by Richard Peabody. London: Serpent's Tail, 1997.

Waldman, Anne. *Another World: A Second Anthology of Works from the St. Mark's Poetry Project*. Indianapolis-New York: Bobby Merrill, 1971.

―――. *The Beat Book: Poems and Fiction of the Beat Generation*. Edited by Anne Waldman. Foreword by Allen Ginsberg. Boston: Shambhala, 1996.

―――. *Out of this World: An Anthology of Writing from the St. Mark's Poetry Project 1966-1991*. New York: Crown, 1991.

―――. *The World Anthology: Poems from the St. Mark's Poetry Project*. Indianapolis-New York: Bobby Merrill, 1969.

Reviews

Beat Scene. 27 Court Leet, Binley Woods, Nr Coventry CV3 2JQ, Warwickshire, England. Tel: (01203) 54 36 04. Full of previously unpublished information. 39 issues have been published to date (Spring 2002).

Chelsea Hotel, A Magazine for the Arts. Issue 10 (1997) is devoted to Larry Keenan's and Gerard Malanga's photos of the Beats. Heidelstrasse, 9, D-79805 Eggingen, Germany. Tel.: 07746 91116.

The Kerouac Connection. P.O. Box 7250 Menlo Park, CA 94026-7250. 30 issues have been published to date (August 2000).

The Kerouac Rag. Edited by Alan Griffey, 43 Chatto Road, Torquay, Devon, TQ1 4HT, England. 2 issues. No 2: Spring 2001.

Audio CD

The Beat Generation. Santa Monica, Calif.: Rhino/Word Beat, 1992. 3 CD.

Burroughs, William S. *The Best of William Burroughs*. Giorno Poetry System. 4 CD.

―――. *Break Through in Grey Room*. Sub Rosa.

―――. *Call Me Burroughs*. Santa Monica, Calif.: Rhino/Word Beat, 1995.

———. *Dead City Radio.* Published by Poly Tone, 1990.

———. *The Elvis of Letters.* TK Records.

———. *Naked Lunch.* Warner Bros.

———. *Seven Souls.* Triloka Records.

———. *Spare Ass Annie & Other Tales.* Published by 4th & Broadway, 1993.

———. *Various Artists 10% File Under Burroughs.* Sub Rosa.

———. and Cobain, Kurt. *Priest They Called Them.* Published by Timken Pub., 1996.

Ginsberg, Allen. *Allen Ginsberg Live in Wuppertal.* S Press.

———. *The Ballad of the Skeletons.* New York: Mercury, 1996. With Paul McCartney, Philip Glass, Lenny Kaye.

———. *Holy Soul Jelly Roll: Poems and Songs 1949-1993.* Santa Monica, Calif.: Rhino/Word Beat, 1994. 4 CD.

———. *Howls, Raps & Roars.* Fantasy, 1993. 4 CD.

———. *Hydrogen Jukebox* (opera). With Philip Glass. Elektra-/Nonesuch, 1993.

———. *Lion for Real.* Mountain Air Books, 1996.

Kerouac, Jack. *The Jack Kerouac Collection.* Santa Monica, Calif.: Rhino/Word Beat, 1990. 3 CD.

———. *Jack Kerouac Reads On the Road.* Rykodisc Label, 78 Stanley Gardens, London W3 7SN.

———. *Readings on the Beat Generation.* Verve.

Kerouac: Kicks Joy Darkness. Salem, MA: Rikodisc, 1997. A tribute by poets, actors and rock stars.

Leary, Timothy. *Beyond Life with Timothy Leary.* Mouth Almighty.

———. *Right To Fly.* Published by Mausoleun Records, 1996.

———. *Turn On Tune In & Drop Out.* Published by Performing Arts, 1996.

———. *You Can Be Anyone This Time Around.* Published by Rykodisc, 1993.

Audio Cassettes

Burroughs, William S. *Call Me Burroughs.* Santa Monica, Calif.: Rhino/Word Beat, 1995.

————. *Dead City Radio.* Audio Cassette. Published by Poly Tone, 1990.

Cassady, Neal. *Drive Alive: Cassady Raps.* Eugene, OR.: Key-Z Productions, 1965.

Ginsberg, Allen. *Holy Soul Jelly Roll: Poems and Songs 1949-1993.* Santa Monica, Calif.: Rhino/Word Beat, 1994. 4 cassettes.

Kerouac, Jack. *The Jack Kerouac Collection.* Santa Monica, Calif.: Rhino/Word Beat, 1990.

————. *Mexico City Blues.* Audio Cassette. Published by Shambhala Publications, 1996. 4 cassettes. Read by Allen Ginsberg.

Knight, Brenda. *Women of the Beat Generation: The Writers and Muses at the Heart of a Revolution.* Read by the Authors with Debra Winger. San Bruno, Calif.: Audio Literature, 1996. 4 cassettes.

CD-ROM

Kerouac, Jack. *A Jack Kerouac Romnibus.* CD-Rom. Penguin.

Mann, Ron. *Poetry In Motion.* Ed. Ron Mann. New York: The Voyager Company, 1992, 1994, 1995. 2 CD-ROM.

Films and Videos

The Acid Test. Eugene, OR: Key-Z Productions, 1990. The legendary acid test. With the Grateful Dead, the Merry Pranksters, Ken Kesey, Neal Cassady, et al.

Allione, Constanzo. *Fried Shoes, Cooked Diamonds.* With Gregory Corso, William Burroughs, Allen Ginsberg, Timothy Leary, Peter Orlovsky, Anne Waldman. Directed by Constanzo Allione. New York: Mystic Fire Video, n. d. VHS Video Edition Published by Baker & Taylor Video, 1987, and Myakka River Pub., 1996.

Antonelli, John. *Kerouac.* Amsterdam: Mystic Fire Video, 1986, 1995.

Aronson, Jerry. *The Life and Times of Allen Ginsberg.* Directed by Jerry Aronson. New York: First Run Features, 1992.

Brookner, Howard. *Burroughs: The Movie*. Directed by Howard Brookner and produced by Howard Brookner and Alan Yentob. New York: Giorno Poetry Systems, n. d.

Burroughs, William. *Commissioners of Sewers*. VHS Video Edition. Published by Myakka River Pub., 1993.

Ferrini, Henry. *Lowell Blues: The Words of Jack Kerouac*. Ferrini Productions, 2001.

Frank, Robert, and Amram, David. *Pull My Daisy*. Narrated by Jack Kerouac, with Gregory Corso, Peter Orlovsky, Larry Rivers, and David Amram. Directed by Robert Frank and A. Leslie. Houston: Houston Museum of Art, 1958.

It Don't Pay To Be An Honest Citizen. With bit parts by Allen Ginsberg and William S. Burroughs. New York: Object Productions/Jacob Burkhardt, 1984.

Kay, Stephen K. *The Last Time I Committed Suicide*. A Roxie release, 1997. Starring Thomas Jane as Neal Cassady, Keanu Reeves and Claire Forlani.

Kerouac. VHS Video Edition. Published by Myakka River Pub, 1995.

Leary, Timothy. *Fatal Skies*. VHS Video Edition. Published by Baker & Taylor Video, 1990.

———. *How to Operate Your Brain*. VHS Video Cassette. Retinalogic, 1993.

———. *Timothy Leary's Last Trip*. VHS Video Edition. Published by Winstar Entertainment, 1997.

———. *Virtual Reality*. VHS Video Edition. Published by Lightworks Audio & Video, 1995.

Lerner, Richard, and MacAdams, Lewis. *What Happened to Kerouac*. Directed by Richard Lerner and Lewis MacAdams. New York: New Yorker Films, 1985. VHS Video Edition published by Vidmark, 1989.

Mann, Ron. *Poetry In Motion*. Produced by Ron Mann Sphinx Productions. New York: Girono Poetry Systems, n. d.

Neal Cassady. In the Back House. On the Road. Eugene, OR: Key-Z Productions, 1990. Contains vintage footage filmed in the prime of the 1960s.

On the Road with Jack Kerouac. Video Cassette VHS, published by Baker & Taylor Video, 1990.

Workman, Chuck. *The Source.* Directed by Chuck Workman. Music by Philipp Glass, Dizzie Gillepsie et al. With Johnny Depp, Denis Hopper et al. Released by Winstar Cinema, n.d., 89 min.

Beat Bookshops (with "Cult Writings" sections)

New York:

St. Mark's Bookshop. 31 Third Avenue, New York, New York 10003. Tél.: (212) 260 7853.

Gotham Book Mart & Gallery. 41 West 47th St. New York City 10036. Tél.: (212) 719 4448.

San Francisco:

City Lights Bookstore, 261 Columbus Avenue, San Francisco, CA 94133.

Cloud House, 1557 Franklin Str. Tél.: (415) 292-5554.

Boulder, Colorado:

Tom Peters. Beat Book Shop, 1713 Pearl Street, Boulder, CO 80302. Tél.: (303) 444 7111.

The Naropa Institute Bookstore. 2130 Arapahoe Avenue, Boulder, CO 80302.

London:

Compendium Bookshop. 234 Camden High Street. London NW1 8QS. Tel: 0171 485 8944. Fax: 0171 267 0193. The best beat bookshop in England, sadly closed in 2000.

————. Books etc. Charing Cross Road. London WC2. Tel: 0171 379 6838.

Belfast:

The Bookshop At Queens. 91 University Road. Belfast, Northern Ireland BT7 1NL. Tel: 0232-666302/662552

Paris:

Un Regard moderne, 10 rue Gît-le-Cœur, 75 006 Paris. Tél: 43 29 13 93.

Virtual Bookshops on the Internet

Those browsing the Internet can view catalogues and purchase books by correspondence from the following beat bookshops:

Fog City Facts & Fiction. P.O. Box 48. Monterrey. CA 93942. tel: (408) 372 4911.
http://www.kerouac.com/

Key-Z Productions, 755 Polk Street, Eugene, OR 97402. tel: (541) 484 4315. Fax: (541) 485 4937.
http://www.key-z.com

Water Row Books. P.O. Box 438 Sudbury, MA 01 776. Tel: (508) 485 8515. Fax: (508) 229 0885.
http://www.waterrowbooks.com

On the Internet

The Beats:

Literary Kicks, by Levi Asher
http://www.charm.net/~brooklyn/

The Beat Generation: Audio and Video Material in the UC Berkeley Libraries
http://www.lib.berkeley.edu/MRC/BeatGen.html

http://www.jackmagazine.com/beatnews/

http://tigger.uic.edu/~dbhale/beat.html

William Burroughs:

http://www.charm.net/~brooklyn/People/WilliamSBurroughs.html

http://www.hyperreal.org/wsb/index.html

http://www.netherworld.com/~mgabrys/william/index.html

Neal Cassady:

http://www.charm.net/~brooklyn/People/NealCassady.html

The Neal Cassady Experience
http://www.geocities.com/soHo/Cafe/1010/index.html

Neal's Denver
http://www.intrepidtrips.com/neal1.html

Allen Ginsberg:

http://www.charm.net/~brooklyn/People/AllenGinsberg.html

http://www.ginzy.com/

Jack Kerouac:
The Kerouac Connection
http://www.angelfire.com/ca2/kerouacconnection/

http://www.charm.net/~brooklyn/People/JackKerouac.html

http://www.jackmagazine.com/beatnews/

Ken Kesey:

http://www.intrepidtrips.com

Key-Z Productions Home Page
http://www.key-z.com/

Timothy Leary:

http://leary.com/

WHO'S WHO?

Charles Bukowski (1920-1994)

Born August 16, 1920 in Andernach, Germany. Grew up in Los Angeles during the '20s. His father beat him. As a teenager suffered a severe form of acne. Drifted across the USA: Philadelphia, St Louis, New Orleans. Numerous jobs. Inveterate drinker. In 1964 he had a daughter, Marina with one of his girlfriends, Frances Smith. Was a postal worker for about 10 years. Published his poems in underground magazines, notably *Ole* and *Open City*. *Notes of a Dirty Old Man* appeared in 1969 and won him an international reputation. Became a cult author in the '70s. Married Linda Lee Beighle in 1985. Published around 40 works, collections of poems and novels. Went to the racetrack every day. Unrepentant gambler. Died of leukemia in 1994. His work's merit lies chiefly in its crudity, realism, challenges, vigour, humour, comical and grotesque aspects, and madness.

Linda Lee Bukowski

Twenty-five years younger than Bukowski. She met Bukowski in 1976 at one of his poetry readings when she owned a small health-food restaurant. Follower of the thought of Indian guru Meher Baba. Marriage in August 1985. Profound saving influence on Buk, who would probably have died prematurely without the stability Linda brought him. They bought a house in San Pedro where they lived surrounded by a tribe of cats until Bukowski's death in 1994.

Linda is Sara in Charles Bukowski's *Women*.

Joan Vollmer Burroughs (1924-1951)

Grew up in Loudonville, New York State. Shared an apartment on 421 East 118th Street with Edie Parker, Jack Kerouac's girlfriend. Became William Burroughs' wife with whom she had a son in 1947, William S.

Burroughs, Jr. Accidental death in 1951 in Mexico from a shot fired by William Burroughs who was acting out William Tell.

She is Jane in Kerouac's *On the Road*.

William Seward Burroughs (1914-1997)

Born in St. Louis, grandson of Burroughs the inventor of the adding machine. Met Lucien Carr and Allen Ginsberg in New York at Christmas 1943. He lived with Joan Vollmer from 1947 onwards. Ginsberg got Burroughs' first novel, *Junky*, published by Ace Books under the pseudonym William Lee. In 1951 he accidentally shot dead his wife Joan in Mexico. Stayed in Ecuador and Peru. Settled in Tangiers where his friends Kerouac, Ginsberg and Orlovksy visited him in 1957. Kerouac retyped Burroughs' *Naked Lunch*, which was published in 1959. He died in Lawrence, Kansas in August 1997.

He is Old Bull Lee in Kerouac's *On the Road* and Bull Hubbard in *Desolation Angels*.

William S. Burroughs, Jr (1947-1981)

Born in 1947 the only child of William and Joan Burroughs. After his mother's dramatic death (see under Joan Vollmer Burroughs) his paternal grandparents brought him up. In 1961 he visited his father in Tangiers— Burroughs was completely indifferent to his son. In New York he became addicted to methedrine. Published his autobiographical novel *Speed* in 1970. Died from drug abuse in 1981.

Lucien Carr

Born in St. Louis. In 1943 became one of Edie Parker's boyfriends when Jack Kerouac temporarily left her to join the merchant marines. Met Allen Ginsberg in 1944 at Columbia University, New York and took him to Edie Parker's place. Introduced him to William Burroughs. Stabbed to death his ex-professor David Kammerer, who was sexually harassing him. Became a good husband and father. Worked at United Press International. Now lives in Washington.

He is Kenny Wood in Kerouac's *The Town and The City*.

Carolyn Cassady (1923)

Born Carolyn Robinson. Childhood in Nashville, Tennessee. Studied at the University of Denver, the town where she met Neal Cassady in 1947. Neal married Carolyn in 1948, after the annulment of his marriage with LuAnne Henderson, who he had married in 1945 when she was 15. They had three children. Carolyn Cassady recounted her ménage à trois with Neal and Jack Kerouac at the beginning of the '50s in *Heart Beat*, a fragment of her memoirs published in 1976, and in *Off the Road* (1990). In the screen adaptation of *Heart Beat* she was played by Sissy Spacek and Neal by Nick Nolte. She has lived in London since 1984.

Neal Cassady (1926-1968)

Born in Salt Lake City. Childhood in Denver. Mother disappeared, father an alcoholic. In 1945 he heard about Ginsberg, Kerouac and Burroughs through his friend Hal Chase. He went to meet them in December 1946. Neal went to New York with his young wife LuAnne. His Joan Anderson Letter (1950) was the determining factor in Kerouac's writing. Encouraged by Kerouac and Ginsberg, Neal began his own autobiography of which he wrote only the first third, hence the title *The First Third*. This work inspired Kerouac to write *Visions of Cody*. *The First Third* was published in 1981 by City Light Books.

In 1964 Neal Cassady drove the psychedelic bus belonging to Ken Kesey and the Merry Pranksters who preached the virtues of LSD from the West coast to the East. Neal died from drug and alcohol abuse and sunstroke alongside a railway line in San Miguel de Allende in Mexico in February 1968.

He is Dean Moriarty in *On the Road* and Cody Pomeray in *Visions of Cody*, two of Kerouac's major works devoted to him. He features as a cult figure in almost all Beat literature (he is Hart Kennedy in J. C. Holmes' *Go*, Houlihan in Ken Kesey's *The Day After Superman Died*, etc.).

Hal Chase

Born at the beginning of the '20s in Denver. He studied anthropology in Columbia University, New York, and shared an apartment with Joan Vollmer in the spring of 1945. During one of his visits to Denver he told Neal Cassady about the group he hung around with in New York: Kerouac,

Ginsberg, etc., that Neal would later join. He now lives near Paso Robles in California.

He is Chad King in Kerouac's *On the Road.*

Gregory Corso (1930-2001)

Born in Greenwich Village. Deserted by his mother, he was placed at a very young age with various adoptive families. Acquainted with reformatories from the age of 12. Discovered literature and poetry at 16 in prison. On his release in 1950 he met Allen Ginsberg who encouraged his attempts to write. Was first published in 1955. His major book *Gasoline* was published three years later by City Light Books in San Francisco. After staying in Europe and San Francisco he went back to live in Greenwich Village. According to his wish, his ashes are buried in Rome, Italy, next to Shelley's tomb. He discovered Shelley's poetry as a young man when he was in jail.

He is Yuri Gligoric in Kerouac's *The Subterraneans* and Raphael Urso in *Desolation Angels.*

Diane DiPrima (1934)

Born in New York. Struck up a friendship with Ezra Pound in 1953. Her first book of poems *This Kind of Bird Flies Backward* was published in 1958 by Hettie and LeRoi Jones. Follower of Zen. Among numerous books, *Memoirs of a Beatnik* (1969) recounts her bohemian youth and in particular a Beat orgy scene (real or fictitious?) with Ginsberg and Kerouac who she met in 1957. She raised five children.

Lawrence Ferlinghetti (1919)

Born in Yonkers, New York State. Studied at the Sorbonne. Went to San Francisco at the beginning of the '50s to found the famous publishing house City Lights and the bookshop of the same name in 1953. Convicted in 1957 for the publication of Ginsberg's *Howl.* He is the author of around 15 books of prose and poetry including *A Coney Island of the Mind* (1958). He lives in San Francisco.

He is Lorenzo Monsanto in Kerouac's *Big Sur.*

Robert Frank (1924)

Photographer of Swiss origin whose work *The Americans* was prefaced by Kerouac and published in 1959. In 1958 Robert Frank filmed the most famous of the Beat films, *Pull My Daisy* (28 minutes) with Ginsberg and Orlovsky playing themselves, Corso playing Kerouac, Larry Rivers playing Cassady and Delphine Seyrig playing Carolyn Cassady. Narrated by Kerouac. Robert Frank is today considered among the greatest photographers.

Allen Ginsberg (1926-1997)

Born in Newark, New Jersey. Son of teacher and poet Louis Ginsberg. Seriously affected by his mother Naomi's mental illness. In 1948 he had a vision of the poet William Blake. Freed himself from the classical forms of poetry in 1954 under the influence of Kenneth Rexroth, William Carlos Williams and Kerouac. In the same year Peter Orlovsky became his life-long lover. *Howl*, published in 1956, made him famous. In November 1958 he wrote the 48-page *Kaddish* in 40 hours under the effect of methedrine and dexedrine, a work inspired by his mother's madness. Charismatic anti-establishment figure in the '60s. In 1974 he founded the Jack Kerouac School of Disembodied Poetics with Anne Waldman at the Buddhist Institute of Naropa in Boulder, Colorado. Lived on the East Side of New York. Died in April 1997.

He is David Stofsky in John Clellon Holmes' *Go*, Carlo Marx in *On the Road*, Adam Moorad in *The Subterraneans*, Alvah Goldbook in *The Dharma Bums*, Irwin Garden in *Desolation Angels* and *Visions of Cody*—all five by Kerouac.

Brion Gysin (1916-1986)

Friend of William Burroughs, author of *The Beat Hotel* that refers to the hotel located at 9, rue Gît-le-Cœur in Paris where Ginsberg, Orlovsky, Burroughs, Corso and Norse stayed from 1957 to the beginning of the '60s. In the hotel Corso wrote his poem *Bomb* in 1958 and Burroughs put the finishing touches to *Naked Lunch* before it was published by Maurice Girodias at Olympia Press in 1959. Burroughs also worked on his cut-up technique with Gysin at the hotel. It is now called Hôtel du Vieux Paris.

Joan Haverty

Kerouac's second wife. See under Kerouac, Joan Haverty.

LuAnne Henderson

Neal Cassady's beautiful teenage wife (married when he was 19 and she was 15). She went with Neal when at the end of 1946 when he made off to New York in a stolen car, then on a Greyhound Bus, with a few clothes and a copy of *Remembrance of Things Past* in his pocket. At the beginning of 1949 LuAnne spent a couple of passionate nights with Kerouac in the Blackstone Hotel in San Francisco where Neal left them to go and get his second wife Carolyn. LuAnne remarried twice. She lives in California.

She is Marylou in *On the Road*.

John Clellon Holmes (1926-1988)

Born in Holyoke, Massachusetts. Met Kerouac and Ginsberg in 1948 in New York. The term Beat generation originated from one of his conversations with Kerouac. His novel *Go* that was published in 1952 was the first to present the Beats because *On the Road* was published in 1957 (although it was written in 1951). Kerouac believed Holmes had stolen his material, although Holmes paid tribute to Kerouac and this roman à clef sold only 2500 copies.

In *Go* Kerouac is Gene Pasternak, Allen Ginsberg is David Stofsky and Neal Cassady is Hart Kennedy. John Clellon Holmes is Tom Saybrook in *On the Road*.

Herbert Huncke (1915-1996)

Born in Greenfield, Massachusetts. Childhood in Chicago. In 1944 in New York he fascinated William Burroughs with his knowledge of the seediest parts of town and introduced him to heroin. Ginsberg and Kerouac encouraged him to write. Poet-thief he "invented" the word "beat" which Kerouac took from him. Author of *Huncke's Journal* (1965), *The Evening Sun Turned Crimson* (1980) and *Guilty of Everything* (1990). Died in 1996.

He is Elmo Hassel in *On the Road*.

Joyce Johnson (1935)

Childhood in Manhattan. In 1952 met Allen Ginsberg through her friend Elise Cowen. Started a novel in 1955 at the age of 20, *Come and Join the Dance*. At the start of 1957 Ginsberg arranged a blind date between her and Kerouac at the time Jack's *On the Road* was published and he became famous. In 1983 she published *Minor Characters* which recounts her life with Kerouac and the Beat generation. Author of several novels including *Bad Connections, In the Night Café, What Lisa Knew: The Truth and Lies of the Steinberg Case*. She lives in New York. Teaches creative writing at Columbia University.

She is Alyce Newman in Kerouac's *Desolation Angels*.

Hettie Jones (1934)

In 1957 married LeRoi Jones (Amiri Baraka). She was white, he was black and their life together was difficult even in bohemian Greenwich Village where she worked for several magazines. LeRoi Jones' involvement in Black Power distanced him from her and drove them to divorce in 1968. She published her autobiography in 1990 *How I Became Hettie Jones* and several children's books. She now lives in the Lower East Side.

LeRoi Jones (1934)

Born in Newark, New Jersey. Married Hettie Cohen in 1957 in Greenwich Village. Wrote and published poems. After Malcolm X's assassination in 1965 he left Hettie, founded the Black Arts Repertory Theatre in Harlem and became a very active black nationalist. He took the name Amiri Baraka when he became a Muslim in 1966. Author of a play, *The Dutchman and The Slave* (1964), of a novel, short stories, musical critiques and a work on the origins of the blues, *Blues People*.

Edie Parker Kerouac (1923-1992)

Grew up in Grosse Pointe, Michigan. Left in 1941 to study at Columbia University. Had a string of boyfriends but a long attachment to Jack Kerouac, introduced by one of the boyfriends Henry Cru. Pregnant, she didn't know whether the father was Jack or Henry. Had an abortion. Edie then met Joan Vollmer, Burrough's future wife, and they took an apartment on 118th Street where Ginsberg, Carr and Burroughs hung out. Jack moved in with her although their relationship was not exclusive. When Lucien Carr stabbed Dave Kammerer to death Jack Kerouac helped him conceal the weapon and was arrested and imprisoned. In the eyes of the law a quickie marriage would sort it out: Edie paid the bail and married Jack with two policemen as witnesses on August 22, 1944. They went to Grosse Pointe where Jack worked until he had paid off Edie's father for the bail money. He then went to sea. An attempt at reconciliation failed and they quickly divorced but stayed on good terms.

Edie is Edna Palmer in Kerouac's *Vanity of Duluoz*.

Gabrielle Kerouac

Married Leo Kerouac in 1915 in Lowell, Massachusetts. Jack was her third child. He always called her Mémère. She died in Florida in 1973 aged 78, four years after Jack's death. Buried next to her husband Leo (1889-1946) and her first son Gerard whose death aged 9 inspired Jack's *Visions of Gerard*.

Gabrielle is Margaret Courbet Martin in Kerouac's *The Town and the City*.

Jack Kerouac (1922-1969)

The most famous of the Beat generation, and rightly so. Born in Lowell, Massachusetts; until the age of 5 he spoke the French of the small immigrant French-Canadian community. At 15 he still had difficulty understanding American when it was spoken too quickly. Gabrielle, his mother, worked from the age of 15 in a shoe factory and called him Ti Jean. His father, Leo, a Canadian emigrant, was employed in a printing works. Jack, the youngest, had a sister, Caroline and a brother, Gerard who died aged 9. Jack made a name for himself at school as an American football player, which got him in to Columbia University, New York. During the war he was in the Navy, and ended up in the Merchant Marines, unable to submit to military discipline. Published his first novel, *The Town and The City* in 1950. Then wrote a dozen books that remained unpublished until he became famous thanks to the publication of *On the Road* in 1957. Married three times: Edie Parker, Joan Haverty (with whom he had a daughter, Jan, in 1952 who he never acknowledged) and Stella Sampas. He died in 1969 from alcoholism and an attack of phlebitis.

Jan Kerouac (1952-1996)

Born in Albany, New York State. Daughter of Jack Kerouac and Joan Haverty. Jack never recognized her as his daughter, only saw her twice when she was 9 and 15, but he allowed her to take his name. Dramatic life. On the road at 15. Drugs, alcohol and sex. Author of two autobiographies, *Baby Driver* (1981) and *Trainsong* (1988) and an incomplete novel, *Parrot Fever*. Underwent dialysis when seriously ill with kidney problems. Died in 1996 due to her illness and alcoholism.

Joan Haverty Kerouac (1931-1990)

Childhood in Albany, New York State. Aged 19 fell in love with Bill Cannastra who she followed to Manhattan. Met Jack Kerouac in 1950 while tidying Bill's apartment. Bill died accidentally decapitating himself leaning out of the metro. Jack and Joan married a few days later. During their short time together Jack wrote *On the Road* in three weeks. Divorce after six months. Joan had Jack's daughter, Jan, whom he never acknowledged. Died in 1990. She wrote *Nobody's Wife*, which was published ten years after her death.

Ken Kesey (1935-2001)

Born in La Junta, Colorado. Kesey attended the University of Oregon, in Eugene. Married Faye Haxby in 1956. In 1960 and 1961, for $20 per session, he was a guinea-pig for tests on psilocybine, mescaline and LSD-25 at Menlo Park Veterans Hospital in Palo Alto. He worked as an aide in a psychiatric hospital. He used this experience in writing *One Flew Over the Cuckoo's Nest*. Published in 1962, the book was hugely successful and was later made into a film by Milos Forman. In 1960 Neal Cassady met Kesey in Palo Alto, California. In spring 1964 Kesey and his Merry Pranksters started a famous trip across the USA on the psychedelic Bus, a 1939 international Harvester with Neal Cassady at the wheel. Unproductive meeting with Timothy Leary at Millbrook Farm. Kesey published his second novel, *Sometimes a Great Notion*.

In 1969 Tom Wolfe (future author *of Bonfire of the Vanities*) published *The Electric Kool-Aid Acid Test*. Kesey was the central character. In 1990 Kesey recounted the odyssey of the psychedelic Bus in *The Further Inquiry* which included numerous photographs.

Philip Lamantia (1927)

Born in San Francisco. One of the representatives of the poetic Renaissance movement in San Francisco. Influenced by Surrealism, he was noticed by André Breton in New York who published his work. His first book *Erotic Poems* was published in 1946. He lives in San Francisco.

He is Francis de Pavia in Kerouac's *The Dharma Bums*.

Timothy Leary (1920-1996)

Liked to tell the story that he had been conceived on January 17, 1920 on the military base at West Point, New York State, during an officers' ball where his father, Tote, quickly seduced Abigail, his future mother. Childhood in Springfield. His father was a doctor-dentist. After Leary's secondary education he spent two years in the military Academy at West Point. Degree at UC Berkeley. Was appointed professor at Harvard University in 1960 where he carried out tests on hallucinogenic drugs, in particular psilocybine. From 1962 onwards, he carried out research on LSD with his colleagues Richard Alpert and Ralph Metzner. In 1963, wealthy supporters Peggy Hitchcock and her brothers, lent Leary the property at Millbrook in New York State so that he could continue his work. In 1969 Tim Leary put himself forward for the post of governor of California against Ronald Reagan. He was arrested and imprisoned for two grams of marijuana. Escaped after nine months. Exiled for two years in Switzerland. Recaptured in Afghanistan, he spent another two years in prison in California. Married four times: Marianne, Nanette, Rosemary and Barbara. He had two children, Jack and Susan, with Marianne; a daughter, Oma, with Nanette; and a step-son, Zachary, with Barbara. Spent the last years of his life in Beverly Hills and died in 1996 from prostate cancer.

Michael McClure (1932)

Poet and author, born in Marysville, Kansas. Attended the poet Robert Duncan's creative writing classes in San Francisco. His first book *Passage* was published in 1956. *Peyote Poem* followed two years later. He used the peyote to assist ecological awareness. He published an autobiography *The Mad Cub* in 1970.

He is Ike O'Shea in Kerouac's *The Dharma Bums*.

Harold Norse (1916)

Began his career in 1939 as W. H. Auden's friend and secretary. In the '40s he became intimate with James Baldwin. In 1944 he lived with Tennessee Williams in Provincetown. During the same year he met Allen Ginsberg. With John Cage he played an important part in Julian and Judith Beck's creation of Living Theater. William Carlos Williams introduced him when he was reading his poems in the Museum of Modern Art in 1952. Struck up a friendship with Pasolini and Moravia. At the end of the '50s he lived in Paris at the famous Beat Hotel, 9, rue Gît-le-Coeur, where Burroughs, Ginsberg and Corso also lived. Returned to Venice, California in 1968 where he formed a friendship with Charles Bukowski. Author of a dozen books of poems and a novel, *Beat Hotel*. His selected poems were published in 1974 entitled *Hotel Nirvana*. He published his autobiography in 1989, *Memoirs of a Bastard Angel*.

Peter Orlovsky (1933)

Born in Lower East Side, New York. Met the painter Robert LaVigne in San Francisco who introduced him to Ginsberg who became his life-long partner. Trip to India with Ginsberg in 1961. In Benares he tried to help a woman with leprosy. This experience inspired him to "Lepers Cry" a poem which features in his book *Clean Asshole Poems and Smiling Vegetable Songs* (1978).

He is Simon Darlowsky in Kerouac's *Desolation Angels*.

Edie Parker

Kerouac's first wife. See under Edie Parker Kerouac.

Gary Snyder (1930)

Born in San Francisco he grew up in Washington and Oregon. During his time at university he got together with Philip Whalen and Lew Welch. He studied Asian languages at Berkeley University and saved up to further his knowledge in Japan. Participated in the famous poetry reading in the Six Gallery in 1955 with Ginsberg who became famous the next day by reading *Howl*. Published his first book *Riprap* in 1959. Author of *Turtle Island*. Lives in Nevada City, California.

He is Japhy Ryder, the central character in Kerouac's *The Dharma Bums*.

Carl Solomon (1928)

Born in the Bronx, New York. Suffered depression after his father's death in 1939. After his studies he joined the United States Maritime Service which introduced him to Europe. He heard Artaud reading his poetry in Paris, took an interest in Dada and Surrealism. Believing he was mad, he went of his own accord to the Psychiatric Institute of New York City and voluntarily underwent electric shock therapy. In the corridor he met what appeared to be another patient and introduced himself as Kirilow, Dostoyevsky's character. The other replied "I'm Michkine." It was Allen Ginsberg. Allen noted some of Solomon's words after his electric shock sessions and put them in to his poem *Howl for Carl Solomon, Howl's* first title. Nephew of the publisher, Wyn, who ran Ace Books, Carl Solomon published Burroughs' *Junky* but turned down Kerouac's *On the Road*. He is the author of *Mishaps, Perhaps* (1966).

Anne Waldman (1945)

Grew up in Greenwich Village in a bohemian family. At 6 she enrolled in the Greenwich Village Children's Theatre where she acted in plays until she was 14. At 17 she met Diane DiPrima. She hooked up with Ginsberg (she lived for a time on his farm in Cherry Valley in the '70s), and with Joanne Kyger, Lew Welch, Philip Whalen, Michael McClure, etc. Travelled in Asia. Keen interest in Buddhism. Discovered Greece and Egypt. Having attended the Berkeley Poetry Festival in 1965 she got involved in The Poetry Project at St. Mark's Church-in-the-Bowery of which she became the director in 1968. In 1974 she established The Jack Kerouac School of Disembodied Poetics with Allen Ginsberg at the Buddhist Institute of Naropa in Boulder, Colorado. Also in 1974 her most famous book of poems, *Fast Speaking Woman*, was published by City Lights. She believes herself to be at the confluence of the Beats, the poets of the San Francisco Renaissance, the Black Mountain School and the New York School.

Alan Watts (1915-1973)

Born in Chislehurst, England. Popularized eastern thought for the western world. *The Spirit of Zen* was published in 1936. In 1958 in an issue dedicated to Zen of *The Chicago Review* he published an article entitled "Beat Zen, Square Zen, and Zen." This issue, which also included contributions from Kerouac, Gary Snyder and Philip Whalen, tripled the magazine's circulation. Watts questioned the Zen character Japhy Ryder (Kerouac inspired by Gary Snyder) in *The Dharma Bums*. He notably criticized Kerouac for mixing Zen effects on the existential and artistic level. He died in Mill Valley near San Francisco in 1973.

Lew Welch (1926-1971)

Born in Phoenix, Arizona. Roommate of Whalen and Snyder during their university studies. Taxi driver in San Francisco in 1959. Met Kerouac when he drove him back to New York, they wrote poems throughout the trip. From this Welch wrote his book *Trip Trap*. The following year he lived with Kerouac in the cabin at Big Sur that Ferlinghetti lent them.

He is Dave Wain in Kerouac's *Big Sur*.

Philip Whalen (1923)

Born in Portland, Oregon. After the war he hooked up with Gary Snyder and Lew Welch. In 1955 he read his poems in the Six Gallery. His meeting with Kerouac and Ginsberg was deciding and confirmed his vocation as poet that had wavered up until then. Author of several books including *On Bear's Head* and *Heavy Breathing*. Became a Buddhist monk in 1973. He lives in San Francisco.

He is Warren Coughlin in Kerouac's *The Dharma Bums*.

BOOKS BY SUN DOG PRESS

Steve Richmond, *Santa Monica Poems*

Steve Richmond, *Hitler Painted Roses*
(Foreword by Charles Bukowski)

Steve Richmond, *Spinning Off Bukowski*

Neeli Cherkovski, *Elegy for Bob Kaufman*

Randall Garrison, *Lust in America*

Billy Childish, *Notebooks of a Naked Youth*

Dan Fante, *Chump Change*

Robert Steven Rhine, *My Brain Escapes Me*

Fernanda Pivano, *Charles Bukowski: Laughing with the Gods*

Howard Bone (with Daniel Waldron), *Side Show—My Life with Geeks, Freaks & Vagabonds in the Carny Trade*